CONTEMPORARY
SOCIAL THEORY

CONTEMPORARY SOCIAL THEORY

Roger Salerno
Pace University

PEARSON

Boston Columbus Indianapolis New York San Francisco Upper Saddle River
Amsterdam Cape Town Dubai London Madrid Milan Munich Paris Montreal Toronto
Delhi Mexico City Sao Paulo Sydney Hong Kong Seoul Singapore Taipei Tokyo

Editorial Director: Craig Campanella
Editor in Chief: Dickson Musslewhite
Publisher: Karen Hanson
Associate Editor: Mayda Bosco
Executive Marketing Manager: Kelly May
Marketing Assistant: Diana Griffin
Production Project Manager: Elizabeth Gale
Napolitano

Media Editor: Nikhil Bramhavar
Editorial Production Service: Jouve India Private
Limited
Manager, Central Design: Jayne Conte
Cover Designer: Karen Salzbach
Cover Image: © Bruce Rolff/Shutterstock

Text Credits: Page 123: excerpt from *Sister Outsider: Essays and Speeches* by Audre Lorde, page 115. Freedom, CA: Ten Speed Press. Used by permission of the C. Sheedy Literary Agency, ©1984 by the Estate of Audre Lorde; page 204: excerpt from *Race Matters* by Cornel West, pages 350–351. Copyright ©1993, 2001 by Cornel West. Reprinted by permission of Beacon Press, Boston.

Library of Congress Cataloging-in-Publication Data

Salerno, Roger A.
  Contemporary social theory / Roger Salerno.
    p. cm.
  Includes index.
  ISBN 978-0-205-45965-0
  1. Sociology.   2. Social sciences—Philosophy.   I. Title.
HM585.S25 2013
301—dc23
                                    2012001183

10 9 8 7 6 5 4 3 2 1

ISBN-10: 0-205-45965-X
ISBN-13: 978-0-205-45965-0

For Sandi, Frances,
Mavis, & Rufus

Table of Contents

PREFACE ix

1 ANTECEDENTS OF CONTEMPORARY SOCIAL THEORY 1

2 STRUCTURALISM AND BEYOND 14

3 HERMENEUTICS AND PHENOMENOLOGY 43

4 POSTSTRUCTURALISM AND SOCIAL THEORY 63

5 EXPLODING THE BOUNDARIES OF REASON: POSTMODERNITY 84

6 FEMINIST SOCIAL THEORY 106

7 CULTURAL STUDIES AND CULTURAL THEORY 132

8 POSTCOLONIAL THEORY AND GLOBALIZATION 150

9 GENDER AND QUEER THEORY 180

10 RACE THEORY 198

SUBJECT INDEX 217

Preface

Contemporary social theory is often looked upon by the uninitiated as a dark, confusing, even distorted rendering of an alien social landscape. Unlike classical theory that basks in the glow of Reason promoted by the European Enlightenment, this theory dwells in a shadowy place—far away from the illumination of certainty. For the most part, the contemporary theory that will be presented here represents a rejection of much of what classical theorists and philosophers have taught us. That is, modern theory frequently rejects the classical notion of an objective reality, its inherent need to discover a universal truth, and its search for a natural order that governs the unified social world. Rather, it reveals a plethora of bizarre, heterogeneous, unintegrated worlds that are *imagined* into existence. These are ephemeral places in which we each live for only a moment with the hope of finding our own truth—perhaps even constructing it.

Many find this new social theory confusing, even threatening. Those who subscribe to the western tradition's notion of an inherent universal truth are frequently disturbed by its implications, regardless of their political or ideological orientations. But for many others, the rich constellation of subjective analyses resonates better with their own experiences, with popular culture, and with the fleeting nature of the worlds in which they dwell for the moment. It is the purpose of this text to explore, describe, and discuss some of these new ways of understanding these strange worlds and, perhaps, to provide a roadmap through this shadowy terrain.

Contemporary Social Theory identifies the important intellectual movements, categories, and paradigms that have given life to many of these new ideas. In doing this, it acknowledges the movement away from Enlightment thought, which proposes a definitive center. It begins with a rendering of the emergence of this movement. It continues with a description of how social and intellectual challenges have affected the production of new theory. And it concludes with an exploration of how these theories have been applied to various social phenomena.

Theories have always emerged from the political, cultural, and social climates that produced them. They have been shaped by powerful institutional processes. At the same time, categories have been developed to encourage and perpetuate production of theory in one particular vein or another. As it exists, the current system of academic scholarship demands this. Frequently, living theorists evolve in their thinking and it is only for the sake of organizing what *appears* to be distinct patterns in their work that they are grouped accordingly here and in other texts. It is the way academics contextualize and categorize social thought to make it more accessible and manageable. Whether a particular theory is considered functionalist, structuralist, poststructuralist, modern, or postmodern is frequently contentious.

One must also keep in mind that many contemporary theorists do not identify their work with any specific category of theory, nor did they ever. In fact they often fail to recognize that such categories actually exist, or are important in any way. For example, Michel Foucault sometimes has been seen as a structuralist, other times as a poststructuralist, and frequently as a postmodernist. Yet, he never identified his work as fitting into any of these divisions. The quintessential postmodern theorist, Jean Baudrillard, rejected postmodernism as a category of theory altogether. And so how scholars categorize theoretical work is often quite arbitrary.

While this book recognizes that ideas often have deep histories, it also advances the view that new theory can be effectively used to assess social and cultural phenomena. Therefore, this book examines the issues that contemporary social theory is likely to confront: the postmodern condition, globalization, postcolonialism, inequality, gender, race, and human sexuality. By seeing how theory is used to frame the world, we gain a better understanding of its potential application.

This text moves from presenting theoretical perspectives and their intellectual development to dealing with those specific subjects to which contemporary theory has been applied. Thus, *Contemporary Social Theory* commences with a brief overview of social theory (Chapter 1) and then examines the intellectual cornerstones of more contemporary thought: structuralism (Chapter 2), hermeneutics and phenomenology (Chapter 3), and poststructuralism (Chapter 4). Then Chapters 5 through 10 deal with contemporary strains of thought, which draw from these new perspectives: postmodernism, feminist theory, global studies, cultural studies, and race theory. These areas each carry a range of theoretical perspectives, and each constitutes a wellspring of current theoretical formulations.

It must also be said that contemporary theory is unsettled. It is still being interpreted and discussed. And new theories continue to emerge. Therefore, this text makes no pretense of providing the final word as to the meaning of the ideas presented; as times change theorists modify their ideas. There are new interpretations. There is also a looseness of meaning built into the theories and concepts developed by theorists we will read about that here. The porous and nebulous quality of such theory often keeps it alive. It gives the reader and critic the power to interpret it—to co-construct it, if you will—to give it meaning for a particular time and place in one's own life.

Something also must be said about the inability of a text like this one to include all relevant and important theorists and all of their significant ideas. Like any theory text, this is a brief survey of the field. It cannot meet the needs of everyone. However, it does attempt to provide the reader with a rich assortment and range of theoretical orientations. Its purpose is to present an accessible genealogy of what has influenced theory both intellectually and historically along the way and to demonstrate its relevance to contemporary issues. In doing this, *Contemporary Social Theory* serves as a tool for those wishing to join in the venture of constructing alternative understandings of their unique social worlds.

SUPPLEMENTS

Instructor's Manual and Test Bank (ISBN 0-205-22543-8): The Instructor's Manual and Test Bank has been prepared to assist teachers in their efforts to prepare lectures and evaluate student learning. For each chapter of the text, the Instructor's Manual offers different types of resources, including detailed chapter summaries and outlines, learning objectives, discussion questions, classroom activities and much more. Also included in this manual is a test bank offering multiple-choice, true/false, fill-in-the-blank, and/

or essay questions for each chapter. The Instructor's Manual and Test Bank is available to adopters at **www.pearsonhighered.com**.

MyTest (ISBN 0-205-22542-X): The Test Bank is also available online through Pearson's computerized testing system, MyTest. MyTest allows instructors to create their own personalized exams, to edit any of the existing test questions, and to add new questions. Other special features of this program include random generation of test questions, creation of alternative versions of the same test, scrambling question sequence, and test preview before printing. Search and sort features allow you to locate questions quickly and to arrange them in whatever order you prefer. The test bank can be accessed from anywhere with a free MyTest user account. There is no need to download a program or file to your computer.

PowerPoint Presentation (ISBN 0-205-22541-1): Lecture PowerPoints are available for this text. The Lecture PowerPoint slides outline each chapter to help you convey sociological principles in a visual and exciting way. They are available to adopters at **www.pearsonhighered.com**.

MySearchLab: My Search Lab contains writing, grammar, and research tools and access to a variety of academic journals, census data, Associated Press news feeds, and discipline-specific readings to help you hone your writing and research skills. In addition, a complete eText is included. MySearchLab can be purchased with the text (ISBN 0-205-87178-X) or separately (ISBN 0-205-87028-7).

ACKNOWLEDGMENTS

No book is a solitary project. This one required a host of comrades, colleagues, students, and acquaintances to complete.

This project started several years ago after a brief discussion with Jeff Lasser, then the sociology editor at Pearson. But it couldn't have been written without the support given to it by a number of friends and colleagues. Two very important people in this regard were Robert Grimwade and Richard Koenigsberg. Both read the manuscript and offered excellent suggestions. Lauren Langman and Jeff Haley also helped in this regard.

While I'd like to thank Rich Lester for his insights into leisure theory and Emily Lester for her expertise in consumer culture, I'd particularly like to thank my wife, Sandi Salerno, who not only gave me important insights, but also provided me with an enormous amount of help as I continued working on this project throughout the past few years. She assisted me in refining and organizing my thoughts. My appreciation is directed to an excellent team I worked with at Pearson. Also, thanks goes to Dyson College at Pace University for providing me with time for this and other scholarly research projects. My students in my classes in social theory were very helpful as well, and I'd like to thank them all.

CHAPTER 1

Antecedents of Contemporary Social Theory

S ocial theory is becoming increasingly difficult to define. At one point in time we could say that social theory was a systematic effort to better understand the world in which we live by examining it through a particular lens or perspective. However, many contemporary social thinkers might find this simple notion quite outmoded. Given the philosophical thrust of current social thought, we can think of social theory as an attempt to better comprehend how and why we construct the social *worlds* in which we live—or, perhaps, discover how and why these worlds are constructed for us to live in.

Social theory has come a long way from the late nineteenth century, when the world was considered to be a place characterized by reason and rules of natural law guiding its evolution—rules that could be discovered with the help of rational positivism and empirical science. But all of this has been challenged. Still, in some other respects, we haven't really moved very far from classical thinking at all. Many of us are still interested in why large groups of people in societies behave the way they behave and what leads them to do the things they do. These concerns were also those of the earliest social theorists—thinkers who even preceded the classical sociologists like Marx, Weber, and Durkheim.

Contemporary Social Theory is an attempt to survey new patterns of social thought and to contextualize new theory that is emerging from older ways of seeing the world. To begin, it is important to examine some of the antecedents of contemporary social theory. How has contemporary theory changed from classical theory, and why has it changed? What are some of the factors that have catalyzed the shift in the way social theorists look at the world?

RUPTURE WITH ENLIGHTENMENT THOUGHT

The European Enlightenment had a profound impact on the development of traditional social thought. Those classical social theorists who helped to build a foundation for contemporary social theory were powerfully influenced by Enlightenment philosophers.

The Enlightenment was an intellectual movement with specific founders and advocates. To locate these early influences, one needs to look to France and to the work of Voltaire (1694–1788), Montesquieu (1698–1755), Rousseau (1712–1778), and Diderot (1713–1784). All were Enlightenment thinkers who helped set an agenda for Enlightenment philosophy and discourse. They saw themselves as living in "the century of the enlightened." Their romance with reason and science laid the groundwork for modern sociopolitical discourse. Many of these thinkers also promoted the ideas that people had "natural rights" and that governments should protect these rights of individuals. In general, Enlightenment thought included the following elements:

- A belief that the universe is fundamentally rational and can be understood through empirical science and reason;
- An assumption that all of nature is knowable and that human experience and thought are the only avenues to this knowledge;
- A belief that knowledge serves to improve human life and that ignorance is the cause of human misery and immorality;
- An expectation that there is both epistemological and moral unity that integrates and governs the world; and
- The thought that there is but one universal, discoverable truth and it alone is the key to endless human progress.

Enlightenment thinkers constituted a small but highly influential group of European males who came from the emerging educated bourgeoisie and helped to bring into existence the continued decline of papal and aristocratic authority. The Enlightenment challenged the Catholic Church's authority as an arbiter of truth and theology as the central means of its discovery (Salerno 2004).

Early social theory, particularly the sociological theory of Auguste Comte, Karl Marx, Herbert Spencer, Emile Durkheim, and Max Weber, was profoundly influenced by Enlightenment thought. Running through their work was a belief that modern science could address the challenges confronted by people and a belief that the world's mysteries could be understood through objective, detached analysis. At the same time, they were influenced by modern philosophical ideas—especially the work of Immanuel Kant, G. W. Hegel, and Johann Fichte. Evident in their work is a sense of the importance of subjective knowing.

For George Hegel, one of the most important philosophers of the early nineteenth century, everything that exists is a product of the mind. And while we might perceive objects to be separate and independent of it, they are not. They are totally dependent on thought for their existence. Therefore, the mind is seen as the source of the objectified world. Not only did Hegel's work help catalyze existential thinking, it challenged some of the foundations of the Enlightenment itself.

But with the failure of the Enlightenment to live up to its promise, the continuation of wars, the institution of slavery in the colonies, the abuses of industrial capitalism, the starvation of millions, and disease rapidly spreading throughout the world, there was a disillusionment with its underlying assumptions and methods and a particular disenchantment with the promise of science. Though Karl Marx defended the advance of reason, by the twentieth century, Max Weber had some serious reservations about it. Modern philosophers like Nietzsche criticized Enlightenment thinking and challenged many of its principal assumptions—particularly the assumption in the ability of reason to make the world a better place.

MARXIST THEORY AND ANALYSIS

While Karl Marx subscribed to most of the Enlightenment's principles, he was highly critical of the bourgeoisie that helped launch this undertaking. It was his firm belief that the bourgeoisie and their heralded nation-states had promoted the advancement and protection of market capitalism as a so-called "rational" means of "developing" society. For him this form of economic system that had been set into place was nothing more than another form of feudalism for the workers who were exploited in the process of generating profits for the owners of the means of production. He refuted Adam Smith's belief that the system was God's will, one divined by an "invisible hand"—and the commonly held belief that capitalism was an expression of natural laws. Marx, who had faith in the Enlightenment's promise of reason, saw it as being distorted by philosophers and theologians alike. Marx contended that society had to change—perhaps even through revolution—if it were ever to progress. Capitalism was a class system, not too dissimilar from those that existed throughout history, wherein it was nurtured and developed by powerful elites who protected and advanced their own rapacious self-interest.

Much of Marx's theory dealt with class struggle in light of enormous inequalities in the world generated not by the aristocracy but through the development of the structure of the capitalistic system and the substructures it both produced and supported—including the state. For Marx, material culture was a direct consequence of capitalism, which promoted an ideology that conditioned people to believe in its redemptive power. For him, capitalism was not only supported by religion, but also became a religion in itself—a system of belief or an ideology that kept society from advancing to a point of greater equality and individual self-actualization. While he saw value and potential in early industrial capitalism, he believed it had become corrupt and reactionary and could not effectively advance the causes of equality and justice, principles that influenced the Enlightenment. Where a few would grow materially rich, now the majority of the world's population would become increasingly poor.

Marx critiqued not only the material devastation of the workers who kept this system alive, but also the existential emptiness and dehumanization that accompanied capital's advance: the *commodification* of life and the devastation of nature. He was fascinated by the sophisticated techniques used by the bourgeoisie to control and distort reality for their own interests. He was interested in issues of global exploitation and the social and political oppression that went along with it in the name of nationalism. His ideas were to have a profound impact on the lives of billions of people. They would inspire revolutions around the world, particularly in the most underdeveloped nations. But they would also inspire new theoretical paradigms dealing with themes of oppression and exploitation.

The legacy of Marx has informed much contemporary social thought. His impact can be found both in structuralist and poststructuralist theory. The structuralist Marx is considered the more mature Marx; it is the Enlightenment Marx that deals with the deterministic structures imposed on society by capitalism and its related systems of exploitation and the political economy. The poststructuralist Marx relates to Marx's earlier work, but most particularly the ideas expressed in his *Economic and Philosophic Manuscripts of 1844*. Here, the phenomenological Marx speaks to us in psychological and humanistic terms. It is here where he addresses such issues as alienation, commodification, and *false consciousness* and their impact on both material and psychic life.

The *structuralism* in Marxism is not merely the implication that the structure of the economic system determines everything else, such as the form of family, the political system, or the values of our culture; it even suggests that capitalism shapes our personalities and how we treat one another as means to ends. While Marx was somewhat deterministic, he more readily saw structures as influencing factors and not ones that negated human autonomy and agency. The individual was seen as capable of transcending these powerfully influential structures and creating revolutionary social change.

FRIEDRICH NIETZSCHE AND THE BREAK WITH REASON

Perhaps one of the most vehement critics of western Enlightenment was Friedrich Nietzsche. As a thinker and social philosopher, he challenged the entire course of western civilization. Nietzsche despised socialism as much as he despised industrial capitalism. He saw both as wedded to the western notion of reason that was corrupt and degenerate.

Nietzsche is most known for his aphorism: "God is dead!" By this he meant that with the advance of science and reason, God has been killed and is no longer the arbiter of truth. The only truth is that which individuals create for themselves and others. Meaning is no longer associated with God but is a human creation. Nietzsche also recognized the relativity of truth and the fiction of its universality. In his view each individual's perspective creates truth for that person; those who have the more powerful wills create worlds others live in. Those who allow others to create a world for them get only what they deserve.

Nietzsche viewed universal truth as conceived by the Enlightenment thinkers as an illusion. It was an artifact from theology's search for divine understanding. Given the differences in the world, there can never be one truth. Thus, the Enlightenment was itself a fraud. There can never be—and will never be—a world without oppression and dogmatism. There will never be the equality, harmony, and cooperation as envisioned by Marx. The world is built on the accrual of power and nothing more. It is power that determines truth. This is what Neitzsche believed the Enlightenment thinkers were after, power through a monopoly on truth. Therefore, Nietzsche advanced the notion that truth and power are one and the same.

Nietzsche believed that art was more compelling than science and that the body was the true source of all wisdom. It is from the body (not the mind) that any sense of reality emerges. He praised the passion of art and its ability to create the universe, to change and reshape the world through theater, music, drama, and poetry. His ideas would not only inspire the *existentialism* of Martin Heidegger and Jean-Paul Sartre but would also go on to influence Gilles Deleuze, Michel Foucault, Judith Butler, Jean Baudrillard, Jean-François Lyotard, and a host of others whose work has been labeled poststructural or postmodern. Many contemporary social theorists look to Nietzsche as a source of theoretical inspiration.

PSYCHOANALYTIC THOUGHT AND THE POWER OF THE UNCONSCIOUS

Few theorists can ever claim the magnitude of influence that Sigmund Freud had on the way educated people saw the social world—particularly in the twentieth century. His ideas not only revolutionized social science, but also had a major impact on art and literature. While he contributed significantly to the burgeoning field of psychology, he had a major impact on philosophy and social theory, too.

Freud's impact on modern thought is often compared to that of Nietzsche, with whom he shared some significant similarities as well as major differences; however, his most important contribution to contemporary social thought was his understanding of the power of the *unconscious* to shape peoples' lives. And while the unconscious mind was not his invention alone, he elaborated on its structure, function, and the early influences that helped form it.

The belief that people were consciously engaged in the world around them was foundational to Enlightenment thought. While Freud did not dismiss this idea, he put forth the notion that the unconscious—a reservoir of repressed unacceptable or unpleasant feelings, wishes, thoughts, urges, and memories residing outside our conscious awareness—influences our behavior and our experience of the world. The power of the unconscious to alter the world for us and make a particular sense of it was a new way of understanding human perception and behavior.

Freud divided psychic life between primary and secondary processes. Primary represented the preconscious mind; secondary, the faculties of egoistic reason. He associated the unconscious with primary process and the conscious mind with secondary processes. It was Freud's contention that the conscious lives of people represent only a fraction of who people are and what they are feeling.

The unconscious houses not only innate biological drives such as sex and aggression, but also experiences, memories, and feelings that did not or could not find conscious expression from infancy onward.

In 1899, Freud published his now classic *The Interpretation of Dreams* in which he suggested that dreams were "the royal road" to one's unconscious. They could be analyzed for their symbolic meaning and could yield to the analyst things that had been hidden away or repressed. Dreams would allow Freud a means of better understanding the problems his patients were confronting. He also saw the psychoanalytic technique enabling a better understanding of the meanings of art.

Psychoanalysis became a set of methods used by Freud and his followers to help unearth the meaning of things hidden away in the dark recesses of the patient's unconscious. It represented a means of reading that which was concealed from both the patient's consciousness and from the therapist. Psychoanalytic methods became important to the notion in contemporary theory that meaning is not as obvious as it might appear. The person doesn't always understand why she or he does something. Hidden away in language and symbols are unconscious motivations and drives. All human actions and products need to be read as well as interpreted.

Psychoanalytic theory became a powerful mode of social analysis. It is central to semiotics, French structuralism, *phenomenology*, hermeneutics, *poststructuralism*, Derrida's deconstructionism, and postmodern theory. The work of Jacques Lacan, Gilles Deleuze, Michel Foucault, and Judith Butler are heavily indebted to Freud, as are French feminist theorists ranging from Simone de Beauvoir to Julia Kristeva. Social theorists like Anthony Giddens, Jürgen Habermas, and Zygmunt Bauman dip frequently into psychoanalysis in their attempts to personalize structural changes taking place in society. While this text has avoided an extensive discussion of psychoanalytic theory, such work today remains vital and constantly nourishes and is nourished by social theory.

THE RISE OF CRITICAL THEORY AS A MODE OF CULTURAL ANALYSIS

Marx's ideas eventually were combined with those of Nietzsche and Freud to produce innovative social and cultural critiques. In Germany, the *Frankfurt school* (a group of radical scholars and philosophers) emerged to critically assess the impact of corporate capitalism on political and social life and to challenge the promise of modernity. Founded at the University of Frankfurt in 1921, this was a group of leftist intellectuals who stressed the importance of history and philosophy in illuminating causes of social ills. It was one of the most influential intellectual movements of the time, and it drew on the work of Hegel, Nietzsche, Freud, Marx, Weber, and others. It attracted the likes of Theodore Adorno, Herbert Marcuse, Max Horkheimer, and a host of close associates, including Walter Benjamin and Erich Fromm. The school had indirect connections to Edward Husserl and his assistant Martin Heidegger, a young philosopher at the University of Freiburg.

Not only was the Frankfurt school exemplary social science, but it was also consummate cultural criticism. It combined sociology, politics, and psychoanalysis with philosophy and cultural critique.

The term *critical theory* was defined by Max Horkheimer in 1937 in his essay, "Traditional and Cultural Theory" (Horkheimer 1937). Here he suggests that critical theory is a type of social theory directed toward both critiquing and changing society as opposed to just explaining it. He viewed it as a radical form of Marxian analysis that called into question both *scientism* and positivism as the sole ways of examining phenomena. Horkheimer studied with the great linguist Edmund Husserl and knew his assistant, Martin Heidegger. In this sense his work had some affinity to the "cultural turn," which will be discussed later.

The Frankfurt school theorists drew extensively from the psychoanalytic theories of Sigmund Freud and Wilhelm Reich as well as from modern German philosophy and linguistics. Unlike classical Marxists, they not only aimed at critiquing capitalism but also critically examined the culture produced by capitalist production and the messages hidden in its products. Influenced by Hegel and Marx, these theorists stressed the alienating features of contemporary societies and human estrangement from nature. Frederich Nietzsche had already challenged the European Enlightenment and the western corruption of reason, as had the renowned sociologist Max Weber. All of these ideas found their way into the Frankfurt school synthesis.

With the student campus rebellions and cultural turmoil of the late 1960s, the Frankfurt school gained a new audience. The New Left was to some extent defined by intellectual leaders such as Herbert Marcuse. But it also was captivated with a left-leaning existential philosophy articulated by the psychoanalytically trained Jean-Paul Sartre. *The New Left Review*, founded in 1960, became an important mechanism for publishing the work of emerging leftist theorists, many of whom we will read about in this text. It would later serve as a launching pad for cultural theory and postcolonial analysis.

Jürgen Habermas, who is considered the heir of the Frankfurt school, has made considerable contributions to social theory. While his work appears to be more conservative than the work of some of his predecessors (he maintains a steadfast commitment to many Enlightenment goals, particularly to the importance of universal reason) he still finds the foundation for much of his thinking in the ideas of Marx and Weber. Yet, Habermas has borrowed much from structural functionalism, systems analysis, and American pragmatism, which no longer find a receptive place in left critical thought. He has been a critical opponent of postmodern theory.

THE LINGUISTIC TURN

While the *linguistic turn* will be covered more thoroughly in Chapter 2, it is important to comment on the significant impact this had on social theory and cultural criticism. Some of the most powerful influences on contemporary social thought are rooted in European linguistics—particularly in the linguistic theories of the Swiss theortician Ferdinand de Saussure (1857–1913). Saussure is seen typically as a founder of modern linguistics, and he is credited by many with what is often referred to in philosophy and theory as the *linguistic turn* which means the emerging acknowledgment of the centrality of language and discourse in the examination of societies. He believed that language was something more complicated than a naming system wherein words were assigned to things. His structural study of language emphasized the relationship of what he called "the sign" to what it signified. We understand this today as the basics of semiotics, wherein a sign (or sound/image) has no true meaning by itself and is given meaning only by being put into a specific context. Saussure distinguished among the components of language, spoken and written words, and the structure built with these components. He was interested in rules of structure. Every system of language, he proposed, has a grammatical structure that gives words their meaning. Each culture has its own unique set of rules. Saussure promoted this idea of structuralism, which asserted that the rules for structure are generated in the human mind, not by an external sense of perception. Such structures are used to make sense of the world. Saussure emphasized that language could be understood only from a synchronic view, looking at the structure of language as a functioning system at a given point in time, in contrast to the diachronic or historical view. His work has influenced the ideas of many contemporary theorists.

A similar emphasis on the subjective emerged in the work of idealist German philosopher Edmund Husserl (1859–1938). Considered the founder of modern phenomenology (the study of the conscious experience of objects), Husserl examined the ideal, or essential, structures of consciousness. He proposed that the world of objects and intentions, or the ways in which we direct ourselves toward understanding and relating to objects, emerges from a "natural attitude" (something internal). Husserl's work is characterized by a belief that objects themselves have certain properties, and in seeing these objects, we come to understand what is inherent in them. How we are intentionally directed toward objects in a sense "constitutes" these objects or "creates" them. This notion becomes the basis for his concept of intersubjectivity. Thus the object ceases to be simply external to the individual—providing indicators about what it is—and emerges as a set of perceptions that imply the idea of a particular object or "type." By bracketing off the outside world and concentrating on subjective consciousness, we are able to avoid unjustifiable claims about their existence. While his phenomenology attempts to identify the uniform features in our perceptions of objects, at the same time it proposes that reality is an attitudinal adaptation toward the things we perceive. Taken together, Saussure and Husserl radically altered the way in which social thinkers saw the world. Their ventures into phenomenology shifted attention away from empiricism as the foundation of modern social thought. Husserl's work influenced not only Freud, but also Heidegger and the Frankfurt school founders.

Born the same year as Husserl, Henri Bergson (1859–1927) became one of France's most important twentieth-century philosophers. His early career was spent as a teacher of philosophy at various *lycées* (the U.S. equivalent of high schools) throughout France. But primarily due to the popularity of his writings, he was appointed chair of philosophy at *Collège de France*. He became an exceedingly influential figure on the existentialism of Heidegger, Sartre, and Merleau-Ponty, and he also influenced the work of Gilles Deleuze and the phenomenology of Levinas. (All of these philosophers will be discussed later in this text.)

Bergson's primary focus was on the subjective nature of consciousness and perception. Like Nietzsche, he believed the body and its vital energy were central to all experience and key determinants of one's unique consciousness. He thought much of intuition and wrote that, more than rational analysis, intuition revealed the *true world* (1903). While human cognition evolved to think in "spatializing" terms, such terms were inadequate for grasping the essential understanding of one's unique reality. It was intuition that enabled one to reach the heart of reality and philosophic truth.

It was Bergson's contention that perception is not merely a cognitive process whose aim is to provide knowledge. Rather, he insisted that perception selects images that have a likely bearing on action. Here perception is viewed as a type of intuition interlaced with memory. It involves a process through which the body is consulted to help determine the meaning of the object through understanding the object's effects on one's body. This can be achieved only by reflecting on its past history with like objects. Thus body and mind converge in this process of perception.

Renowned German philosopher, leading contributor to existential phenomenology, and one-time Nazi, Martin Heidegger (1889–1976) had been a student of Edmund Husserl. The central philosophical question that concerned him was, "What is it to be?". This further led him to question the quality of Being. Heidegger saw people as thrown into a world that they had not made. Still, it was a world consisting of potentially useful objects—both cultural and natural objects. According to Heidegger, the individual is in constant danger of being submerged in the world of objects and everyday routine. There is a constant sense that he or she will be swallowed up in a crowd. This feeling of dread (*Angst*) brings the individual to a confrontation with death and the seeming meaninglessness of life. Only by confronting this can an authentic sense of Being and of freedom be found. Heidegger also proposed that, although the individual is not the master of his or her own origin, there is a capacity to undertake authentic actions that validate one's distinctive capacities. There is an authentic self that is defined by a potentiality for action and an orientation toward the future (Becoming). Heidegger's work became highly influential in the turbulent years of the 1960s. But at the close of that decade, his ideas, as well as those of Jean-Paul Sartre and other existentialist thinkers, fell into disfavor. A new, linguistically based structuralism arose in France to challenge it, which displaced this paradigm with a more deterministic approach and dismissed the notion of authenticity. The work of structuralist anthropologists, such as Claude Levi-Strauss, proposed that all culture was merely a reflection of the structures of the mind. Structuralism, however, appeared too deterministic for these times. By the early 1970s, the value of *structuralism* was also being challenged.

Foucault, Lacan, and Derrida (all of whom were structuralists at one time) ushered in a wave of what was to be called by some post-structuralism. Poststructuralism was a rejection of the rigidity of structural analysis and the determinism that appeared to be part of it. It also attacked the Enlightenment and its grand theoretical pretensions. In its place was a Nietzschian brand of critical theory. Reading social theory was a challenging venture as ideas clashed and merged. It was a time of cultural, economic, and political turbulence and considerable confusion.

THEORY AND SOCIAL MOVEMENTS
OF THE 1960S AND 1970S

One cannot fully comprehend the emergence of contemporary social thought without recognizing the powerful influence of the social movements of the 1960s and early 1970s as responses to world events. Particular reference must be made to those movements promoting antiracism, gender equality, and environmental and human rights. The civil rights movement, the women's movement, and the movement for gay and lesbian social justice need to be emphasized here. These movements were to shape the theoretical discourse for decades to come. Historical events taking place during this period—most specifically the civil rights movement in the United States and the wars in Vietnam and Algeria—highlighted issues of colonialism and racism throughout the world. The women's movement and the gay liberation movement challenged traditional notions of gender and sexuality. During these times (1960–1970), sociology, particularly radical social theory, often best articulated a deeper understanding of such events.

In France, the Paris Uprising in May 1968 had a major impact on French students, professors, and other workers. Students and unionized workers disrupted the normal flow of life through major demonstrations and occasional riots for more than twenty-five days, bringing the city to a halt. Barricades were built by thousands of people who amassed in the streets and called for economic reform and social justice. All this threatened the stability of the French government.

Social turmoil of the late 1960s forever changed the process of constructing or conceptualizing social theory. A rapidly increasing cycle of fragmentation, consolidation, and identity politics began to invade theory building. The structure/agency pendulum that had emphasized the importance of structure in the determination of social outcomes now swung in the other direction; it was conflict and agency that seem to matter more. Prior to the 1960s Marxist theory was hardly ever invoked as a means of explaining social phenomena. Now it appeared to have answers (Young 1999). Vast social movements unnerved those on the right and emboldened those on the left.

Contemporary social theory became just that—theoretical attempts to make sense of what was happening at the current time. Unlike Durkheim and Weber, who focused on the historical significance of grand societal trends, new theorists became blatantly ahistorical (MacRaild and Taylor 2004). The new theories looked at the struggles for power and the established mechanisms of dominance and control. Neo-Marxist thought contributed heavily to these early analyses.

The writings of W. E. B. DuBois inspired a new generation that spoke in terms of "black power." But even more, theory was articulated by street corner orators such as Malcolm X and novelists such as Richard Wright and James Baldwin. The women's movement also was indebted to the cultural shifts they helped to mobilize. Simone de Beauvoir not only articulated women's issues, but she walked the walk. Her focus on the otherness of women and deep philosophical insights into domestic oppression inspired succeeding generations of women, just as the literature of Virginia Wolf had done the generation before. It would not be unusual to see the great existential philosopher Jean-Paul Sartre marching against the war in Vietnam, or other public intellectuals marching to ban the cold war buildup of nuclear weapons.

Social movements of the 1960s and the 1970s focused on the importance of identity: What does it mean to be a woman? What does it mean to be black? What does it mean to be lesbian or gay? Much theory during this time attempted to address these questions by creating political agendas for these individual demographic groupings. The trouble was that such so-called identity groups were not very homogeneous. They were frequently internally divided into sub-groups. Conflicts ensued within these groups. Who spoke for whom and with what authority? Contemporary theory needed to address this.

TRANSDISCIPLINARITY: EVAPORATING BOUNDARIES

While social theory was traditionally associated with sociology, this is no longer the case. By the 1970s, disciplinary boundaries were becoming more porous. Cultural studies, black studies, women's studies, and gay and lesbian studies began to take shape in academia drawing from traditional disciplines such as history, literature, philosophy, and anthropology. They borrowed not merely from one discipline but rather from several simultaneously. Often methodology was borrowed from one field or another. Sometimes there was little in the way of a clearly articulated method. Fragmentation and specializations within disciplines helped to nourish this new interdisciplinary direction. Postcolonial studies and cultural studies were discrete areas of the academy by the 1980s. Each new area put forth its own unique theories that crossed traditional disciplinary lines. Social theory was now often simply referred to as theory. It could be cultural, feminist, psychoanalytic, or literary. It could be racial or ethnic; its method could be ethnographic or quantitative. The drive for some sort of grand, unified social theory embedded in one discipline was evaporating. In some respects this was due to the powerful influence of poststructuralism and its rejection of the perceived rigidity of Enlightenment thought.

Within the past few decades, the value of rigid disciplinary boundaries has been the subject of academic challenge and debate. While theory has become exceedingly fragmented, it has also become less wedded to discipline. Just as one easily crosses the border established between sociology and psychology, it has become equally possible to cross from literature into anthropology or into history. This "border crossing" occurs not only in the social sciences and humanities; it is also happening to an ever greater extent in the natural sciences. As the humanities and natural and social sciences more fully recognize their interdependencies, crossovers from one curriculum to another occur more and more often: from psychology into neurobiology and into philosophy and literary criticism. New theory must come to terms with this. While *transdisciplinarity* recognizes and even celebrates these border crossings, it is still often wed to discipline-specific paradigms that are difficult to translate for someone from another discipline. The production of new theory is in need of venues that can accommodate transdisciplinarity. And there are new eclectic or *hybrid* venues emerging all the time.

In this sense, transdisciplinarity offers liberation from disciplines characterized as "rigorous, aggressive [and] hazardous to master" (Frank 1988, p. 100). Yet disciplines still exist; they have been around for a while and will probably remain a bit longer as a means of organizing work and ideas. For cultural historian Joe Moran, what distinguishes interdisciplinarity from transdisciplinarity is that interdisciplinarity offers "a co-operative alternative to the old fashioned inward looking cliquish nature of disciplines" (Moran 2002 p. 3). Here old disciplines remain intact but recognize the contribution of other disciplines. Researchers in one field find ways of communicating and sharing ideas with people in another field. Transdisciplinarity in contrast connotes the crossing of many disciplinary boundaries to create a more holistic approach to the subject matter. It is not hierarchical and is more egalitarian in its outlook, but at the same time is less wedded to strict disciplinary research protocols. It is easy to understand that topics such as class, race, and gender can best be explored by more than one discipline. However, this does not mean that disciplinary boundaries are useless.

For anyone who ventures forth to examine newly emerging theory, there needs to be an awareness that social theory often becomes more opaque and less orderly. This is especially true for contemporary theory. It frequently confounds the reader with obstructions built of jargon that must be scaled. Without some appreciation of this type of difficulty, the project can be daunting. But there is great promise in transdisciplinarity. Contemporary theory no longer seems bound to strict adherence to one set of methods, which in the past often confined the creative range of its output. Its openness provides an invitation to celebrate a rich diversity of ideas without attempting to confine these ideas to a disciplinary box.

KEY TERMS

commodification A term used by Marx to describe how everything in capitalistic society becomes a commodity or product with a price or market value attached to it.

existentialism A twentieth-century philosophy that claimed that people were both free and alone in the world and thus responsible for their own lives and actions.

a virtual chain of people who were connected by this ritual. Malinowski interpreted the structural importance of this in promoting status distinctions, friendly relations among the islanders, and other types of more utilitarian exchanges. This particular study profoundly influenced Marcel Mauss's work, *The Gift* (1990), originally published in *L'Année Sociologique* in 1924.

Marcel Mauss had done extensive work on gift exchange in traditional societies. Following the lead of Malinowski, it was his contention that forms of gift exchange were related to social structure. He was instrumental in turning the attention of modern sociologists to ethnography and exerted great influence on the work of anthropologist Levi-Strauss and phenomenologist Maurice Merleau-Ponty, both of whom were influenced by the work of Karl Marx.

Malinowski was among the first anthropologists to attempt to see the relevance of noneconomic trading. He also was the first to use Freudian psychoanalysis cross-culturally, examining the applicability or lack of applicability of the Oedipus complex in other cultures. Alfred Radcliffe-Brown (1881–1955), another anthropologist, focused his studies on social structures and how they functioned in traditional society. In his major work, *Structure and Function in Primitive Society* (1952), he provided a rationale for analyzing social structure's relation to culture. His field work in the Andaman Islands and in Australia helped to provide ground-breaking contributions in the study of kinship. Out of his work, the field of structural-functionalism blossomed. He became an important figure in anthropology beginning in the 1930s, influencing the work of Gregory Bateson, Robert Redfield, and Erving Goffman. By the 1950s, sociologists such as Talcott Parsons had become popular by detailing the relationship between social structure and human action.

For Durkheim, and later for Radcliffe-Brown and Parsons, the individual was constituted by his or her place in the social system. All people could be traced back to specific structures that made them what they were—human outcomes of a system of social structures, situations, and human networks. Durkheim was a pioneer in this regard. His study of language, myth, and religion was his way of better understanding the dynamics of social cohesion, an interest that drove him his entire life. For Durkheim, people were primarily products of their society's collective conscience, as he called it. Few thoughts or sentiments could be developed outside social structures, certainly none outside language. Durkheim and his nephew Marcel Mauss (1872–1950), who gained renown as an anthropologist, looked at myth, ritual, and exchange activities in preliterate societies as elementary forms of language. These were codes that they believed could reveal the very nature of culture itself and could enhance one's understanding of the cognitive structures that helped to create them.

PARSONS AND SOCIAL STRUCTURE

In the 1930s, Harvard had emerged as the most prominent center of a new American sociology. Its emphasis was on a home grown, structuralist perspective. The work of Vilfredo Pareto, an Italian economist, assumed particular importance there and influenced rising stars such as George Homans, Joseph Schumpeter, and Talcott Parsons. Pareto had proposed a dynamic equilibrium evident in economies of healthy societies. Though a liberal, Pareto often toyed with socialist ideas but rejected them in favor of a free market economy. At Harvard in the 1930s and early 1940s, there arose a group of scholars who were often referred to as the "Pareto Circle". They took great interest in the writings of this sociologist/economist. Pareto posed an alternate structuralist view of society to that which had been established by left-leaning intellectuals of Europe. Interestingly, Pareto was bestowed with honors by the fascist regime of Mussolini just prior to his death.

Parsons, who had been influenced by Durkheim and Mauss, was also influenced by Pareto. He attempted to move structuralism in sociology back to a more conservative perspective. While acknowledging that structure was essential in social life, he contended that the frameworks or structures that comprised societies functioned primarily to produce patterns of interaction that maintained order. His emphasis on function, social order, stability, and equilibrium is what set his theories apart from many others at the time.

Parsons leaned heavily on a systems theory approach, which became popular in the 1950s and 1960s in the United States. Systems theory was indebted to the work of biologists such as Ludwig van Bertalanffy (1901–1972), the creator of General Systems Theory. According to this theory, actors are viewed as rational, goal-directed entities who work together in an almost mechanical fashion to achieve identifiable ends. This system was an ambitious paradigm that could be applied not only to biological organisms, but also to cybernetic machines and social systems. Such a perspective became particularly popular in the area of organizational theory—looking at how organizations maintain themselves in the face of disrupting internal and external forces. It also was central in the development of computer theory, particularly systems analysis.

One of Parsons' central concerns was the maintenance of order in society. Why didn't societies simply fall prey to the innate destructive disposition of the people who comprised them? He was interested in why people acted in a restrained fashion. In his work, *The Structure of Social Action* (1937), he saw human action as engendered by each society's norms and values. He viewed societies as self-regulating and sustaining systems of action. He described societies as goal-seeking systems that were comprised of a highly complex set of patterned human social behaviors that were associated with a particular physical environment. Parsons developed his own method to identify and analyze important system behaviors, which he called the AGIL Paradigm. This paradigm was a model used to assess what he saw as "functional imperatives" that kept all systems alive and well. AGIL stood for Adaptation, Goal Attainment, Integration of its components, and latency, or the period of maintenance. In Parsons AGIL Paradigm, adaptation had to do with a society's ability to interact with and to be sustained by its environment. The availability of natural resources might be an example of this process while goal attainment was the actual identification and ability to achieve the goals it had selected for itself. A society also needed to integrate any conflicting values so that there was harmony and order. Only in this way could goals be achieved. Finally, a society had to maintain order and stability in order to progress. Thus, any challenge to this progress had to be integrated or isolated so that order could be maintained.

Zygmunt Bauman (1978) describes Parsons' work as an extension of Edmund Husserl's phenomenology. However, unlike Husserl, who organized his ideas around transcendental subjectivity, Parsons organized his ideas around the transcendental actor. While he placed a theoretical emphasis on subjective consciousness, Parsons is primarily known as a theorist of social action and social systems. He saw action as basically rational and oriented toward an end. For him, everyone who acts has choices and operates within a framework of values supplied by society.

Parsons' work also built on the anthropology of Malinowski and Radcliffe-Brown in that it focused primarily on the relationship between structure and function with each subsystem contributing to the whole. It was also in keeping with the Pareto framework of social action theory in sociology. The Parsonian project aimed at discerning and describing how the interrelationships among the various social system and subsystem components (social, personal, cultural, biological) helped to order and stabilize societies. His work in this area of structural functionalism took him further away from his original interest in studying the production of human action. Drawing upon his training as an economist, Parsons constructed a theory of exchange wherein the various components of society contributed to one another to promote overall societal functionality. In this sense, society was some sort of organic machine, with its components working harmoniously to reproduce themselves. All societies needed to be mindful of those imperatives that kept them functioning: adaptation of each system to its broader environment, goal attainment within each system, integration of the various elements of each system, and latent pattern maintenance and tension management of each system.

It was Parsons' aim to construct an integrated theory of grand scale that could synthesize that which came before. While his chief influences were Max Weber and Emile Durkheim, his work was exceedingly more pragmatic. Emerging at the time it did, Parsons' work eschewed more radical elements of left conflict theory and pushed the notion of order and social stability. It shaped a whole generation of American sociologists in the 1940s and 1950s. He became chair of Harvard's sociology department in 1944 and was elected president of the American Sociological Association in 1949.

And while his work had an appeal in post–World War II United States, it was seen as failing to predict the social upheavals that would characterize the 1960s. Even in light of this, Parsons' work influenced sociology, particularly U.S. structuralist theory, for decades to come. His venture into the understanding of social processes and their relations to social structure was to lend itself to empirical applications.

LUHMANNIAN STRUCTURALISM

Similar in some ways to Parsons, and certainly no less prolific, was the German social theorist Niklas Luhmann (1927–1998). Luhmann was influenced by structuralists such as Malinowski and Radcliffe-Brown. He even studied with Parsons at Harvard in the early 1960s for a short while. Like Parsons, he drew on biological models, including systems theory. He views systems as comprised of real actions based on shared meanings and interpretations, and all actions are the result of institutionalized and consensual expectations. Unlike Parsons, however, Luhmann thought that consensus was not critical. Society appeared to be orderly despite the different value orientations of its members. In place of consensus, he posited that communication was much more essential. All social systems are communications systems. All socialization is processed through interpretation, and all social interpretation is predicated on communication. Thus, he believes systems are based on shared meaning (Luhmann 1984, p. 243). And while he agreed with Parsons that societies were comprised of systems, he did not believe that there has ever been one single, holistic system striving for equilibrium.

Luhmann looked at any system as defined by the boundary between itself and its environment. And for him, there was always a clear distinction between the system and its environment created by its boundaries. Outside the system is an environment seemingly characterized by meaninglessness and chaos to those within the system itself. While a system might use information or resources from that which is external to it, each system remains separate and distinct. All systems establish meaning within themselves, and they incorporate information from the external environment that, in turn, is digested and utilized.

Luhmann contended that society is comprised of several systems with overlapping and related parts. Systems in this sense include institutions such as education, politics, economy, and religion. All of these systems overlap and each is defined through its communication system. A significant difficulty in modern society is that the existence of any social system no longer depends on consensus or shared values. Very little exists in terms of a commonly lived life. Therefore, there is a much greater emphasis on compartmentalization, which means no system determines what happens in another system. Given this condition, conflicts are localized and prevented from spreading to other systems. Crisis in economy will not necessarily mean crisis in religion. In actuality, religion might assist in coping with that crisis. In a sense, this can be a built-in safety mechanism.

Luhmann's work puts a great deal of emphasis on trust as the basis for social order. He sees trust as particularly important in modern society where there are increasingly complex interdependencies. Not everyone can know everything, and one must rely on stranger-experts to build one's home and ensure its safety, to educate one with skills for survival, and fix one's subways, buses, railways, and cars. Thus the complexity of modern social systems requires considerable trust; but this dependence on others can equally engender mistrust.

STRUCTURAL INTIMACIES

Structuralism was perceived as the optimal means for understanding societies. And it was not much of a leap from perceiving structures external to the individual that guided social behavior to considering internal structures as responsible for social outcomes. The psychic aspects of structure had already been explored in psychology by Wilhelm Wundt (1832–1920) in the late 1800s. Like the sociologists who were interested in the workings of the basic components that comprised societies, Wundt was interested in the elements and structures constituting human consciousness and reducing them to their simplest sensate components. Wundt's student, Edward B. Titchener, more fully developed this structuralist perspective in psychology. Titchener (1929) hoped to discover and describe the structure of the mind in relation to the primitive elements of mental experience and functioning through the use of "scientific introspection," often using himself as the subject. He also believed he could capture and classify these components of mental cognition through cognitive experiments.

Sigmund Freud (1856–1939), in contrast, was central to the exploration of the structure of the unconscious mind. One's behavior could tell us much about the hidden unconscious. For Freud, the id, ego, and superego constituted basic psychic topographical structures and were central to social behavior.

As we will see in the next section, linguists such as Ferdinand de Saussure (1857–1913) worked to establish the earliest connections among culture, consciousness, and language. In this respect structuralism was an extension of the **Enlightenment Project** and the drive to categorize, classify, and find hidden causes for things. The Enlightenment Project was an attempt to prove that some sort of reason, some kind logic, guided everything and that there were discernible rules for it all. Unlike the critical theory of Marcuse, Adorno, and Horkheimer, structuralism rejected humanism and held onto positivism. Simply put, it was an attempt to pry open nature to reveal its hidden determinants.

STRUCTURALISM AND THE LINGUISTIC TURN

In the previous chapter, we saw that contemporary social theory has many roots, some planted more deeply than others. In this chapter, we now examine what is often referred to as the *linguistic turn* in structural theory. Such a turn constitutes brand new growth, not merely offshoots of existing thought. But to examine this topic, we need to discuss some of the intellectual history that brought about such a revolutionary approach to theory construction.

The linguistic turn refers to a relatively modern paradigm in philosophy, the humanities, and the social sciences that privileges language as the creator of the social world. While this notion has many sources, its genealogy can be traced back to the linguistic work done by early so-called structuralists such as Ferdinand de Saussure (1857–1913). But before examining some of his essential contributions to this revolution in social theory, it is important to recognize that such a revolution in social thought cannot be attributed to any single person, idea, or event. It is safer to say that the beginning of the twentieth century saw language as having potential not only to connect and divide the peoples of the world, but also to give meaning to that world.

Ludwig Wittgenstein (1889–1951), a student of Bertrand Russell at Cambridge University, inspired much of this linguistic turn in modern philosophy. He was profoundly interested in how sentences logically structured meaning and, in a sense, reality. For him, only words in the form of a logically constructed sentence could produce a thought. All thought had to emerge from language, and language set the boundaries of one's world. All meaning appeared to come from the use of words. All modern problems were seen as problems of meaning and language. According to Wittgenstein's major work, *Tractatus Logico-Philosophicus* (1922), the science and logic of language enables us to address these problems.

There are many different readings of Wittgenstein, many different interpretations of what he said. And there are at least two Wittgensteins: the earlier, more formal one guided by logic and mathematics, the one who believed language to be a clear and perfect expression of reality, and the later, a less formal one, the one who saw language as less ordered by established rules and more guided by play. His ideas changed significantly as he matured. Nevertheless, he was only one of several influences on the growing importance of language in philosophy and social theory. He was deeply concerned with structure. Saussure, who more directly influenced the course of modern social theory, was another important influence.

Ferdinand de Saussure (1857–1913) was a Swiss linguist who moved to Paris to teach ancient languages. His work profoundly influenced Wittgenstein. Though he never formally wrote on linguistics, he lectured extensively on the subject in his later life. His famous book, *Course in General Linguistics* (1910–1911), was a collection of his lectures that was edited by his students. Saussure asserted that words have little or no meaning if we take them out of context and can mean different things depending on how they are arranged in sentences. This was a challenge to traditional linguistics, which proposed that language was a unified field of study and that language was nothing more than a process of naming or labeling things.

Claiming that there are many histories of language, that there was no single history of language, Saussure went on to look carefully at the structure of language and how meaning was developed. He suggested that phonetic contrasts (how things are pronounced) allowed people to distinguish between words. We needed to be trained to listen to and decipher how speech is articulated in order to make sense of it. It was his assumption, though a mistaken one, that the sound representing the word had something to do with its historic meaning. It was his belief that the *rules* for language construction existed cross-culturally and operated at an unconscious, primal level. Phenomena such as **binary oppositions** were linguistic universals (i.e., hot versus cold, sweet versus sour, etc.). He attributed this to how our brains are structured. Accordingly, he insisted that structures existed at this deeper level of the unconscious and predisposed outcomes that enabled a system of classification and communication.

His science of **semiotics** or semiology examines not only how meaning is constituted, but also how the rules of language (such as grammar) determine how sentences and, in turn, meaning could be structured. For Saussure, all social meaning is constituted through signs and the relationships between and among them. He considered the **sign** as the basic unit of communication. It could be almost anything: a word, a sound, an object, a picture, and the like. It had to be significant to the culture in which it could be found. Saussure then broke the sign down into two components. One component was the *signifier*, or the physical form of the sign, be it the word, the photograph, or whatever else. The second component of the sign, he called the *signified*, which is the mental concept people of the culture associate with the signifier. Together, these constitute a sign. Fashion can be an example of this. Always what we wear is a sign. It has two components. For instance, the tie a man puts on is a signifier that conveys a meaning. The meaning it conveys is what it signifies (such as power). Taken together, the tie (signifier) and what it says (the signified) are a sign.

Saussure had a profound influence not only on philosophy and linguistics, but also on art and social science. However, the modern currents of structuralism are credited to the work of Roman Jakobson (1896–1982) and Noam Chomsky in linguistics and to Claude Levi-Strauss (1908–2009) in anthropology. Jakobson was in some ways a bridge to Levi-Strauss in that he attempted to connect the mental structures of language to kinship relations. He believed that the study of language allowed one to discern the basis of social formations. Levi-Strauss came into contact with Jakobson when he was teaching in New York during World War II.

The structural anthropology of Claude Levi-Strauss had a major impact on both the social sciences and the humanities. He borrowed heavily from Saussure, Jakobson, and later Chomsky, and concluded that deep mental structures both determined the form of language and conditioned cultural and personal outcomes. The nature and aim of such structures became the project of modern structuralism and modern linguistics. This was the basis of modern structuralism in the humanities and social sciences. Poststructuralism was a radical departure from this.

Levi-Strauss asserted that it was the aim of *his* structuralism to discover "unsuspected harmonies," which comprised formal universals reflecting the nature of human intelligence. These were referred to as "deep-structures". An example might be binary oppositions, which he saw as a primal element in all human thought and language. While Durkheim, Marx, and others had been looking at surface reality, this was a structure that went much deeper. He relied heavily on Saussure and drew on Freud to establish his unique approach. For Levi-Strauss, natural structures of the mind condition people cross-culturally to think in certain ways. And these inherent structures that determine language, also determine what type of culture people will create. He saw this evidenced in art, rituals, and customs.

In this type of structuralism, the unconscious internal rules guiding both language and behavior were seen as more important than the individual's conscious choices that also were guided by them. The individual was in this way minimally significant. For Levi-Strauss, the ultimate goal of human science was to "dissolve" the individual actor. Structuralism, in this sense, became inextricably linked to antihumanism. The person was seen as a direct result of these deep structures. This view, of course, put Levi-Strauss in direct opposition to existentialism as espoused by Sartre, his contemporary, whose humanistic philosophy saw the human condition as characterized by inordinate individual freedom resulting in groundlessness and anxiety.

Levi-Strauss's most significant work, *Anthropologie Structurale* (1958), focused on his new method. In this work, he proposed four elements that were to become central to structuralism. First of all, structuralism was to examine the unconscious infrastructure of all cultural phenomena. Second, it was to see all elements of the infrastructure as relational (not independent). Third, structuralism needed to be concerned with the system and not the individual. And fourth, it was to discover the laws underlying the organizing patterns of phenomena. In a sense, Levi-Strauss was successful in moving social theory toward the area of cognitive science that was primarily concerned with mechanisms of human thought. The human was viewed merely as a product of such inherent mechanisms, trapped by them in some ways even determined by them.

Levi-Strauss' structural anthropology was also an extension of semiology, which was established by Saussure. All human cultures had structures similar to language, and it was the work of the structural anthropologist to discover those cognitive structures that determined social activity and to understand the elements that comprised these structures that gave culture its meaning. Levi-Strauss must be credited with radically shifting the course of social theory in the twentieth century away from humanism. Levi-Strauss' position was that, by studying culturally interrelated signs, one could better understand the structure of relationships in any society. In fact, he believed the study of artifacts, rituals, roles, or anything taken in isolation lead nowhere unless one sought to understand how such things were internally interconnected. All such interconnections were seen as binary in nature as well as providing permanent, organized categories of experience.

ALTHUSSER AND MARXIAN STRUCTURALISM

Another version of structuralism was advanced after World War II by one of Levi-Strauss's brightest students, Louis Althusser (1918–1990). Althusser was a French philosopher and communist who helped to reinvent the works of Karl Marx. While Marx was considered by many as both a structuralist and a humanist, Althusser rejected the latter vision of Marx by suggesting that Marx's earlier, more humanistic work dealing with phenomena such as individual alienation was less mature (Althusser 1969). Althusser himself saw structure as the primary determinate of all social activity. He posited that all of the existing structures of society (eg. market, family, religion, and others) could be seen, in turn, as shaped by ideology that indoctrinates the individual from birth. For Althusser, ideology is an imaginary relationship of individuals to their material conditions of existence. Like Marx's notion of false consciousness, it exerts its power of domination by turning people into subjects and leading them to believe that they are autonomous actors when, in actuality, they are shaped by hidden ideological processes. In capitalistic societies, people's lives are scripted for them by the system's inherent and hidden ideology. This was indeed a pessimistic view.

Althusser borrows heavily from the work of Levi-Strauss in promoting the notion that all signifying processes are related to ideology, which shapes not only language but also myths, art, and rituals. Thus, ideology is embedded in the colonized mind, deep within the psyche. It becomes essential to personal consciousness and produces social structure (Althusser 1970). It is an imaginary relationship of individuals to their real conditions of existence. While individuals still view themselves as self-determining actors, they are actually turned into subjects and conditioned to reproduce the ideology that holds them in check. All along they assert that they are free, but under capitalism they never get the chance to be so.

For Althusser, all consciousness is inscribed in ideology. By ideology, he means codes or frameworks used to understand society. Mass media, which encodes the dominant ideology, produces narratives or texts that "interpellate the subject." This notion of interpellation is a rather complex one, but simply put, Althusser posits it as a "hailing" or "calling out" to someone, in this case, the object to whom the message is seemingly directed. This process is one that grabs the attention of the individual by signaling him or her and then making the individual engage in the practice of ideological construction—seeing the self as the consumer of the message or a subject, as a participant in the ideological process. Ideology creates roles and functions for people in society to occupy and act on. Thus everyone is called on to support a system that is against their own interests and promotes their own oppression.

Althusser depicts the system of capitalism as both *interpellation* and indoctrination of its subjects. While different components constitute the system, all (such as media, religion, education) are interconnected through ideology promoted by the state, what he refers to as the Ideological State Apparatus. The ideology is enforced by what he calls the Repressive State Apparatus, which consists of the military, the police, and prisons and works in a more coercive and violent fashion.

The structuralism of Althusser, which has a lineage stretching back to Saussure and Marx, gained considerable influence in the early 1970s. However, by the late 1970s, after he murdered his wife, many of his ideas fell into disfavor. His intractable structuralism was seemingly an obstacle for the more subjective tendencies in theory. Nevertheless, his work was continued and reformulated by his most brilliant student, Michel Foucault.

SEMIOTICS OF ROLAND BARTHES

In addition to his influence on the anthropology of Levi-Strauss, Saussure's ideas revolutionized literary criticism. Roland Barthes (1915–1980), an important French literary critic and sociologist, argued that literature, like other forms of communication, was a system of interpretive signs. Borrowing extensively from Saussure and significantly influenced by the work of Levi-Strauss, Barthes proposed that literary criticism was a science that needed to subscribe to the same investigative principles as structural linguistics. He attacked traditional criticism as bourgeois. He viewed it as hiding its own ideology or simply being unaware of it.

Barthes's work in semiology made extensive use of concepts developed by Saussure as well as Levi-Strauss to interpret the meaning of signs in literature, art, advertising, and in various aspects of popular culture. As a leftist intellectual, he hoped to "demystify" the reactionary elements inherent in that culture through interpretive processes. Some of his major works were published in French in the 1950s and included *Mythologies* (1971) and *Eiffel Tower and Other Mythologies* (1979); Barthes referred to them as "critical interrogations of the obvious." In these works, he questions hidden meanings underlying popular images displayed in film, television, magazines, fashion, the tabloid press, and cultural icons. It was his sense that there were messages in all of these that were not overt. Perhaps they were even unconsciously communicated. Nevertheless, they seemed to be powerful. While not discussed extensively today in textbooks on social theory, Barthes is critically important. His work is very much connected to that of Levi-Strauss and, of course, Saussure, yet he expands on the anthropological use of semiotics by taking it into the contemporary social realm and showing how myths become taken for granted as facts of nature in modern societies. He used his sharp understanding of language and sociology to demystify and to discuss the relationship of a multilayered culture that surrounds each individual to ideology. Like Althusser, he claimed that ideology holds a key place in the understanding of culture. Toward the end of his career, however, Barthes moved away from Saussurian structuralism. One of his more significant works, an essay entitled *"Death of the Author,"* was published in 1968. In it he proposed that the reader, not the author, brought essential meaning to any text. Focusing on the possible meaning given to a work by its author was a futile enterprise resulting in little of consequence. It was the reader who gave meaning by placing the text into a social context. This was to bring his work more in line with the emerging paradigm of poststructuralism as advanced by Jacques Derrida and others. It was also in tune with the new political emphasis of agency.

Psychoanalysis was also responding to the linguistic turn. In the 1940s and 1950s, Jacques Lacan, a French psychoanalyst trained in the Freudian tradition and a friend of Salvador Dali, Georges Bataille, Pablo Picasso, and other celebrities, began dabbling into the work of Levi-Strauss and connecting these ideas to those of Sigmund Freud. While Talcott Parsons was gaining much attention for his work in structural-functionalism, Lacan was giving lectures and organizing seminars in Paris to promote the ideas of Levi-Strauss. In attempting to break down false distinctions between self and society created by language, he moved psychoanalytic theory that much closer to sociology.

Borrowing from Hegel, Lacan saw language as the means through which the social world and the natural world were separated from one another. Through language, people became increasingly estranged both from nature and from one another. Language fragmented the world as well as the self. Like Barthes, Lacan saw language as incapable of accurately representing the world. Because words have multiple meanings, he proposed that the unconscious plays a very important role in how we use language. Words can cover up what is intended; they can also distort meaning. But slips of the tongue, jokes, and dreams are often ways in which hidden meaning is revealed.

Like Freud, Lacan proposes that dreams are a form of discourse hidden from the conscious mind. They are open to interpretation. But he takes this a step further by proposing that, like language, dreams are governed by linguistic mechanisms, particularly *metonymy* and metaphor. He is not as interested in the hidden message of the dream but rather the means by which the dream communicates.

JACQUES LACAN'S STRUCTURALISM

While most scholars currently view Jacques Lacan (1901–1981) as a poststructural theorist, it is important to recognize the impact that Levi-Strauss had on his work. As a psychoanalyst influenced by the linguistic turn and the work of Levi-Strauss, Lacan wanted to bring Freud's work closer to a place that could be integrated with this new discovery of the role of language in shaping the unconscious. Lacan sensed that Freud had already recognized (to some extent) that the unconscious was linguistically based. Without the work of Saussure, however, he was not able to articulate this idea. Lacan suggested, as did Levi-Strauss, that the unconscious was structured like a language. But he went further. Rather than seeing the unconscious governed by repressed instinctual desires, he viewed it as governed by the order of signifiers or the placement of words and symbols.

Lacan became central to the structuralist movement in a number of ways. Most importantly, he saw language as key to psychic life, and in this sense believed the unconscious to be structured like a language. It was his contention that the individual was *parle-etre* (the subject of speech) by which he meant that every aspect of the person's life, a life imbued from infancy with language, is a reflection of that language and all conscious life is perceived through the meanings that language bestows upon one's sensations. Only the unconscious is liberating because it is the initial registry without language—without words.

In 1953, however, Lacan dissociated himself from structuralism (Dosse 1997, p. 121). While he had originally subscribed to the structuralism of Levi-Strauss and Jakobson, he began to move further away from the belief that a science of linguistics could be applied to discover the unconscious.

By the mid-1970s, structuralism was in its death throes. It had come under attack by a host of brilliant intellectuals who saw the so-called logical tools of linguistic analysis as a dead end. It was also a victim of the social activist movements of the late 1960s. Structuralism was viewed by these new intellectuals as too closed off from social change, too disparaging of human initiative and rebellion. It was seen as static and ahistorical; many claimed that it reified social reality. Structuralists frequently engaged in grand theoretical speculations that were unverifiable, untestable. They disregarded the significance of power relations in the construction of meaning and in the use of words. Lacan and poststructuralism will be considered in more detail in Chapter 4. Lacan's work was to revolutionize how the unconscious was viewed in the last half of the twentieth century.

DID STRUCTURALISM FAIL?

More than twenty years ago, Anthony Giddens announced that both structuralism and poststructuralism had become "dead traditions." While they originally displayed promise and originality, they both failed to generate radical change in the way theorists understood things (Giddens 1987, p. 195).

Many would argue that structuralism did not fail at all. But this depends on the type of structuralism one is considering. The use of Saussurian structuralism in the social sciences might have already seen its apex. Nevertheless, sociologists today continue to see the structures of society as the object of their discipline's study. Survey courses in sociology usually start with a definition of social structure and then describe the components of the system (statuses, groups, roles, institutions, and networks) and their function in this abstract model. These elements of society are frequently seen as working together to maintain harmony and order. So most sociologists view the components of society as part of an overall social system. Viewing societies as social systems with interrelated parts can be traced back to the work of Herbert Spencer, Emile Durkheim, and later to Talcott Parsons and Robert Merton.

As already mentioned, Marx's work was exceedingly structuralist. Not only did he view the structure of capitalism as conditioning the development of material culture, but he also contended that it led people to see the world and view their place in it in a particular way. For him, the external structure conditioned one's perception and one's psychic world.

But certain types of structuralism fared worse than others. The heft of Parsons's structural functionalism gave way to a resounding collapse in the 1970s under the weight of European influences on theory, particularly the thrust of French structuralism and poststructuralism, which seemed less mechanical and more flexible. Most European theorists had already dismissed grand theoretical assumptions on which the Parsonian model was built. Structural functionalism was highly mechanistic. An attempt was made by Jeffrey Alexander (1984) from Yale to salvage what was left of the Parsonian paradigm and spark a renewed interest in Parsons' work. His reappraisal was eloquent and directed to closing some obvious gaps and flaws in the Parsonian approach (Alexander and Colomy 1990, pp. 39–43). But this bold effort at creating a "neofunctionalism" had few takers, even in the reactionary political climate of the 1980s when it was developed.

Still, it is important to see the relevance of other structural theory in dealing with macro-order issues such as advanced urbanization and globalization. For the most part, these theories still lean heavily on positivism and are broad in scope. They are frequently akin to the fields of economics and political science. Take, for instance, global theory advanced by Immanuel Wallerstein. In the mid-1970s, his *world systems theory* became very important as a means for understanding the currents of world development and underdevelopment and relations between wealthy states and those dependent on them. Unlike structural functionalism, its aim was much more limited. It still maintains a significant place in contemporary global studies. Yet, the most successful structural theories have moved away from grand theoretical modeling.

CONTEMPORARY STRUCTURAL THEORY: CRITIQUES OF CAPITAL ACCUMULATION

While sociologists have been deserting linguistically inspired structural theory in ever-increasing numbers, they have not abandoned structuralism per se. We will take up some of these structural theories in greater detail in the latter part of this text, but it is important to understand (through some examples) how contemporary structural theories rely on the past, whereas historicism has little or no place in cultural and linguistic structuralism, which tends to remain ahistorical.

Immanuel Wallerstein's work collapses the boundaries between sociology and the other social sciences. He posits a view of the world that is very structural but historical at the same time. This is quite different from linguistically driven structuralism. While Wallerstein's work gained greatest popularity in the 1970s, his theories still provide an important perspective from which to assess the processes that have come to be called globalization. He is contemporary in that his work has kept evolving. He is indeed a structuralist, but he is not concerned with deep structures that Levi-Strauss brought to the social sciences. His structures are the immediate scene on which human relations and struggles for power are played out. For Wallerstein (1974), the world is a broadly delineated economic entity not confined to political or cultural boundaries. This is a system with a unique division of labor, a set of geographic boundaries, and a specific life span. His notion of a world system is comprised of different subsystems—member groups and constituencies made up of a powerful core or center, a semiperiphery, and a periphery. Much of his structuralist conceptualization emerged from his work in postcolonial Africa and his Marxian or conflict orientation to social processes. Rather than discussing the bimodal relationship of powerful to less powerful states, imperial empires to postcolonial and colonial ones, he instead focuses on purposeful underdevelopment of peripheral areas by those nodes in command of inordinate economic and military power. Theories like his help sociologists to better conceptualize dynamic world processes.

Similar, more contemporary theories, grounded in macro-ordered structuralism, have attempted to grapple with issues of global dominance and the exercise of hegemonic power over the past few decades. Most of these theories have emerged from philosophers and social scientists. David Harvey, Saskia Sassen, Zygmunt Bauman, Anthony Giddens, Ihab Hassan, and Alex Callinicos all have approached globalization using different perspectives while still leaning heavily on structural explanations. Chapter 8 will be devoted to some of these ideas. Structural theory still permeates not only descriptions of macro-oriented global structures but local ones, too. Theories of community structure, organizational structure, and group structure often attempt to explain human action through assessing how things are organized and the mechanization of social relations.

RATIONAL CHOICE AND NETWORK THEORY

An important outgrowth of American structuralism was rational choice theory. Like Parsons' functional structuralism, *rational choice theory* has its roots in utilitarian economics, particularly in the ideas advanced in the Pareto Circle at Harvard. This theory assumes that action results from individual decision making, and that such decision making is a product of reason, which is driven by innately self-serving behavior.

In sociology, rational choice theory is frequently associated with exchange theory because it sees society as a social marketplace wherein tangible and intangible goods and services are exchanged. However, this perspective has not been as warmly received in sociology as it has in fields like political science or psychological behaviorism. Part of the reason is its relatively conservative view of society and its intellectual debt to capitalist free-market ideology. Still, even some structural Marxists support this perspective.

Not all exchange theory is rational choice, however. Many sociologists and anthropologists have recognized, since the studies of Bronislaw Malinowski and Marcel Mauss, that all exchange does not mean an attempt to somehow maximize profit. Many nonrational elements of exchange involve things such as custom, tradition, or even habit. Exchange is often part of a system of reciprocity that holds society together.

George Homans (1910–1989), an important sociologist in the early 1960s, was a pioneer in attempting to link exchange and rational choice theory in explaining social relations using behaviorist theory from psychology and basic economics. He asserted that people rationally wanted to maximize their rewards and minimize their hurt in their relations with others. It was obvious that he was greatly influenced by the behaviorist B. F. Skinner (1904–1990), who had gained considerable renown in the United States at this time.

Homans developed his exchange theory based on fundamental behaviorist principles in psychology and classical economics. In the late 1950s and early 1960s, Homans looked at social behavior as exchange. And he viewed exchange as the means through which social order was maintained. Focusing on the group, Homans contended that all interpersonal behavior is predicated on maximizing the outcome of each individual actor. Competition, cooperation, conformity, and authority rest on individuals' assessments of costs and benefits of all interpersonal relations.

Sociologist Peter Blau (1918–2002) developed a theory that was more or less a follow-up to Homans' exchange theory. Instead of focusing primarily on interpersonal elements of exchange, he looked at social structure and how it emerged as a consequence of these interactions. People seek attachment to others because they perceive such connections as rewarding. His primary aim was to describe the development and organization of groups and other social structures based on these exchanges. In fact, it was his sense that sociology's primary project should not be explaining individual behavior but explaining how the structural context of the social environment influences people's life choices (Blau 1975). In some ways he rejected rational choice while promoting "exchange" and at the same time admonishing sociologists to focus their sights on social structure, not individual behavior (Blau 1964; Molm 1997). Like most exchange theorists, however, Blau viewed societal-level structures as resulting primarily from individual choices, underscoring the notion that most structures are the result of people pursuing their own ends.

Another important architect of this type of theory was the renowned sociologist, James Coleman (1926–1995). Coleman was interested in applying social theory to public policy issues, and he found rational choice theory to be attractive to both liberal and conservative policy makers in the United States. The Coleman Report issued in 1966 promoted public school integration through a system of busing. This was the application of a perceived *Pareto optimum* to resolve the school segregation issue in the 1960s and 1970s. Based on his research, he found that, while black students would gain significantly from being sent to predominantly white schools, white students would not lose as much by being sent to schools in predominantly black neighborhoods. A number of municipalities embraced the report's recommendations with disastrous consequences. Coleman believed that nearly all social problems were predicated on interactions that could be reduced to individuals competing with one another for scarce resources, such as quality education.

Rational choice theory has also been closely aligned with mathematical and economic sociology and other methods of devising a calculus for human behavior. While adhering to a structural perspective, the approach here is a micro-order one as opposed to a macro-order one. Thus, critical choice theory is an attempt to scale back the ambitiousness of theoretical discourse.

STRUCTURALISM AND NETWORK ANALYSIS

Social network theory is a form of structuralism made popular in the 1960s and 1970s; it continues to have an important place in social theory today. Not exceedingly different from the systems approach to social relations, social network theory attempts to assess and interpret the structures of human interactive relations through diagrams and analyses of social interconnections, particularly in the area of communications. Social network theory maps human interrelations graphically and then describes the significance of these connections. Here the attributes of an individual are far less important than the individual's connections to others and the quality of these connections. As with most structural theories, the position of individual agency is frequently assigned less importance than to one's position within a network. It is hoped that by examining human connections, predictions of social outcomes of the individual and/or group can be made.

Network analysis claims to focus on the study of structure. A descendant of Durkheimian functionalism and British anthropological structuralism, its sense of deep structure is not some unspoken, unconscious, or mystical order inherent in the human psyche manifested in behavioral outcomes (Maryanski and Turner 1991). Network analysis views deep structure as "regular network patterns beneath the surface of regular social systems" (Wellman 1983, p. 157). Network theorists speak in terms of *ties* and *nodes*—a language quite foreign to most critical theorists. While its roots can be traced back to the anthropology of Radcliffe-Brown and others, it leans heavily away from hermeneutics and subjectivism. It places a much greater emphasis on quantitative methodologies and model building and might have more in common with exchange theory. Nevertheless, it has crossed paths with other structuralism on occasion.

Nearly all proponents of network analysis still adhere to the notion that structure is the primary object of sociological investigation. This approach is not meant to focus on the macro order at the expense of the micro order. Both large-scale structures and more intimate ones are deemed critically important. Still, network theory appears to be in the traditionalist camp. It is more favored by pragmatists and utilitarians. It is far more attuned to the positivist tradition in sociology.

Social network theorists measure flows and activity between nodes using the concept of degrees, or the number of direct connections a node has. Claude S. Fischer (Fischer, Jackson, Stueve, and Gerson 1977) of the University of California at Berkeley was an early proponent of network theory. He saw the usefulness of network analysis applied to the study of communities and cities. In fact, Berkeley's sociology department became somewhat of a center for such study when it recruited Manuel Castells, who explored global information networks.

Harrison C. White, working at Columbia University, had a profound impact on the direction network analysis would take. Throughout his career, which spans nearly fifty years, White has been involved in articulating theories of social structure ranging from kinship patterns in Australian aboriginal people to the modern structure of economic markets. His most recent work has attempted to identify those networks responsible for social control.

It is White's position that social structure both constrains and determines human behavior, including the behavior and control of large organizations and markets. Perhaps one of his most notable contributions to network analysis is the concept of vacancy chains in organizations. In his now classic *Chains of Opportunity* (2008), White identified the emergence of "holes" in organizational structures when people vacated their positions. These vacancy chains are thought to provide pathways for corporate career mobility. Vacancies, or jobs themselves, are considered every bit as important (if not more important) than the people who occupy them. For White, these chains give the organization a particular character, which allows advancement and job mobility. And within this framework White applies probability theory to predict the direction of flows and organizational change. While one cannot adequately summarize the expansive work of sociologists like White, such theorists still struggle in the realm of empiricism to apply models to predicting outcomes and have been met with varying degrees of success.

Bruno Latour (1987), a French sociologist and anthropologist, took network analysis in a very different direction. Actor network theory (ANT) is a theoretical perspective developed by Latour and Michel Calon, his colleague at École de Mines de Paris, where they studied the philosophy of science in the 1980s. ANT is an outgrowth of their work. For them, science is not fundamentally different from other social activities. Unlike other network theorists, they see no division between the natural world and the socially constructed one in that anything that lends itself to scientific analysis is a construction of human activity, especially scientific analysis itself. All of this is influenced by and created through symbolic meaning. ANT attempts to study (and map) the relationships among people, their ideas, and their things (their material objects). Alternately referred to as material semiotics, enrollment theory, and the sociology of translation, ANT has been much more a method of research than a theory. Still, ANT has come closer to incorporating into its analysis elements of poststructuralism that have continued to remain outside the more traditional forms of network analysis.

Despite the growth in the popularity of network analysis in the late 1990s and the first decade of the twenty-first century, it still has not received a place at the theoretical table. Part of the reason has to do with its position as a method that is both esoteric and outside the realm of cultural studies—an area that has significant representation in more contemporary sociology. Cultural studies readily embraces French structuralism and poststructuralism but remains skeptical of quantitative analysis and of positivism in general. Both characteristics are associated with network theory. In spite of Latour's attempt to bridge the divide, not much progress has been made in its integration into the mainstream.

Two important proponents of network theory, Mustafa Emirbayer and Jeff Goodwin (1994), have identified key weaknesses in the network literature. Recognizing the failure of network analysis to adequately explain issues of culture and social psychology, they have devised a relational paradigm that attempts to connect social network research to these important areas. Their recognition of the need for structuralism to better explain individual agency offers a chance for network analysis to become more fully integrated into more general theoretical discourse.

NARRATIVE AND SOCIAL THEORY

Narratology has assumed an important place in both social theory and research methods. If we were to look at prestructuralist anthropology and sociology, we would find a textual richness in how stories of human experiences were told and recorded. Cultural anthropology and the Chicago school of sociology of the 1920s are often full of rich and brilliant narratives of people's "own stories." Certainly, psychoanalytic theory and its focus on case presentation has long emphasized the personal narrative co-constructed by the analyst and the analysand. But under the structuralist banner, narratology has provided a perspective that challenges the early humanist inclinations of these disciplines. For the structuralist, narrative is less the story itself than how the story is constructed. It focuses on how meaning is shaped and assembled through the act of relating a story—through the use of narrative elements.

Vladimir Propp (1968), in his examination of Russian folktales in 1928, found that all of these narratives shared common characteristics that appear to remain constant over time. A finite set of actions are performed in all narratives, and a limited number of story elements can be found. Narratology attempts to discern the personal and psychological factors that drive actors and the issues and tasks they confront.

In a broad sense, narratology is any systematic study of narrative. As a term of distinction, it did not come into existence until 1969. Narratology was primarily a product of a mid-twentieth century structuralism that sought to comprehend recurrent patterns, themes, and elements of a human story. It was most certainly a product of the linguistic turn and the work of Saussure and Levi-Strauss. It sought to assess the taxonomy of the story by looking at the arrangement of its components.

Nearly all theories of narrative distinguish between *what* is narrated—that is, the story being told and *how* it is narrated and the *form* the narrative takes, which is often called the narrative. A narrative need not always be a verbal narration. It can be a picture, a film, a performance, or even a dream. For the purpose of analysis, it is distinct from the story—a sequence of events (eg., a storm, a murder, a funeral) involving characters who are agents of change, victims, bystanders, and the like. Therefore, great artistic works often constitute narratives as such.

Roland Barthes (1975), who recognized the origins of narratology in the work of Aristotle, took a leading role in constructing narrative theory embedded in the structuralism of his day. For Barthes, "no one can produce a narrative without referring himself to an implicit system of units and rules" (p. 238). Barthes saw Saussurian linguistics as providing the tools for the assessment and interpretation of narrative. He spoke of analysis in terms of *levels* and *units*. He posited that these levels and units are universal to every narrative. Levels are stratified ranges at which things happen that constitute ranges of analysis and understanding. For Barthes, however, units of narrative analysis are less linguistic than they are connotative. Every narrative has levels that enable one to explore meaning, levels or units that lend themselves to analysis. He views everything in the narrative as important: "It is not so much a matter of art (on the part of the narrator) as it is a matter of structure" (p. 244). Everything in the narrative has a purpose—everything in it is significant. Answering a telephone in the story or not answering the phone is a significant element as is any description of the phone itself. He breaks these down between functional and indexual elements. The functional units or levels have much to do with moving the story forward chronologically—this happened and then that. But the indexual speaks to a saturation of detail, a richness of subtle elements. However, Barthes warns that one should see temporality as a separate component of narrative and as something that can itself be analyzed for meaning. It is different from the logical relationship between story elements. Characters themselves constitute functional elements that need to be assessed for meaning. They represent *agents of action* or non action, but without them the narrative does not move along. This is true even when the actor is not explicit. Barthes also tells us of the critical importance of the narrator and to whom the narrative is given.

By the early 1970s, structuralism had reached its peak. Derrida was striking out against the rigidity of the formulaic endeavor. Barthes was to recognize the importance of the intersubjective in his assessment of narrative. In its more structural form, however, narratology was given little space in the human sciences. If it were not for Paul Ricoeur (1913–2005), structuralist narratology would not have been as widely accepted as a method of analysis in the social sciences and might have died an abrupt death. However, Ricoeur was an intellectual who could easily synthesize and integrate complex materials and see value in ideas that others might discard. Ricoeur's publication of *Time and Narrative* (1990) was a case in point. In this work, Ricoeur saw these two elements as intrinsically connected: narrative expressing time and time expressed through narrative. His theory of narrative is a reworking of Aristotle's notion of *mimesis*—"the desire to know," and "learning from inference." In contrast to one *mimesis*, he proposed three movements or stages. *Mimesis* is the prenarrative stage at which people perceive the world in a prefigured or nonstory form; it is where the world is already articulated in terms of signs and rules and norms, a social reality already mediated through symbolic representation. Mimesis2 is the stage at which the prenarrative form is configured into narrative form through what Ricoeur refers to as ***emplotment***: the folding together of events, characters, and dialogue into some sort of plot that makes story-sense. Finally mimesis3 represents the means through which narrative transfigures our ideas of the world. It is the point at which the plot is contextualized or decontextualized; it is a new creation that allows the person to understand his or her surroundings. This is how one makes sense of the world. For Ricoeur, the primary concern of narrative is coherence and structure and how narrative provides a critical determinant of action.

THE LEGACY OF STRUCTURALISM: THE STRUCTURE/ AGENCY DIVIDE

The structure-agency dualism animates much social theory today. That is, structuralism, as an impersonal set of social mechanisms versus the power of the autonomous actor to generate change, has produced a wealth of theoretical discourse. For die-hard structuralists, most social life is an outcome of social structure. Individual agency is seen here as a consequence of it. In this sense, the individual is a structural construction. Opposing this position are approaches such as phenomenology, interactionism, ethnomethodology, and other forms of social constructionism that emphasize the power of individual agents to construct and reconstruct their own social worlds, or at least to interpret them by interacting with similarly situated others. Of course, there is a middle ground wherein these two positions are viewed as complementary to one another. Interacting individuals are seen as creating these structures, which in turn impose themselves on the individuals who created the structures. In this sense, interaction is always viewed as a dynamic interactive process.

Nevertheless, debates continue in the social and behavioral sciences as to which position should be granted greater legitimacy. The structure-agency debate is frequently carried forward in the concept of *essentialism versus social constructionism*. Essentialism basically means that it is possible to discern the essence of anything objectively. Essentialists tend to believe that all objects, including human beings, have essential properties or essences. This notion is often attributed to Plato's theory of ideal forms. It is likely that an essentialist today would also be a structuralist. Social constructionists, on the other hand, reject the notion of fixed essences in social life; instead, they promote the idea that humans create the social world in which they live—a world that is ever-changing. Such thinkers tend toward poststructuralism.

The essentialist versus the social constructionist debate in sexual studies, for instance, is an outcome of how much social theory has been divided between two opposing camps. In this debate, essentialists still adamantly hold the position that sexual preference is an innate biological pattern that is somehow universally present in nature, and while there might be a certain number of people in all societies who are not heterosexual, those who are not are somehow preordained to be the way they are—genetically or otherwise. And then there are social constructionists who contend that sexual preference is merely a consequence of social dynamics and social control. What is normal and abnormal is viewed as socially constructed, as is every bit of sexuality itself. In some sense, this debate clearly reveals the importance of ideology that Althusser discussed in his work. First, whether one's sexual orientation is important has to do with ideology, consciousness, and power relations. Then one needs to assess whether a binary approach to the subject is or is not equally ideological.

Structuralism is alive and well in much of the social sciences. It remains a powerful force in sociology. Structuralists contend that cognitive frameworks as well as institutionalized norms structure the action of people in the social system. In some way, although people believe that they are helping to structure their own world, they are merely playing out their scripted assignments as actors in the system and helping to reproduce it. But such a position has been radically challenged by feminist theory and queer theory, which we will address in Chapters 6 and 9, respectively.

ANTHONY GIDDENS AND STRUCTURATION

Anthony Giddens's structuration theory promotes the importance of understanding society in terms of both structure and agency. Giddens contends that neither the individual nor the structures comprising society are in any way alone capable of explaining human behavior. He views all human action as embedded within some kind of social structure. But structures themselves are both a medium and a consequence of human actions that constitute them. He posits that structures create particular social practices that are arranged over time and space, but such practices cannot be viewed merely as the outcome of these structures. In this case, structures might be understood as rules and resources that comprise a social arrangement. They are the result of the dialectical interplay between structures and those who comprise them and individual responses to them. Giddens refers to the modality of a structural system, by which he means the ways in which structures are translated into human action. Accordingly, he identifies three types of structures present in all social systems (1) *signification*—how language produces meaning, (2) *legitimation*—how order is produced by social norms and rules, and (3) *domination*—how power emerges from the control of resources.

While Giddens sees people as fashioning themselves and their societies through language over time, he is critical of those structuralists, like Levi-Strauss, who see societies as structured *like* language. Rather, Giddens sees action structured through rules, which are in some ways the means through which we also establish and structure language. While some of these rules are specific and codified, others are taken for granted. Legitimation also draws on rules that have been established to justify human action. He sees most social action as rule-governed, but not everyone interprets rules in the same way. The same goes for the implementation of rules. Rules are often applied to situations and events in creative and transformative ways. Nevertheless, these rules, along with associated resources, are developed through interactive processes and constitute the institutions that constrain our actions. He argues that, because of the constant modification of interactions over time, it is impossible to establish theories of structural causation (Giddens 1987, p. 227).

Domination is an important means through which the system is ordered, especially where competition thrives. By domination, Giddens means power in a generalized sense. He is speaking about a transformative capacity to intervene in a given set of events and alter them. Mostly, this has to do with the control of resources, both allocative and authorative. While the first relates to material resources, the second is related to human activities themselves. Domination is significant in describing how the structure is ordered through rules and maintained.

For Giddens, structures are both constraining and enabling. They are not simply brought into existence by those who comprise them; they are continually being re-created by them. Structures are not rigid but are relatively flexible; they are often changing their form. Both consciousness and structure are produced by human interactions. Giddens refers to this re-creation as the *recursive* character of social life.

Giddens' focus is on a reconception of terms like *agency versus structure* and how they are used. He does not view society as a social structure or as the totality of individuals' actions. Instead he views society as a structuration process wherein individual actions both structure and are structured by these interactive processes. He focuses on the importance of reflexivity. By *reflexivity*, he means that actors are conscience beings having the ability to understand what they do when they are doing it (Giddens 1984).

Structuration theory requires that neither structure nor agency be given primacy. Giddens himself understands its limitations. Still his work has been criticized for the conflation of structure and agency as well as for giving significant preference to individual agency.

BOURDIEU'S HABITUS AND FIELD

Pierre Bourdieu's appraisal of structure and agency is expressed in his model of habitus and field (Bourdieu 1977). For Pierre Bourdieu (1930–2002), habitus represented the internalized mental, cognitive, and somatic structures that people use to interpret and assess the world. Many of these dispositions are socially acquired, gained unconsciously through experience in one's social environment.

Habitus is neither fixed nor rigid; it is neither rational nor logical. Rather, it is the product of one's personal and social history. It has a high degree of flexibility and interpretive creativity, despite the fact that it is a product of the social structure that it comes to represent.

For the individual, habitus establishes a set of personal and social parameters in terms of what is thinkable and unthinkable. It reproduces an internalized logic, and for nearly all people reading this text, it is the logic of capitalism. All of one's formative personal experiences are inscribed in it. In a sense, they are incorporated. Personal deportment, outlooks and opinions, and even bodily posture are derived from cultural conditioning and absorbed into the habitus. In a sense, it becomes an instrument for building a class-based society. It is simultaneously a producer and product of habitus.

Bourdieu envisions field as a structured system of social positions occupied by individuals and institutions. Each field has its own logic, its own belief system, and is comprised of a hierarchy of individuals who occupy power relationships to one another. It is here that the struggle over resources occurs. A society is primarily comprised of a collection of interrelated fields. Each of these has its own internal dynamics, with internal and external struggles for resources.

Inherent in Bourdieu's description of field is an internal order held together through some form of symbolic violence—struggles to control the resources that constitute the field. His theory attempts to provide a middle ground between structure and action, but in doing so, leans far more to the structuralist side. Habitus and field are also means by which Bourdieu attempted to theoretically navigate a course between the subjectivist cliff of phenomenology and the objectivist valley of structuralism. For his theory to work, he needs to reject extremes in order to develop his theory of action.

SOCIOLOGY AND POSTSTRUCTURALISM

Classical perspectives in sociology were usually classified as functionalist, conflict, or interactionist. These categories can be directly attributed to the concerns of the theorists who helped shape early sociology. They have historical relevance. Functionalism, as exemplified in the work of Emile Durkheim, saw society as comprised of social institutions, each of which performed a set of functions. Functionalists viewed society as constituting a system of interrelated parts that were self-regulating. Functionalism, like structuralism, focused on social infrastructure and not the individual actor.

Conflict theory, most associated with the work of Karl Marx, looked at issues such as the clash of classes emerging from market capitalism and the industrial revolution. While it also focused on the structures of societies, theorists such as Marx privileged economics and the power of capitalism. Conflict theory, like functionalist theory, tended to be theory on a grand scale. It took a very broad view of the social landscape.

In the early 1900s, a focus on individual perception was advanced by theorists such as George Herbert Mead and W. I. Thomas, who taught at the University of Chicago. Influenced by German romantic philosophers, these theorists maintained the notion that perceptions of interacting subjects played a key role in creating a type of truth, a type of reality. The importance of hermeneutics in sociology is very much connected to this perspective.

In many respects, poststructuralism was a breakaway faction of structuralism. Theorists such as Derrida were certainly influenced by the linguistic turn. But while most rejected the majority of Saussure's ideas about language, they found themselves still subscribing to one: that words themselves have no meaning; rather, it is the context in which they appear that gives them meaning. Obviously, there is recognition here in the existential notion of the meaninglessness and absurdity of life, but this is transformed into the meaninglessness of language taken out of context. While the structuralists saw meaning as conveyed by rules of structure, the poststructuralists generally asserted that it was the participant who constructed meaning. Instead of a search for hidden rules and structures, the poststructuralists attempted to examine just how meaning was socially constructed and how people interpreted the world. This was a shift from an emphasis on the signified to a focus on the signifier.

For the most part then, the poststructuralists see no objective reality at play, no essential form of stable structures determining outcomes. Poststructuralism investigates the instability of language and signs. Poststructuralists see no universal truth, but rather many truths. Language needs to be challenged as a power that oppresses people, imprisons them, and sometimes sets them free. It is not a conveyor of ultimate truth.

Poststructuralism today has gained enormous popularity in literary studies and has become an essential category of contemporary social theory. While many sociologists were not influenced by this perspective, many of the more contemporary social thinkers have been. Imbedded in poststructuralism, however, is structuralism itself. But before moving on to a more thorough assessment of poststructuralism, it is important to look at two of its major influences—hermeneutics and phenomenology. Both will be discussed in Chapter 3.

KEY TERMS

binary oppositions Two seemingly antagonistic concepts: good versus evil, black versus white, straight versus gay, male versus female, etc.

Enlightenment Project An 18th century intellectual movement begun in Europe aimed at establishing a rational, progressive, and cultivated society based upon the empirically discovered and/or logically deduced laws of human nature.

death of the author A poststructural notion developed by Roland Barthes in which he proposed that the reader, not the author, brought essential meaning to any text.

deep structure An abstract underlying structure that is the basis for other less salient structures.

emplotment A term developed by Ricoeur to describe the folding together of events and characters into a plot.

essentialism versus social constructionism The debate in philosophy and social theory about whether set, essentially inherent characteristics make people what they are or if they are constructed socially.

homeostasis A process through which a system maintains its own stability through internal equilibrium.

interpellation A term used by Althusser to mean the creation of a subject by someone in authority calling out to that subject, identifying it as such. The subject here is a person.

linguistic turn A relatively modern paradigm in philosophy, the humanities, and the social sciences that privileges language as the creator of the social world.

metonymy A figure of speech wherein one word is used to stand in for another word or phase. For instance, one might say, "The crown" to stand for "royalty," or "Washington" to stand for the U.S. federal government.

networks The structural linking of people and/or things through time and space.

network analysis The examination of the way people are linked together in social relationships. Network analysis views these social relationships in terms of ties and nodes: *nodes* are the individual actors; *ties* are the relationships between them.

Paretooptimum An exchange or action wherein no-one could be made better off without making someone else worse off.

parle-etre A concept of Lacan that proposes that every aspect of the person's life, a life imbued from infancy with language, is a reflection of that language and that all conscious life is perceived through the meanings that language bestows upon one's sensations. Only the unconscious is liberating because it is the initial registry without language of all experiences.

rational choice theory An American outgrowth of American structuralism and utilitarian economics that assumes that action results from individual decision making and that such decision making is a product of reason, which is driven by innately self-serving behavior.

reification The making or treating of an abstraction as though it were something real and concrete.

sign An analytical unit composed of the signifier and the signified.

signified The mental concept people of the culture associate with the signifier.

signifier The physical form of the sign.

semiotics The study of symbols and signs that are grouped into sign systems.

structure The organization of a group or society that may define its conditions and qualities.

structure versus agency The debate in philosophy and social theory about the nature, character, and limits of the individual's ability, or inability, to determine her or his own personal outcomes.

world systems theory An important theory developed by Immanuel Wallerstein as a tool to understand the currents of world development and underdevelopment—relations between wealthy states and those dependent on them.

adhering to a scientific worldview, holding that the sociologist needed to gain an understanding of the inner life of others through empathy, or *Einfühlung*. For Weber, *Verstehen* meant a systematic interpretative process that embraced an empathic understanding in which the sociologist places him- or herself in the life of the observed.

Hermeneutics entered the social sciences primarily through the work of Schleiermarcher and Dilthey. Dilthey also influenced Martin Heidegger's notion of hermeneutics and contributed to the early rise of existentialism and eventually poststructuralism. In terms of sociology, it would be difficult to conceive of the work of Max Weber, Georg Simmel, George Herbert Mead, Alfred Schutz, Harold Garkinkel, or Erving Goffman without him (Bakker 1999, p. 46). In the United States, what has come to be called symbolic interactionism had its origin primarily in the work of George Herbert Mead, W. I. Thomas, and Herbert Blumer. While Blumer is credited with coining the label, the ideas behind symbolic interaction had been around for a very long time.

George Herbert Mead (1863–1931), who had been a student of William James (the pragmatist at Harvard) taught in the philosophy department at the University of Chicago along with John Dewey. Both came into contact with William Isaac Thomas, a graduate student of sociology there. Mead put forth the notion that social reality was constructed by people interacting with one another. For him, like others schooled in linguistics, language was quite slippery—meanings could never be precise. Therefore, what words people choose to use and how people choose to hear these words might have little in common. Perception is always paramount. Beyond this, people are constantly playing roles—performing, if you will. These performances are based on what they perceive these roles to be—how they are interpreted. Thomas came to Chicago from a professorship at Oberlin. He already held a doctorate in literature and language but wanted to switch his career to sociology. In pursuit of a doctorate at the University of Chicago, he took courses with both Mead and Dewey, and was seen as having a significant influence on their work and ideas. By 1895, he was teaching alongside both and was on his way to becoming the founder and architect of Chicago School of Sociology.

Thomas understood the importance of texts and their meaning. He had studied in Germany, was familiar with Dilthey's work, and was well acquainted with the scholarly debates concerning empathetic research. His own work was to reflect his prioritizing of the situation and the personal perspective from within it. To present the reader with a human portrait of the Polish immigrant, he borrowed extensively from letters written by immigrants living in the United States to those abroad, from diaries, and the like. He understood fully the importance of the individual perspective in shaping the reality of the experience. In fact George Mead studied under Dilthey between 1889 and 1890 at Humboldt University in Berlin (Cook 1993, pp. 21–22). On his return to the United States, he incorporated much of Dilthey's work into his own. Thus, Mead and Thomas had already laid groundwork for introducing a more subjectivist orientation into American sociology. However, their work was to be eclipsed by a greater emphasis in the field on structure.

Herbert Blumer (1900–1987), who also studied at the University of Chicago, learned much from men who had been influenced by the German thinkers. But while he studied with Mead, Thomas was already gone from the University of Chicago when he came there to take his degree. So was Dewey. Although Blumer did not write very much, he was instrumental in helping to shape the American symbolic interactionist perspective. Still American sociology, particularly at the University of Chicago, was steadily trending toward greater empiricism.

FROM SYMBOLIC INTERACTION TO THE LIFE-WORLD

Symbolic interaction was an assortment of relatively sophisticated ideas on the importance of subjective perception filtered through American pragmatism. Blumer attempted to give it form as a unique American perspective. Essentially, this line of thought descended from German post-Enlightenment thinkers. Because of the position of the University of Chicago and its tools of intellectual dissemination, it became a central category of social theory. Out of Chicago was to emerge Erving Goffman, who had studied with Blumer and was indirectly influenced by Mead, but who was most profoundly influenced by the British anthropologists such as Alfred Radcliffe-Brown (Collins 1986). The notion of hermeneutics was viewed as a bit too subjectivist and incapable of lending itself to American empiricism. The same might be said for phenomenology, which never really caught on in American intellectual circles in its less pragmatic forms. Still symbolic interaction was the closest Americans came to a sophisticated, subjective theory. It combined social psychology with pragmatism in an attempt to explain the social construction of both the self and the other.

Phenomenology and hermeneutics have become central, however, to the construction and study of contemporary social theory. The world has changed radically from the turn of the twentieth century and the introduction of symbolic interaction theory in the United States. In many ways, America was separated from the European world and continental philosophy out of which more radical perspectives were launched. Many of these had to do with Marxism, structuralism, or psychoanalysis. Some had to do with the works of Kant, Hegel, or Nietzsche. Most of these ideas were vitally connected to the shifts in philosophical thought that hardly saw the light of day in the United States. In many ways the United States resisted such theory as too exotic and too left leaning.

It should be remembered that European philosophy and social theory took time to be translated and penetrate American scholarly circles. By the 1960s, the structural-functionalism of Parsons was the most popular theory in the United States. It was home grown. And there were attempts to export it to places that were consumed by ideas generated by Levi-Strauss, Althusser, and Sartre. This met with limited success. Even in the United States there were rumblings by leftist theorists, such as Alvin Gouldner (1970), that social thought was in trouble and that American structural-functionalism was a dead end.

Phenomenology was hardly on the American sociological radar when Peter Berger and Thomas Luckmann published their seminal *The Social Construction of Reality* in 1966. It was not so much a groundbreaking work, but it was a book that opened the eyes of many American theorists and challenged preconceived notions in the social sciences in general and sociology in particular. This book, more than any other, helped shift the perspective away from a shallow form of positivism and Parsonian sociology. And it was *The Social Construction of Reality* that championed phenomenology to a highly skeptical American academic audience.

Berger and Luckmann had both been students and later colleagues of Alfred Schutz, who inspired their work. They taught alongside him at the New School for Social Research in New York in the 1940s and 1950s. Schutz's most important work, *The Structures of the Life World* (first published in German in 1932 before he immigrated to the United States), was not translated into English until 1973.

Berger and Luckmann's book was an Americanized translation and reformulation of Alfred Shutz. Shutz had gained an influential position in Germany as an investment banker and economist by day and a philosopher by night. He had a personal acquaintance with Husserl. He was first and foremost a member of a right-wing faction of political economists who formed an intellectual circle around Ludwig von Mises in Vienna. While his take on Husserl's work was more grounded in social science, Husserl still recognized him as a phenomenologist. He is viewed by many as having synthesized the ideas of Dewey, Mead, and Husserl and having developed a phenomenology acceptable to Americans—a more accessible version of it with an emphasis on pragmatic action.

Although there are many versions of phenomenology, Edmund Husserl is generally credited with developing the phenomenological movement in the early 1900s. His stress on language and perception helped pave the way for a new type of understanding. To begin with, phenomenology is seen as the descriptive study of experiences. It was part of Husserl's philosophical project (his phenomenology) to gain certain and irrefutable (a priori) truths on which all knowledge of the world rests. This he would refer to as *first philosophy*—a type of thought on which all knowledge was based, from which all knowledge would advance. His philosophy was predicated on achieving apodictic (based in logic) certainty through the method of Cartesian doubt wherein nothing could be taken for granted. Descartes believed that one's senses could be lying and therefore sought a truth beyond what the body could perceive. He had hoped to study the world free from doubt.

Philosophy was viewed by Descartes and Husserl as an a priori science dealing with rational concepts and necessary truths. In constructing his philosophical approach, Husserl rejects naturalism and what he calls psychologism, wherein psychology and introspection form the foundation of philosophy. His philosophy of phenomenology is descriptive. It describes the world as it truly is—a world of things, a world of phenomena. Any object, value, or notion of which one is conscious is a legitimate target of phenomenological inquiry and description.

Husserl sees positivism as predicated on a meager foundation, such as "taken-for-granted" assumptions and presuppositions. He saw phenomenology as calling into question all the assumptions on which positivist knowledge rests.

For him, getting to the foundational core of things was to question how assumptions were made. It was not his intention necessarily to reject assumptions. To do this, he subscribed to reductionism—a shift of attention away from factuality and particularity toward universal qualities that constitute the essence of things. This shift would mean a reliance of intuition, which in a Cartesian sense was a direct awareness of what it is.

However, truth comes from insight and not from ordinary and natural generalizations. The quest of all phenomenology is to discover the inherent essences of the *appearances* of objects that comprise the world (the things themselves), as they are registered in one's consciousness. To do this, Husserl suggests a type of bracketing off of the natural and ordinary attitude toward things—a bracketing off of daily activity, eliminating doubt and skepticism and things considered to be self-evident. Thus, one enters into what he sees as a *life-world*—a place where objective thought and doubt are suspended. This life-world is a place of pure subjectivism. He calls for a transcendental-phenomenological reduction. Once we begin this type of exploration, we develop a transcendental ego, or pure consciousness. in which everything eventually can be seen as an object. Thus, the natural world, which is his target of exploration is a world comprised of objects. For Husserl, the phenomenologist needed to look at how objects that are taken for granted in everyday life constitute themselves in consciousness (Stewart and Mickunas 1990). Thus, phenomenology turns away from objects in the world and turns toward the subject as giving meaning to the world.

The big difference between Husserl and Heidegger, or Husserl and Schutz, was that Heidegger and Schutz rejected much of Husserl's early phenomenology, which was a quest for certain meaning attained only through bracketing-off the taken-for-granted life-world. Unlike Hursserl, both Heidegger and Schutz saw the everyday life-world as the source of all meaning, not the obstacle to attaining pure meaning, not something that prevented achieving certain meaning, as contended by Husserl. It was attempting to better understand the taken-for-granted life-world that eventually was the foundation for late Husserlian thought and the starting point for Heidegger's and Schutz's phenomenological work. Husserl's earliest work appeared almost mystical and cultist; the notion of a transcendental consciousness was a consciousness of exception associated with pure reason. Few would ever have the ability to attain it. Such problematic elements of Husserl's work were smoothed over and modern phenomenologists saw all meaning emerging from interpretation. This was indeed a position that could be more easily sold to U.S. academics. It was far less elitist and more democratic in a populist sense of the term.

ALFRED SCHUTZ AND SOCIAL THEORY

Alfred Schutz (1899–1959) had been influenced by Husserl's writing and saw the potential in phenomenology for being a method of social investigation. Coming to the United States in 1939, he saw value in connecting the phenomenological world to American pragmatism.

Schutz's work with the Vienna Circle (von Mises's group) had encouraged him to take a very close look at the contributions of Max Weber. He saw in Weber's notion of *Verstehen* the potential for explaining behavior in the social world and how meaning was constructed therein. The central problem he saw in Weber was his failure to come to grips with this issue philosophically. For Schutz, people are continuously involved in the project of making sense of the world in which they live, and they do this through interacting with others. Through these interactions, meaning and consciousness are acquired.

Schutz contends that sociology needs to uncover what he views as *typifications* through which individuals intersubjectively organize their actions and produce commonsense knowledge. In other words, people have a sense of the world and objects in it; they have their own experiences from which they draw to frame new perceptions. Actors have stock knowledge that allows them to make cohesive sense of the world. Objects that constitute the world are perceived through their typicality—anticipated qualities that come from past experiences. In fact, this notion of typification is loosely drawn from Plato. People have a sense of what a table is and therefore know one when they see one. But one's typification and the real thing are not one and the same. In some sense Schutz sees this typification as being related to Weber's notion of *ideal type*.

Borrowing from Husserl, Schutz contends that taken-for-granted assumptions underlie most every day practices of people, and these assumptions tend to be hidden in plain sight, just like typifications. People see other people in this way. They see people as having general qualities something like their own. For Schutz, social theorists need to comprehend how people come to understand one another intersubjectively as people and how they make sense of their social world, how they establish order out of seeming chaos, and how they create the life-world. He asserts that, unlike the positivist, who collects facts that represent real objects, the phenomenologist explores mutually constructed meaning through attempting to understand the actor's position in the world and his or her situation in it. Of critical importance here is the actor's intention, which can explain much. Here conceptual and linguistic analysis, hermeneutical method and praxis, historical and critical methods, and logic and qualitative interviews come into play (Wilson 2002).

Schutz believes that in the *intersubjective* life-world, rather than the world of the mind (which is often the world of sociologists and philosophers), actors both create meaning and are constrained by preexisting meanings. He sees typifications as the means through which people (common sense actors) organize their world of things and ideas. This everyday knowledge of everyday people, a knowledge based on subjective typifications, seems to constitute the basis of all interactions in the life-world. But he recognizes that this knowledge is always in flux, and that living in the life-world enlarges and modifies our knowledge of it.

It is from this that Schutz develops his notion of action. He is careful to distinguish *acts* from *actions*. Acts are completed actions. Actions are intended—directed toward the future and predicated on typifications. Experience from past actions or acts provide, for what he refers to as the "knowledge at hand," enabling people to project from the past into the future. The actor learns from past experiences and projects these experiences into the future, believing that he or she can accomplish this new task based on an experience of doing something like this before. The meaning of the act is always grounded in time or temporality. Meaning is essential to the act itself and always directed toward achieving certain imagined goals. Thus the imagined goal is the projected act. It is also time-transcendent in that it is not based on current ego-awareness but rather on past acts and visions of outcomes. For Schutz, the actor makes a choice among the various imagined courses of action to achieve an imagined goal. This process is constituted by a plan, which consists of means and goals. And it is only through awareness of such plans that an outsider can ascertain social phenomena. To ascertain the meaning of plans, one needs to grasp the knowledge-at-hand, which is comprised of typifications. It is Schutz's further assertion that most of the typifications that comprise the knowledge at hand are in reality social constructions. They have little to do with the actor's personal awareness and more to do with societal constructions such as laws, customs, regulations that are frequently distant from the personal level. He sees these social constructions as constituting ideal types in a Weberian sense.

Schutz's social theory proposes that there are three basic ways by which intersubjective awareness or understanding of social reality is achieved by actors of the life-world: *the "we" relationship, the "thou" relationship*, and *the "they" relationship*. By *the "we" relationship*, Schutz means that actors are both aware of each other and know that this awareness exists in the other. Through communicative action, they come to understand their respective meanings, which enable them to understand one another's motives for action. Nonreciprocality of awareness constitutes what he calls *the "thou" relationship*. Here, the actor's awareness of the other actor's motive is not reciprocated and therefore communication is relegated to so-called objective and anonymous types of meaning. Frequently this is the bureaucratized or instrumental form of behavior. However, there is an even more anonymous type of social relationship. Schutz refers to this as *the "they" relationship*. To grasp the meaning of an actor's motives in this relationship, one must rely on ideal typical constructions, or what is referred to by Schutz as course-of-action types. This basically consists of typical motives ascribed to certain types of actors. A second type of "they" relationship is one wherein individuals are seen as functioning in specific personal roles.

Actors appear to be reactive elements locked into a structuralist formulation wherein decisions to act are based solely on typifications. Schutz does not fail to recognize that unique events do occur. But expectations of future occurrences seem to deny the possibility that any future occurrences are radically unique to an individual or might yield radically different outcomes. In a sense, this typically structuralist position mitigates against any radical form of change. In fact, Schutz contends that the "knowledge at hand" that constitutes the basis of all human action is not really individually constructed, but rather prescribed by society, specifically by the in-group subculture (culture of the group within the larger group) to which the actor belongs. And such knowledge is unquestionably accepted there. There is something inherently conservative in his position that keeps the world operating in a state of equilibrium. And there is something lacking in the commonsense actors who constitute the life-world (Koppl 2001, p. 186).

Schutz's action theory is a relatively controversial notion, one that seems to have evolved from his associations with the Austrian school. For Schutz, all people act and all acting people "choose". They deliberate and choose to buy one thing and not another, to go here and not there, for example. Here, he borrows from pragmatists such as Dewey to support this notion. He believes that people design a plan for themselves, a project, and imagine the consequences based on their plan. Thus, people are planning animals. They see the end before they select the means. Schutz sees the life-world as comprised of rational free actors—maximizing their decisions and learning from past decisions.

Some have argued that Schutz's phenomenological theory is not phenomenology at all (at least in the philosophical sense of the term) and that his work was really a distortion of both Husserl and Weber (Best 1975; Zaret 1980; Prendergast 1986; Campbell 1996). Schutz's attack on Talcott Parsons' action paradigm was also seen by Parsons himself as a distortion of his work (Giddens 1979). Still Schutz did help to pique the American interest in interpretive social research and theory of social construction. One of his strongest supporters was Harold Garfinkel, a student of Talcott Parsons at Harvard, who used Schutz's work to develop *ethnomethodology*, which became popular in the 1960s.

ETHNOMETHODOLOGY

A truly Americanized translation of phenomenology was developed by Harold Garfinkel (1917–2011) and popularized in the late 1960s. Weak on theory but strong on theatric method, Garfinkel's approach gave relief to sociologists seeking an alternative to boring empirical positivism and the staid but heady theory of Parsons. Keeping within the conservative tradition of American sociology, ethnomethodology gathered a strong group of followers. In some ways this method was a return to what sociologists loved most—a study of people and their day-to-day activities.

While Garfinkel had been tinkering with ethnomethodology since the 1940s, it was the popularization of Schutz's phenomenology that helped jumpstart it. In 1967 he published *Studies in Ethnomethodology*, in which he described ethnomethodology as the "investigation of the rational properties of indexical expressions and other practical actions as contingent ongoing accomplishments of organized artful practices of everyday life" (Garfinkel 1967, p. 11). In other words, it was a systematic attempt to organize, classify, and understand unremarkable human interactions and to show how these both constitute and explain the social order.

In ethnomethodological practice, sociologists attempt to uncover, demystify, and identify taken-for-granted assumptions about the micro-ordered social world—a world of personal interactions. Garfinkel had wanted to uncover what he called background assumptions, to make explicit Schutz's idea of knowledge-at-hand and typifications. Actors are viewed as nonreflexive and unaware of what they most take for granted. Most human interaction is routine. Garfinkel's work is closely related to structural anthropology, but without much of the intellectual weightiness. He wanted to know how and why people do what they do, what they actually mean when they say something, and toward this end he developed a variety of techniques, such as examination of colloquy. In examination of colloquy, actual verbal exchanges are recorded on the left side of the page; what was understood by the words is listed on the right. For instance:

I got new shoelaces for my shoes.   *As you will remember I broke a shoelace on one of my brown oxfords the other day so I stopped to get some new laces.*

The point here is that many things are left unsaid in colloquy that are intended. Another version of this is when colloquy is challenged as though the listener does not receive the unstated but necessarily implied information. For example, if someone said, "I got new shoelaces for my shoes," the ethnomethodologist would challenge the meaning content. "What do you mean?" Does it mean "I went to a store and paid money for a new pair of brown laces for my brown shoes because I broke a lace on my brown oxfords on Tuesday?" Or does it mean more or less than this? Garfinkel extracted from this type of exchange key rules used to organize and weigh information.

Again, such a small space in a text on social theory does not permit elaboration of some of Garfinkel's more interesting or important methods and ideas. But there appeared to be a lot of room for slippage in his approach, which brought a wealth of reaction to ethnomethodology, some of which was highly critical (Atkinson 1988).

The failure of Garfinkel's ethnomethodology and Schuzt's phenomenology to account for the revolutionary ferment of the 1960s underscored their emphasis on human conformity, or what some saw as "going along." The political and cultural upheavals sweeping the world were not part of their discussions. Still, as an analytic tool, ethnomethodology retains an important place in sociology today.

MAURICE MERLEAU-PONTY

Although there were some subtle references, little *explicit* philosophy entered into Garfinkel's ethnomethodology, certainly not much of the imported stuff. In fact, the accusation has been made that ethnomethodology was steeped in ideology (Gleason and Eban 1976). It was Maurice Merleau-Ponty (1908–1961) who helped to radicalize philosophical phenomenology and infuse it into the ongoing discourse on structuralism and poststructuralism.

Merleau-Ponty was a very close friend of Jean Paul Sartre—the renowned existentialist. Along with Sartre, he was the co-founder and editor of *Les temps modernes* from 1945 to 1952. *Le temps modernes* was a journal publishing cutting-edge ideas in social thought that were written and read by some of the leading French intellectuals of the day, including Levi-Strauss, Lacan, and Foucault.

Merleau-Ponty would eventually break with Sartre and join forces with the structuralists, whose ideas were in ascendancy.

Merleau-Ponty's central work, *Phenomenology and Perception* (1962), focuses on an effort to come to terms with the challenges of empiricism and rationalism in Cartesian philosophy. In his work, he is highly critical of objective thought, which he views as a second-order expression of the world. Still he is not dismissive of science. He wants to find a way of connecting it to phenomenology. In *Phenomenology of Perception* he attempts to come to terms with Husserl's transcendental phenomenology as well as Martin Heidegger's work in existentialism. In spite of his strong background in psychology, Merleau-Ponty asserted that perception was *not* a product of sensations, but rather a primordial openness to the life-world. He viewed the body as a permanent condition of experience reflective of a perpetual openness to that world. Our bodies are made up of the same stuff as the world around it; it is familiar with that world. He rejects the mind–body dualism promoted by Descartes and in its place posits the notions of ***corporality of consciousness*** and ***intentionality of the body***. He views both as elements of these elements as parts of the preconscious. His work places an emphasis on the physical and biological as the basis for perception. Consciousness is not something he viewed as emerging only from one's mind.

The basis of a person's contact with the world was thought to be through one's body and not through a consciousness that was somehow removed from external stimuli, as was proposed by the positivists. Rather, consciousness is seen as the body projecting itself onto the world. It provides sort of a bridge between subject and object. In moving through the world, the body provided objects one encountered with a presence. The presence of such objects was confirmed by one's perception and the perceptions and behaviors of others. This presence was constituted by what Merleau-Ponty viewed as an intersubjective experience. By intersubjective, he meant that perception is only confirmed by others and cannot be confirmed subjectively. However, such perception of the world of objects is never definite; it is always open and ambiguous. For Merleau-Ponty, perception originates in the external stimuli as discovered by the body, and there can be no objects in the actor's world without perception of them. All perceptions end in objects. Merleau-Ponty rejected Husserl's transcendentalism. For Merleau-Ponty, belief in the world was the person's existential commitment. All objects become objects through encounters with them; they are products of human intentionality in that they need to be dealt with and cannot be ignored.

Merleau-Ponty was critical of the classical approach to the human sciences, especially sociology, that emphasized empiricism and naturalism. "[S]ociology always spoke as if it could roam over the object of its investigation at will—the sociologist was the absolute observer. What was lacking was the patient penetration of its object, communication with it" (Merleau-Ponty 1962, p. 115). He rejected much of the work of Emile Durkheim—especially Durkheim's contention that social facts existed in the world and could be discovered through positivism. He viewed Durkheim's theory of society as particularly flawed and his notion of social cohesion and collective consciousness unfounded. However, he found greater resonance with the work of Marcel Mauss and later with Claude Levi-Strauss. He believed that it was the anthropologist Levi-Strauss who offered the human sciences a closer path to phenomenology. Here was a blatant rejection of positivism and a move toward a more phenomenological position.

In the place of the Durkheimion belief in the centrality of community, Merleau-Ponty substituted the primacy of intersubjectivity—what he saw as the living relationship and tension among individuals (Merleau-Ponty 1962, pp. 114–115). In fact, he rejected what he viewed as the sociological imperative at that time, especially Durkheim's attempt to find the meaning of society in the social cohesion produced by religion rather than finding it in interpersonal understanding. Mauss and Levi-Strauss seemed to give a glimmer of hope to the human sciences, finding their way out of their ontological dead-end pursued by Durkheim. For Mauss, society was a totality where phenomena give mutual expression to each other to reveal the same theme (cited in Schmidt 1985, p. 49).

Merleau-Ponty did not reject the concept of a social fact out of hand, but he adamantly dismissed Durkheim's notion that related such facts to cause and effect. He saw the social fact as an intersubjective construction—an efficacious system of symbols. But he could not agree with the subject/object stance of sociological investigation.

Compared to Schutz, Merleau-Ponty operated within the realm of French Marxism and radicalism. His difficulties with Sartre over politics aside, he was disgusted by the Soviet Union's betrayal of Marxist humanist principles. Though he deplored Soviet Marxism and was highly critical of it, he never yielded his belief in the need for a classless society, nor in the corrosive impact of capitalism on the general social well-being. He found in Marxism an invaluable critique of modern capitalism and a promise for the future: "Marxism is not just any hypothesis that might be replaced tomorrow by some other. It is the simple statement of those conditions without which there would be neither any humanism . . . nor any rationality in history. In this sense Marxism is not a philosophy of history; it is *the* philosophy of history and to denounce it is to dig the grave of Reason in history. After that there can be no more dreams or adventures" (Merleau-Ponty, 1969 p. 153).

Merleau-Ponty's phenomenology went on to strongly influence the work of numerous social theorists, and had a particularly profound effect on the work of Pierre Bourdieu, who will be discussed later.

PAUL RICOEUR: THE TEXTUAL UNDERSTANDING OF SOCIAL LIFE

Like Merleau-Ponty, Paul Ricoeur's earlier work can be classified as an existential phenomenology. In a broad sense, his was a search for a clear understanding of the existential notion of being and insights into who we are. Paul Ricoeur (1913–2005) was schooled in theology and biblical hermeneutics, and he drew frequently on these ideas. His work firmly crossed over into the secular realm, establishing a dialectic between science and subjectivism—the material world and the phenomenological one. Ricoeur's social theory places great emphasis on textual readings. And as noted previously, he promoted narratology as an instrument of analysis that could provide exceptional insights.

Ricoeur (1971) contributed greatly to the human sciences, especially in his hermeneutic anthropology. Here, one comes to see how he understands the construction of meaning through reading texts (in its broadest sense). It was Ricoeur's contention that structural linguistics could provide the basis for the construction of critical interpretive theory rooted in the logic of the human sciences (Ulin 1992). Like Dilthey, he asserts that the search for meaning is closely tied to issues of time and history. Hermeneutic anthropology has focused on the intersubjective processes of understanding and recognizes time as a critical variable for interpretation (Agar 1980).

Essential to Ricoeur's work is also the notion that meaningful human action can be considered a text and is subject to the same hermeneutic rules of analysis. Through objectification of human action (like objectification and fixation of writing), action becomes part of discourse and constitutes a delineated pattern that needs to be interpreted. Ricoeur posits that action (a) has the propositional structure of a locutionary act; (b) can be detached from its agent (just as a text can be detached from the author) and can therefore develop consequences of its own; (c) transcends its relationship to the initial situation that brought it about, and in so doing is emancipated from that context; and (d) is an open work, which means that it is open to interpretation by all—no one is more privileged than any other in interpreting it.

Ricoeur wanted to tackle what he and others have viewed as the dialectical nature of *Erkären* (explanation) and *Verstehen* (understanding) in the social sciences. This is seemingly the same sort of antagonism between empirical description and subjective interpretation that has long divided human science methodologies. Ricoeur's position is that a theory of textual analysis can provide an intersubjective approach to understanding all meaningful human action—an approach that is capable of transcending such divisions.

Perhaps Ricoeur's notion of the **hermeneutic circle** best represents the effort to connect subject/object as well as the quantitative and qualitative ways of explaining and understanding all meaningful action as well as all discourse. The circle is one of awareness that moves from naïve understanding to a deeper comprehension, in which the interpreter understands only parts of the text in relation to the whole and then moves on to understand the whole of the text in relation to its parts.

Ricoeur made a serious effort to link his hermeneutics to the human sciences with rather mixed results. In a series of lectures given at the University of Chicago in the fall of 1975, he established an ideology/utopia framework for understanding most classical social theory and what Lacan referred to as the *Social Imaginary*—the symbols, laws, institutions, and values that are common in a particular society. Although the paradigm of ideology/utopia was supposed to give these lectures some degree of coherence, it appeared to restrict Ricoeur's treatment and focus of essential contributors to social theory, including Marx, Weber, Mannheim, Geertz, Althusser, Habermas, and others. Nevertheless these lectures give us important insights into his unique understanding of the social and human sciences.

Ricoeur proposed that every society participates in a *sociopolitical imaginaire* that represents symbolic or mythic discourses that serve to guide social and political behavior of a group. Through the telling and retelling of their own stories, cultures create and re-create themselves. He saw the *imaginaire* as consisting of two elements: the social imaginary of ideology that reaffirms a society's identity by articulating its foundational symbols and forms the basis of a shared identity, and the social imaginary of utopia that provides a redescription of social life—one that calls into question the existing imaginary and provides an alternative that challenges the existing ideology. The tension between these two is fundamental to Ricoeur's social theory. Accordingly, he views the enterprise of hermeneutic human science as rearticulating ideology while finding a way to bring utopia closer.

EMMANUEL LEVINAS

Perhaps one of the most influential figures in modern phenomenology was Emmanuel Levinas (1906–1995). He was born to a relatively poor Jewish family in Kovno, Luthuania, and moved to France in 1923. At the University of Strasbourg in France, he studied psychology with Charles Blondell and sociology with Maurice Halbwachs (a student of Henri Bergson who had developed the concept of collective memory). It was Halbwach's contention that memories, despite their personal nature, could never exist outside a social context and that they are always constructed and edited against a backdrop of collective narratives. In 1928, Levinas went to Freiburg University to study with Edmund Husserl and Martin Heidegger. He is often credited with introducing Husserl's work to France and has been also credited with popularizing the work of Heidegger. Like Merleau-Ponty, Levinas was another source of existential phenomenology.

Levinas's objective was to develop a philosophy that would challenge the ethically neutral tradition of ontology. His is a phenomenology of the lived experience in the world, one that explores the meaning of intersubjectivity that begins with an encounter with another (*autrui*) and recognition of some personal aspect of the self through the existence of the other. But it negates the existence of neither the subject nor the object. The subject welcomes the other. Levinas rejects an ontology that attempts to reduce the Other to the Same, or to merge the Other with some mythical Totality. He finds this homogeneity, this totalism, to be characteristic of western Enlightenment thought. In his work, he senses a narcissism that guides this ontological disdain for otherness and craves homogenization. Levinas recognizes the value of otherness and does not shirk a human responsibility to know it in all of its differences, to welcome it and to celebrate it—to come to terms with it. This challenge to the ethos of Sameness pushes Levinas's philosophy into the realm of ethics. Such ethics have little to do with a code of morality or set of values; instead ethics represent the challenge to Sameness.

Levinas believed that the ethos of Sameness is manifested in a couple of ways. First, Otherness is frequently robbed of its uniqueness by being approached only on the terms of the self. The self looks at the other only from its protected perspective. He refers to this as egology, which promotes a sameness in the world that does not exist. Second, the self and the other are viewed as aspects of a total system; thus, the other is denied a reality of his or her own. Here, Levinas points to Heidegger's notion of Being that transcends the recognition of difference, seeing each actor as a mere manifestation of that Being. Finally, Levinas views perception of another as a threat to desired homeostasis and therefore there is an attempt to synthesize this Other into the mythical whole so it can no longer be a threat to stability and order.

This mythical totality or wholeness concerns Levinas. For him this aspect of Enlightenment thought has led to totalitarianism, domination, racism, and the like. "Therein without their knowledge individuals are reduced to bearers of forces which command them without their knowledge. Individuals borrow from this totality their meaning" (Levinas 1969, p. 21). This puts him at odds with important essentials of structuralism. Furthermore, it identifies him as a radical humanist. He views the first philosophy of ontology as a philosophy of power. Here, there is need for synthesis and domination.

C. Fred Alford (2002) draws a number of similarities between Levinas and the Frankfurt school thinkers, particularly Horkheimer and Adorno. (One might also add Fromm.) Alford suggests that these theorists challenge in their work the western emphasis on escape from difference. They recognize the closely held western belief that difference or otherness constitutes a major source of alienation and fear. Both the Frankfurt school and Levinas see ideology as a means used to address such fears. They concern themselves with the means used to dissolve difference. Still Alford rejects the value of Levinas as a critical social theorist because Alford views Levinas' interest as verging more on the mythical elements of hermeneutics rather than on grounded reason—on nonbeing as opposed to Being.

The spiritual elements of Levinas' work are often thought to be associated with his study of the Talmud. The tragedy of the Holocaust took much of his family. He himself served time in a prisoner of war camp during World War II. His turn to Judiasm occurred after the war. Throughout his Talmudic writings, the notion of Transcendence persists. Here, one can see the spontaneity of responsibility for another. But Levinas also promotes what he views as an inherent responsibility in all people for all others. His notion of subjectivity is a welcoming of otherness; it is the good host to the other and responsible for its well-being. Goodness, peace, love, and generosity are not values in themselves; they come from our encounter with the other. At each of these encounters, we can choose love or hate, peace or war, or other things that rest in between. In his phenomenological writings Levinas develops a theory of unlimited obligation (Blum 1983). He is rejecting the individualistic tradition of ethics espoused by thinkers such as John Rawls, where people act to maximize benefit to themselves. Accordingly, all people have a moral claim on all others.

Levinas believes that typical methods of social research offer little in the way of real understanding. Only an ethical approach can offer a tangible alternative to positivism. He rejects self-based transcendental phenomenology that posits a transcendental ego—one that focuses on Being. Instead he proffers one that is focused on nonbeing or the infinite.

THE STATUS OF SOCIAL PHENOMENOLOGY

The relevance of phenomenology to social theory has been strongly challenged by Zygmunt Bauman and Pierre Bourdieu. But this again depends on what one means by phenomenology. Certainly, one can find little in the way of a strong bond between Husserl's ideas and modern social phenomenology, even existential phenomenology (Best 1975). Heap and Roth (1973) have shown that most social theorists (particularly sociologists) use phenomenology metaphorically and not in the way it was used by Husserl and other philosophers. Hans Seigfried (1976, p. 256) refers to this as "knife-and-fork" phenomenology. Nevertheless Bauman has long contended that the subjective turn in sociology was a detour from "society-centered theory" and a radical turn toward "self-centered theory." This is not to imply that Bauman rejects phenomenology completely, however. It is his belief that the trail blazed by Husserl in phenomenology posits a hermetically sealed "pursuit of true meaning," one that is isolated from the potentially "polluting" influences of the social and political events taking place in the world. Bauman dismisses the Husserlian notion of a "pure consciousness" where all understanding is anchored (Bauman 1978, p. 232).

While Bourdieu is criticized for using an expanded and vague conceptualization of Merleau-Ponty's phenomenology (Throop and Murphy 2002; Endress 2005), he has suggested that his phenomenology views society primarily as a product of emergent human actions. He believes that phenomenology does not explain how the lived experience is produced by the internalization of previously externalized structures, and he believes that it furthermore relegates all human action to a person-to-person interaction—ignoring those broader structural constraints that shape both action and outcomes. This is related to his use of the notion of habitus. However, it seems to him that phenomenologists give the actor an exaggerated degree of agency with an overstated degree of intentionality and consciousness when much action is neither conscious nor intentional. Here he includes nonintentional somatic dispositions similar to those described by Merleau-Ponty. He rejects phenomenological reductionism as an intellectual drive to ignore human connection to the natural world. He also criticizes most phenomenologists for their failure to look into what he views as the ultimate reduction, which is the examination of social conditions that provide the basis for reductionism.

Bourdieu's simultaneous rejection and embrace of phenomenology emerges from his own sincere belief that human practices are primarily economic and take place within a structured field constituted by symbolic capital and economic interests. At the same time he emphasizes reflexivity in his work, which only brings him closer to the phenomenological perspective. In fact his notions of habitus and field emerge in some ways from a reading (some would say a misreading) of Husserl's phenomenology. His notion of reflexivity has much in common with Husserlian theory as well. He is certainly a promoter of the importance of the unconscious in social theory. But it is his disdain for an ungrounded subjective interpretation of social processes as method for social inquiry that is far less than enthusiastic.

If anything, social theory might be thought of as having cannibalized some of the more valuable elements of Husserlian phenomenology and ignored or discarded the rest. Although the term *phenomenology* is still in frequent use, philosophical phenomenologists would probably fail to recognize it in its varying social and cultural forms. Elements of Husserlian phenomenology enter into the work of some of its most powerful detractors. Cognitive theorists have been attempting to develop new phenomenologies such as neurophenomenology or naturalized phenomenology since the late 1990s, with varying degrees of success (Varela 1996; Gallagher 1997, 2006; Roy et al. 1999; Petiot et al. 2000). Like other paradigms that transmute into another life, and one after that, it is unlikely that, with the emphasis on subjectivity in social theory, phenomenology will soon fade from view.

Harvie Ferguson (2006) has called for a more intense dialogue between philosophy and sociology on this matter. He claims that phenomenological sociology can hold the key to many of the ontological challenges confronting both disciplines. He calls for these disciplines to break free from their restricted methods and to focus on human experience.

KEY TERMS

corporality of consciousness Maurice Merleau-Ponty's assertion that one's awareness is not limited to language; rather, language is merely an extension of one's body, which plays a critical role.

Einfühlung (literally: empathy) The notion developed by Max Weber for a way to gain positivistic understanding of the inner life of others through empathy.

ethnomethodology (1) A systematic attempt to organize, classify, and understand unremarkable human interactions and to show how these both constitute and explain social order. (2) To uncover, demystify, and identify taken-for-granted assumptions about the micro-ordered social world—a world of personal interactions.

exegesis An extensive and critical interpretation of an authoritative text, especially a text that is considered holy or sacred.

first philosophy The name given by Aristotle to the study of the principles, first causes, and essential attributes of being. Husserl saw phenomenology as a "first philosophy" or a foundational philosophy from which all knowledge proceeds. Phenomenology was seen as the means of describing "things themselves" as constituted in consciousness.

hermeneutics Interpretation of texts. This term was often applied to biblical interpretations, but it can actually be traced back to ancient Greek philosophy and early studies of rhetoric. For our purposes here, hermeneutics became a method used by philosophers, particularly social philosophers, to examine not only texts and other media of communication but also to survey institutions and human behavior. For existential philosophers it became a means to investigate the meaning of human existence.

ideal type A model, developed primarily by Max Weber, that serves as a systematic representation of a social phenomenon in its ideal-typical form for the purpose of explaining or representing that phenomenon and comparing it actual cases.

intentionality of the body According to Merleau-Ponty, the physical body contains intentions that are free from conscious decisions.

intersubjective A term having many meanings, all of which imply a break down in subject/object distinctions. The sharing of mutually subjective understandings by two or more people.

life-world A concept developed by Husserl and used by Schutz to mean a taken-for-granted scheme of everyday routines.

phenomenology A theory originated by Edmund Husserl and whose purpose is to discover the inherent essences of the appearances of objects that comprise the world (the things themselves) as they are registered in one's consciousness.

hermeneutic circle Ricoeur's idea of a circle of awareness that moves from naïve understanding to a deeper comprehension, in which the interpreter understands only parts of the text in relation to the whole and then moves on to understand the whole of the text in relation to its parts.

social imaginary A concept developed by Lacan to mean the symbols, laws, institutions, and values that are held in common in a particular society.

sociopolitical imaginaire Ricoeur's notion of symbolic or mythic discourses that serve to guide social and political behavior of a group. The discourses consist of two elements: (1) the social imaginary of *ideology* that reaffirms a society's identity by articulating its foundational symbols and forms the basis of a shared identity, and (2) the social imaginary of *utopia* that provides a redescription of social life.

the "they" relationship Developed by Schutz to describe a relationship in which, to grasp the meaning of an actor's motives, one must rely on ideal typical constructions or what is referred to by Schutz as course-of-action types. This basically consists of typical motives ascribed to certain types of actors. A second type of "they" relationship is one wherein individuals are seen as functioning in specific personal roles.

the "thou" relationship Developed by Schutz to mean a nonreciprocal relationship of awareness between actors.

the "we" relationship Developed by Schutz to describe a relationship in which the actors are both aware of each other and know that this awareness exists in the other.

typifications Developed by Alfred Schutz to describe the means through which people (commonsense actors) organize their world of things and ideas. The creation of social constructions based on essential assumptions about an object.

Verstehen (literally: understanding) A concept developed by Max Weber, it is a way to gain access to the thoughts and social position of another through conceptually placing oneself in the position of the other.

SOURCES

Alford, C. Fred. 2002. "The Opposite of Totality: Levinas, and the Frankfurt School," *Theory and Society*, Vol. 31, No. 2, pp. 229–254.

Agar, Michael. 1980. "Hermeneutics in Anthropology: A Review Essay," *Ethos*, Vol. 8, No. 3, pp. 253–272

Atkinson, Paul. 1988. "Ethnomethodology: A Critical Review," *Annual Review of Sociology*, Vol. 14, pp. 441–465.

Bakker, J. I. 1999. "Wilhelm Dilthey: Classical Sociological Theorist," *Quarterly Journal of Ideology*, Vol. 22, Nos. 1 & 2, pp. 43–82.

Bauman Zygmunt. 1978. *Hermenuetics and Social Science*. New York: Columbia University Press.

Berger, Peter L., and Thomas Luckmann. 1966. *The Social Construction of Reality*. New York: Doubleday & Co.

Best, R. (1975). "New Directions in Sociological Theory? A Critical Note on Phenomenological Sociology and Its Antecedents," *British Journal of Sociology*, Vol. 26, No.2, p.133–143.

Blum, Ronald Paul. 1983. "Emmanuel Levinas' Theory of Commitment," *Philosophy and Phenomenological Research*, Vol. 44, No. 2, pp. 145–168.

Campbell, Colin. 1996. *The Myth of Social Action*. Cambridge, MA: Cambridge University Press.

Collins, Randall. 1986. "The Passing of Intellectual Generations: Reflections on the Death of Erving Goffman," *Sociological Theory*, Vol. 4, No. 1, pp. 106–113.

Cook, Gary A. 1993. *George Herbert Mead: The Making of a Social Pragmatist*. Chicago: University of Chicago Press.

Endress, Martin. 2005. "Reflexivity, Reality, and Relationality: The Inadequacy of Bourdieu's Critique of the Phenomenological Tradition in Sociology," in M. Endress, G. Psathas, and H. Nasu, eds., *Explorations of the Life-World: Continuing Dialogues with Alfred Schutz*. Dordrecht, Netherlands: Springer.

Ermarth, Michael. 1978. *Wilhelm Dilthey: The Critique of Historical Reason*. Chicago: University of Chicago Press.

Ferguson, Harvie. 2006. *Phenomenological Sociology, Experience and Insight in Modern Society*. London: Sage Publications.

Gadamer, Hans Georg. 1975. *Truth and Method*. Trans. by G. Burden and J. Cumming. London: Shed & Ward.

Gallagher, Shaun. 1997. "Mutual Enlightenment: Recent Phenomenology in Cognitive Science," *Journal of Consciousness Studies*, Vol. 4, No. 3, pp. 83–107.

Gallagher, Shaun. 2006. *How the Body Shapes the Mind*. New York: Oxford University Press.

Garfinkel, Harold. 1967. *Studies in Ethnomethodology*. Englewood Cliffs, NJ: Prentice Hall.

Giddens, Anthony. 1979. "Schutz and Parsons: Problems of Meaning and Subjectivity," *Contemporary Sociology*, Vol. 8, No. 5, pp. 682–685.

Gleeson, Denis, and Michael Erban. 1976. "Meaning in Context: Notes Toward a Critique of Ethnomethodology," *British Journal of Sociology*, Vol. 27, No. 4, pp. 474–483.

Gouldner, Alvin. 1970. *The Coming Crisis of Western Sociology*. New York: Avon.

Heap, J. L., and Roth, P. A. 1973. "On Phenomenological Sociology," *American Sociological Review*, Vol. 38, No. 3, pp. 354–367.

Koppl, Roger. 2001. "Alfred Schutz and George Shackle: Two Views of Choice," *The Review of Austrian Economics*, Vol.14, No. 2–3, pp. 181–191.

Levinas, Emmanuel. 1969. *Totality and Infinity, An Essay on Exteriority*. Trans. by A. Lingis. Pittsburgh, PA: Duquesne University Press.

Merleau-Ponty, Maurice. 1962. *Phenomenology and Perception*. Trans. by C. Smith. New York: Humanities Press.

Merleau-Ponty, Maurice. 1964. *Signs*. Evanston, IL: Northwestern University Press.

Merleau-Ponty, Maurice. 1969. *Humanism and Terror*. Boston: Beacon Press.

Petitot, Jean, Francisco Varela, Bernard Pachoud, and Jean-Michel Roy. 2000. *Naturalizing Phenomenology: Issues in Contemporary Phenomenology and Cognitive Science*. Stanford, CA: Stanford University Press.

Prendergast, Christopher. 1986. "Alfred Schutz and the Austrian School of Economics," *American Journal of Sociology*, Vol., 92, No. 1, pp. 1–26.

Ricoeur, Paul. 1971. "The Model of the Text: Meaningful Action Considered as a Text," *Social Research*, Vol. 38, No. 3, pp. 529–562.

Rochberg-Halton, Eugene. 1986. *Meaning and Modernity: Social Theory in the Pragmatic Attitude*. Chicago: University of Chicago Press.

Roy, Jean Michel, Jean Petitot, Bernard Pachoud, and Francisco Varela. 1999. "Beyond the Gap: An Introduction to Naturalizing Phenomenology," in J. Petitot, F. Varela, B. Pachoud, and J. M. Roy, eds, *Naturalizing Phenomenology*. Stanford, CA: Stanford University Press.

Schmidt, James. 1985. *Maurice Merleau-Ponty: Between Phenomenology and Structuralism*. New York: Macmillan.

Schutz, Alfred. 1973. *The Structures of the Life-World*. (*Strukturen der Lebenswelt*.) Trans. by Richard M. Zaner and H. Tristram Engelhardt, Jr. Evanston, IL: Northwestern University Press.

Seigfried, Hans. 1976. "Descriptive Phenomenology and Constructivism," *Philosophy and Phenomenological Research*, Vol. 37, No. 2, pp. 248–261.

Stewart, David, and Algis Mickunas. 1990. *Exploring Phenomenology*. Athens: University of Ohio Press.

Throop, C. Jason, and Keith M. Murphy. 2002. "Bourdieu and Phenomenology: A Critical Assessment," *Anthropological Theory*, Vol. 2, No. 2, pp. 185–207.

Ulin, Robert C. 1992. "Beyond Explanation and Understanding: Anthropology and Hermeneutics," *Dialectical Anthropology*, Vol. 17, No. 3, pp. 253–269.

Varela, Francisco. 1996. "Neurophenomenology: A Methodological Remedy to the Hard Problem," *Journal of Consciousness Studies*, Vol. 3, No. 4, pp. 330–350.

Wilson, E. D. 2002. "Alfred Schuts: Phenomenology and Research Methodology for Information Behavior Research," Paper delivered to the Fourth International Conference on Information Seeking in Context, Universidad Lusiada, Lisborn, Portugal, September 11–13.

Zaret, David. 1980. "From Weber to Parsons and Schutz: The Eclipse of History in Modern Social Theory," *American Journal of Sociology*, Vol. 85, No. 5, pp. 1180–1201.

CHAPTER 4

Poststructuralism and Social Theory

While structuralism came crashing down to earth in the 1970s, it did not disappear. Some would say that it merely picked itself up, dusted itself off, and changed its appearance and nomenclature. But this would be a simplistic exaggeration. Certainly, some elements remained quite viable and were incorporated into what has become known as poststructuralism, but other parts of structuralism passed away with the smoldering protests of the late 1960s.

Poststructuralism, like structuralism itself, was part of the linguistic turn. However, it moved considerably away from the binary subject/object field of reference that was so pronounced in structuralism, and it made a radical turn toward intersubjectivity, privileging neither subject nor object. If any one detail stands out in distinguishing it from structuralism, it is that it rejected the Enlightenment notion of the subject—one endowed with the capacities of reason, consciousness, and action, and whose center consisted of an inner core that first emerged when the subject was born and unfolded with its development (Hall 1996).

In poststructuralism, the subject is decentered. It stands no ground. Subject/object binary is under constant attack, as are all binaries. Rather than viewing people as products of structures (internal or external), the poststructuralists see both the subject and the object as potential agents of change—different from each other yet also similar. While making use of structuralist tools of linguistic analysis, it takes a divergent path, which had much to do with the work of people such as Jacques Derrida and Michel Foucault.

DECONSTRUCTION AND THE SOCIOLOGY OF JACQUES DERRIDA

Jacques Derrida (1930–2004) was a key figure in this turn toward poststructuralism. He had already made a name for himself in structuralist circles and was personally acquainted with Michel Foucault, Roland Barthes, Jacques Lacan, and

Louis Althusser. Derrida was born in Algeria and was the son of Sephardic Jews. He later studied in Paris at the renowned *Ècole Normal Supérieure.*

Decentering the subject was an essential aspect of Derrida's social theory. Although he was deeply influenced by Husserl's phenomenology as well as Heidegger's existentialism, Derrida could never bring himself to accept the validity of the subject/object binary or to concede the potential power inherent in the object. Derrida rejected Saussure's notion of difference that contends that each sign is distinct from another. He argued that there was no such thing as pure difference and that each signifier not only contains elements of the other but needs to be defined by it. He rejected all binaries and posited in the place of difference the notion of *différance* as a means of explaining the relationship between the written signs or, as he calls them, *tracers. Différance* is a word he used to combine the idea of defer, or being somehow present while having been omitted (such as a trace), and differ, or being distinct or discernibly different. All words, all signifiers, have traces of other words. Thus, he opposed the notion of a distinct and separate meaning that structuralism assigns.

While structure was important for Derrida, he asserted that it determined nothing. This view was made clear throughout his work. He fully subscribed to the notion that words in themselves have no meaning; it is the context in which they are placed that gives them meaning. And it is perception that is crucial here. Derrida takes the existential notion of the meaninglessness of life (inherent in existentialism) and translates it into the meaninglessness of language. The participants in discourse construct meaning. Thus, meaning can never be singular. It is the product of an interactive, intersubjective exchange. There is constant slippage in language as it is spoken, heard, written, and comprehended.

Phenomenology had an important influence on him. Therefore it is not surprising that Derrida had been significantly affected by the work of Husserl early in his career and later by the work of Merleau-Ponty, even though he would often deny this influence. It has been suggested by at least one critic that Merleau-Ponty's phenomenology helped to open the door for Derrida's deconstructionism (Reynolds 2004). In fact, it is Derrida's radicalization of the phenomenological notion of experience that both separates his work from Husserl and other phenomenologists such as Heidegger and simultaneously connects his work to phenomenology. It was Derrida's intent to move beyond a phenomenology that posited a self-presence, a presence in the here and now, which underlies phenomenological metaphysics and existentialism. There is no pure now, no lingering presence in deconstructionism. The present can never be captured and brought under control. Therefore, there can be no present self, only future selves. This is a direct rejection of Husserl's notion of temporality. For Derrida, any attempt to capture the here and now in language is destined to fail because everything is either *in the past* or is *to come.* Temporal existence forever eludes us, and the meanings of words are always changing, always slipping away.

In Derrida's semiotics, there is similarly a real shift in focus from the signified to the signifier. Rather than a search for rules and structures that produce outcomes, Derrida and other poststructuralists search for the ways in which meaning is constructed by those who use language. They look at how people interpret the world through what they think, say, and do. Unlike Levi-Strauss's structuralism, which privileged the spoken word over the written one, Derrida's *deconstruction* dismisses this approach as romanticism. There is no concern with the power of deep structures; rather, deconstructionists are most interested in how meaning is socially constituted. Derrida and other poststructuralists attack the notion of structure, of universal truths that supposedly shaped an objective reality. Instead they see language as unstable, always flawed, subjective, never exact. It is never seen as the means of acquiring truth.

Deconstruction takes direct aim at the binaries associated with structuralism. It reveals the biases inherent in hierarchies of opposites: white/black, smooth/rough, cooked/raw. It aims to undermine the binary hierarchy, subvert the favored first term (the privileged of the two), thus enabling the reader to liberate meaning from words that might not have been intended. Its aim is to reveal ambiguities, to free up meaning so that it can be easily subverted.

Derrida also attacked the structuralists as privileging a certain ethnocentric view of nature over culture. This was not only related to Levi-Strauss's contention (taken from Saussure) that spoken language was much closer to nature and therefore much purer than the written form, but also that primitive societies were thus closer to truth. For Derrida, there was no true nature, no pure nature, and that all so-called truth was a linguistic construction. He proposed that there is "nothing outside the text." Thus, Derrida favors a particular form of hermeneutics—a position in which naturalism is rejected in favor of interpretation. For him, human life was to be read like a text. To make sense of it, one needs to resort to "thick description." There are no determinate meanings, only the infinite interplay of signifiers, only texts and interpretation of interpretations.

Derrida's deconstructionism is a means through which he dissected a world of language, a world created by words. But beyond this, he saw deconstruction as a tool for uncovering false logic through which embedded social institutions maintain their power. This is very much in line with his Marxist orientation as well as a Nietzschean one. While Derrida hoped to illuminate the unstable nature of language, his thesis was a radically political one. This politics was deemphasized by Yale's literary elites, who saw him primarily as a literary critic and not a social one. But it is within his sociology that we can find some of his most brilliant insights.

Ben Agger (1994) sees Derridean sociology as a rejection of both positivism and grand theory. The sociological radicalism of Derrida is embedded in his opposition to western logocentrism, the flat-out supposition that all intellectual problems can be solved through science and philosophy because these incorporate certain foundational *first principles* that do not need to be contested. In fact, Derrida rejects the whole notion of first principles as ludicrous because all such principles have to rely on language, particularly written language. Ben Agger posits that: "Deconstruction becomes critical social theory and cultural studies . . . when we move beyond literary texts to all 'social texts,' whose secret authorship can be revealed and contested. Hence, one can 'read' film, architecture, advertisements, music, and science politically" (Agger 1994, p. 503). Derrida's outright rejection of logocentrism is a challenge to sociological positivism, which assumes that empiricism can be put to use to address intellectual problems through applied methodology. Deconstruction challenges the method and its contended first principles. It opens debate by challenging the underlying narrative.

Ben Agger contends that this attack on foundational causes and first principles is the greatest challenge to classical sociological theory and its grand-scale orientation. Deconstruction is not a competing paradigm; rather, it is a method of assessing these paradigms by converting them into readable texts that can be pulled apart and radically challenged. The politics of this sociological stance is indeed revolutionary. And some have classified it as a postmodern critique. Derrida does not deny this intent. As a young man he had been influenced by existentialism, structuralism, psychoanalysis, and Marxism. However, this was not Marxism in any classical sense. Derrida rejected all grand theory and essential elements of the Enlightenment that guided Marxian principles. By the end of his career, he embraced what some have referred to as "Marxism without Marx" (Derrida 1994; Bedggood 1999). Derrida claims to be the inheritor of Marx's radicalism, without necessarily subscribing to most of his ideas on political economy.

FOUCAULT AND THE CULTURAL TURN

One of the most celebrated social theorists of the last quarter of the twentieth century was Michel Foucault. While he died more than a quarter of a century ago, his impact on contemporary theory has been profound.

To understand Foucault, it is important to gain a picture of the context in which he evolved as a theorist. Born on October 15, 1926, in Poitiers, France, he emerged from a middle-class family. His father was a surgeon, and he attended the École Normal Superieuer in Paris, one of France's premier institutions of higher learning. He studied with both Maurice Merleau-Ponty and Louis Althusser. He was a nonhumanist and was significantly influenced by the work of Frederich Neitzsche. But he was also well versed in the works of Marx and Freud.

Foucault was a vocal and articulate structuralist, and he joined forces with Claude Levi-Strauss, Roland Barthes, Jacques Lacan, Jacques Derrida, and others to challenge the intellectual dominance of existential humanism. Like many structuralists, he abandoned the Marxian notion of class and capitalistic exploitation for an alternate theory of power and discourse. Yet he was a member of France's communist party, gained celebrity status as an iconoclastic intellectual, and participated in the student and worker strikes of 1968.

It is important to recognize the impact that phenomenology and existentialism (advanced by his teacher, Merleau-Ponty) had on Foucault's early work. It was Merleau-Ponty who filtered Saussure into a structuralist phenomenology, which later was picked up by poststructuralists. Merleau-Ponty's emphasis on the body and its function in history and discourse greatly influenced Foucault's work.

Foucault's early concern with deep structures placed him squarely in the structuralist camp. Here, all human phenomena are seen as part of the language system. Language is seen as vital to an integrated network of social control. He was less interested in the actions of human beings than he was in the mechanisms established to control their behaviors. And for this he turns to examine human sciences (such as sociology, psychiatry, medicine, and criminology) and their imposition of *tyrannical reason*. It is reason that makes people into subjects, an idea he took from Althusser.

To Foucault (1982), power is the means through which reason is instituted. It is the ultimate principle of social reality. He locates all power in discourse. It is his position that power rests not within people but within institutional arrangements that have been defined and established by language. While Marx talked of power only in terms of material production, and Freud addressed it in terms of human biology and psychic repression, Foucault looks at the connection of power to knowledge. Foucault does not see all power vested in the hands of an elite social class, nor view it as emanating from a solitary sovereign or a state. Rather Foucault asserts that discourse defines and produces objects of our knowledge. It also constructs subjects and positions. Like Derrida's notion of the all-encompassing text, there is nothing outside discourse for Foucault. But what does he mean by discourse?

Discourse must be viewed as a group of statements that provide a language for a particular topic or issue. It "constructs" the topic in that it governs the way it can be meaningfully discussed or approached. In fact, it creates the topic. We cannot enter into a discussion of anything until we accept the terms by which it is to be discussed. Thus, we must yield or submit to this power that has defined the legitimacy of our discussion. It can be suggested that those without an ability to enter into the discussion have little or no power. But power enters into every realm of life. Much of his later work is an examination of the history of its use. It is the power of discourse that defines sexuality and even the human body. It is the power of discourse that defines who we are.

Foucault makes extensive use of Nietzsche's term *genealogy*. By this he does not mean a history of a family. Rather, genealogy is seen as a method for exposing those elements in society that appear to be natural, without history of development, without struggle. Things are taken as axiomatic, and taken for granted at face value, such as sexuality. He refers to such presuppositions as *epistemes*. The intent of genealogy is to expose the inherent falsity in these and to reveal the role of power in establishing truth.

It is important to clarify *Foucault's notion of truth*. For Foucault, all truth is entrenched in power. One cannot achieve truth without it. Power is truth's articulation. Much like Nietzsche, Foucault posits a world in which truth is guarded and power is often hidden. Foucault's attack on the Enlightenment is also reminiscent of Nietzsche's, and in some ways similar to Max Weber's. It was both Weber's and Nietzsche's contention that reason and rationality became an oppressive means through which access to power was granted and held. Truth could be revealed only through reason. That which was reasonable and rational was strictly controlled by elites who occupied institutionalized positions of influence and training. Anything or anyone considered to be nonrational (such as a young child) was subject to the strictest observation, was placed under the will of authority, and therefore became the object of coded discipline and education. This subjugation would include both the body and the mind.

Foucault's studies of the asylum, the prison, madness, and sexuality enabled him to move from a structuralist position to a more poststructuralist one. In each of these works, power and knowledge construct the discourse, which in turn creates subjects. It molds subjects, yet it does not completely dissolve agency. Foucault both rejected the modernist notion of individualism and disputed the idea that all oppressive power flows from one primary source, such as capitalism. Power and discourse are ubiquitous. They create new modes of activity, yet there is always resistance. Foucault saw this resistance as somehow confined because it never occupies a position of "exteriority as it relates to power" (Foucault 1990, p. 95). Such ambiguity has led to numerous interpretations of his notion of resistance (Hartmann 2003).

Foucault refused the label of structuralist as he did that of poststructuralist. Still, certain elements in his work have prompted his readers and critics to classify him at times as both. His early embrace of structuralism in *The Order of Things* (1970) and later in *The Birth of the Clinic* (1975) calls into question his later denouncement of that approach. Foucault was concerned with the structures of knowledge and knowing. He also embraced structuralist jargon in his early work and in 1967 gave an interview in which he posited that the aim of his work was to "introduce the analyses of a structuralist style into those areas where they haven't penetrated until now, that is to say into the domain of the history of ideas, the history of connaissances, the history of theory" (in a 1967 interview in *Dits et ecrits, Vol I*, pp. 580–584). Yet he never seemed to subscribe completely to such a perspective. His archeology of knowledge was a denial of the structuralist quest to discover essentials in life. There are no essentials, he proposed, only the way things appear to us at a particular point in time.

For much of his later work, he took a deconstructive approach, especially in his study of the connection between knowledge and power, searching out and interpreting newfound meaning within social relations where power might rest. In a poststructuralist sense, Foucault does not embrace the myth of the European Enlightenment as a noble attempt to discover universal scientific truths to advance humanistic causes. For him, it was a method to produce new mechanisms of social control and human subjugation. Thus, he pushed away from the structuralist position, from its reliance on positivism as a value-free method of unlocking secrets of the universe.

Foucault's work is no mere exploration of sociological phenomena; rather, it is an exploration and description of how knowledge has been used to shape the world of human relationships—how it has become a base of power and control through a system of classification, observation, and finally, manipulation. Like Freud and Nietzsche, Foucault is concerned with the internalized methods of regulation and control. In so doing, he moves us away from the seeing oppressive power as external to the person and helps us see how each is part of this oppressive system.

In some ways, Foucault's work is a continuation of the Frankfurt school concern with domination, the oppressiveness of reason, and the repressive uses of science. However, in being influenced by the linguistic turn, phenomenology, and structuralism, he moves away from leftist humanism. His creative approach is far and away one of the most eclectic.

In recent years Foucault's work has been under attack by those who see themselves as "post-Foucaultians" (Dean 1994). While he spent considerable time and effort describing oppressive cultural, political, religious, and socioeconomic hegemony, Foucault gives his readers no insight about how to question and confront these forces and constantly deemphasizes the power of individual agency and contested meaning. He seems purposely to overlook individual will and instead focuses on constructing the image of monolithic systems of control, and in a sense he helps to reproduce the discursive system he articulates so well.

JACQUES LACAN'S POSTSTRUCTURALISM

Like Foucault, Lacan also began his intellectual career as a structuralist. Twenty-five years Foucault's senior and nearly thirty years older than Derrida, he had already become an intellectual celebrity in France by the 1950s. Structuralism was very important at this time and made its way into the popular culture in the late 1950s and early 1960s with the publication of Levi-Strauss's most significant works.

When structuralism was "the new thing," it was viewed as the challenge to Sartre's seemingly sappy, humanistic existentialism. Certain nodes of intellectual discourse were fed up with Sartre's politics, his romance with communism (his embrace of Fidel Castro), and his attempts to connect intellectual life to the lives of the common people (Minahen 1997). His ideas were attacked viciously by Foucault, Lacan, and Althusser. Theory was becoming more and more antihumanist as men such as Althusser rejected Marx's earlier work dealing with dehumanization and alienation. And Lacan rejected the humanistic notions of Freud in the hope of developing a mathematical equation to represent the unconscious. But alas, this was impossible. French structuralism was rather short-lived. It could not stem the tide of political and cultural revolution taking place in the world.

Jacques Lacan (1901–1981), who was born in Paris on April 13, 1901, was France's most celebrated psychotherapist. Like Foucault, he grew up in a middle-class family and attended a Jesuit school as a youngster. He trained in medicine at Saint Stanislas College and took a clinical residency at Sainte Anne's Hospital, where he came into contact with the renowned psychiatrist Gaëtan Gatian de Clerambault, who supervised his psychiatric training. He worked at Sainte Anne's until 1964. After being trained as a psychoanalyst, he began a thriving but unconventional clinical practice and was therapist to a host of celebrities, including Pablo Picasso. He hobnobbed with cultural elites and was connected to the dada movement in art.

Lacan began his career in theory by attempting to reformulate Freud. Much like Derrida, and Foucault, he was influenced by the popularity of Saussure's work. He was also influenced by Levi-Strauss (his contemporary), who was in turn influenced by him. He gained recognition for himself by emphasizing the importance of language in understanding human psychology, particularly that of the unconscious. Because words convey multiple meanings, he believed that they were often used to convey things that were unintended.

While it was his early hope to systematize psychoanalysis and make it more of a psychological science with the use of semiotics, he eventually abandoned this course, much like Barthes had done, and Derrida before him. It was obvious to Lacan that language could not be seen as inflexible, as Levi-Strauss had earlier implied. In the years to come he would shift his understanding of language, how it operated within the psyche, and how symbols could be transformed in the unconscious.

With the exception of the Frankfurt school, Lacan's work moved psycho-analysis that much closer to sociology in the sense that it attempted to break down the false distinctions between self and society created by language. He saw language as creating the self. Like Hegel, he viewed language as the means through which the self became objectified—separated and alienated from others. Words were responsible for fragmenting both the world and the self.

In many ways Lacan's work is a continuation of the Hegelian tradition that entered American social sciences in the sociology of George Herbert Mead and, to a lesser extent, Charles Horton Cooley, the symbolic interactionist. These social theorists were also concerned with the notion of self, its fragmentation, and its subjective interpretation. However, unlike them, Lacan anchored his idea to both the structural anthropology of Levi-Strauss and Freudian psychoanalytic thought. Lacan's work also was a continuation of the Frankfurt school's reformulation of Freud. While Marcuse and Horkheimer (also influenced by Hegel) saw subjectivity as a product of capitalism and its bureaucratic order, Lacan viewed it as a result of language.

Lacan posited that the individual came to be *self-recognized* at what he terms the mirror stage, between six and eighteen months of age. This is when the child sees its reflection in the mirror and comes to perceive an alien self staring back. He saw this as the time at which language is developing. Thus the child detects a fissure between him- or herself and the rest of the natural world. While language seems empowering, it forever removes the child from direct experience with its world. This disconnection is to shape its very future. The desire to be reconnected to some amorphous primal reality drives the child forward into life, unconsciously longing for a reconnection. In fact Lacan sees this longing for connection as the basis of all desires. This notion is in line with object relations theory in psychoanalysis.

Central to Lacanian analysis is the recognition of what might be called three orders or registers of being: the Imaginary, the Symbolic, and the Real (Clark, 2004). At the mirror stage, the child falsely assumes that he or she is the image seen in the mirror. However, this is actually not the case. There is a child that is inseparable and indistinguishable from an all-encompassing oneness—a premir-ror stage from which the child started and to which it can never return. This is to say, the Real child or natural child rests as part of something inherent in nature and does not stand alone. This Real is the oneness to which Hegel subscribed. The Real is outside consciousness as well as the unconscious because it exists outside language itself, and cannot be articulated; it is outside the Symbolic order. The self at the mirror stage is what Lacan calls Imaginary, a mirage of an alienated individual structured by the Symbolic, by language. This is the reflection rather than the Real. It is language that imposes and indoctrinates the child into the registry of the Symbolic order. But this order is inextricably intertwined with the Imaginary one, which drives the child's deep neonatal longing for connection. However, language of the Symbolic order is the initiation into a new alienated world of rules, the world of the father. For Lacan, this is the metaphor that stands in place of Freud's Oedipus complex. Language is the powerful tool of male domination, and to accept the language is to resolve one's "complex." Lacan refers to this as taking *the-Name-of-the-Father*. Not only does the child take on language in order to be connected, but he or she also takes on laws and the imposition of restrictions on desire as posited by patriarchal authority. Certainly, Lacan displaces the oedipal striving of the child with a striving for connectedness and stability that is resolved only through taking on the language and law of the father.

What gives Lacan a seat at the poststructuralist table is his reading of Freud's work as literature rather than science; his emphasis on the ephemeral nature of language; and his deconstruction of sex, domination, and desire. He makes a significant effort in his writing to depose the subject from the privileged position it held in Freudian analysis. However, it is Lacan's attack on the *phallocentrism* inherent in Freud's notion of sexual desire and his imposition of a more symbolic version of it that radically alters the classical analytic framework. Lacan believes this lack to be a desire for connectedness. Still, like Freud, he views lack and desire as underlying most human anxiety and as the central engine of psychic life.

While Lacan has been claimed both by structuralists and poststructuralists, and exhibits characteristics of each, his work becomes the jumping-off point for poststructuralist assessments of contemporary society. And while his ideas are rarely used by sociologists, Lacan contributes some of the most important theoretical insights into psychoanalytic sociology. His notions of how self and identity are constructed are essential to a broader picture, not only of early socialization but also of the deeper strivings in our world for connection. Thus his work has become pivotal to feminist theory, communication theory, and consumer studies.

POSTSTRUCTURAL FEMINISM

Feminist theory owes much to this revolution in thought. But French feminist theory has had a particularly intimate connection to poststructuralism. It was both influenced by it and simultaneously helped to create it. American and British feminists were latecomers in this regard. The women's movement of the 1970s, particularly as it came about in the United States and Britain, took off in a somewhat more utilitarian direction. Feminist theory, as connected to social change, is more fully examined in Chapter 6.

In France, while the work of Foucault and Derrida had broad appeal in the social sciences and humanities, Lacanian thought was most fully developed in feminist theory, literary criticism, and psychoanalysis. One of the most prominent contributors to poststructuralism has been French cultural theorist Luce Irigaray.

Born in Brussels in 1932, Irigaray received her academic training in psychology, philosophy, and linguistics, and taught linguistics and philosophy throughout Europe. She was a student of Jacques Lacan in Paris in the 1960s, remains an active feminist voice, and is a significant influence in the field. Two of her most important works, *The Sex Which Is Not One* (1977) and *The Speculum of Other Women* (1985), developed rather radical positions on sexual difference.

In her first book (originally publish in French in 1974), which actually came out of her graduate studies in philosophy, Irigaray derides what she sees as the phallocentric position developed by Freud and Lacan. She proposes that, throughout the development of western civilizations, the control of discourse has rested in the hands of males. This masculine perspective has shaped our understanding of the world and dominated the development of modern cultures (Irigaray 1985). Women were viewed by philosophers as merely reflections of men, or men without penises. Irigaray uses the terms *self-same* to represent men and *other* to represent women. Men are always self-conscious subjects and women always nondiscursive objects. The word *speculum* in the title of her book takes on several meanings: from its Latin use, *mirror,* to an instrument used in gynecological examinations.

In *The Speculum of Other Women*, it is Irigaray's contention that western philosophy, beginning with Socrates, and later in the psychoanalysis of Freud, became an instrument for objectifying women and establishing phallocentrism as the basis for a dominant Symbolic order. Irigaray asserts that women have been defined historically not only as *others* but as "mothers" in both ancient thought and in psychoanalytic theory. While men are seen as related to culture, women are viewed as connected to nature. In being relegated to this role, women occupy the inferior, complementary position. They have been locked out of the dominant discourse.

Irigaray attacks Simone de Beauvoir for her advocacy of sexual homogenization, wherein she contends that men and women are equal and one and therefore deserve equal rights and protections. Instead Irigaray posits a significant difference that inherently separates the sexes and promotes the notion that womankind is an alternative to mankind.

Nevertheless, Irigaray contends that language is phallocentric and has not historically allowed for expression of female sexuality from a woman's point of view. In examining and deconstructing the position of boys and girls at the oedipal stage of development where language is Firmly acquired, she takes aim at the use of both Freud's and Lacan's notion of identity formation being based purely on masculine norms. She objects to this exclusion of the feminine and to the privileged *oneness* of the male perspective. And she counters Freud's, and indirectly Lacan's, imagry of the phallus around which the psyche develops with her own metaphor of the labial lips of the clitoris and vagina in female identity formation.

For the phallus to represent both power and desire is to write women out of the picture completely. Her counter argument is that *labial lips* represent the complexity and dynamics of feminine signification and challenge the dominant male paradigm in psychoanalysis.

The logic and relative closure of the male syntactic system allows Irigaray to challenge the rigidity of language as patriarchal. Poststructuralism becomes a tool to liberate women from the confines of phallocentrism, which privileges the phallus as the essential starting point in the development of language. The complexity of female sexuality and the fluidity of feminine communication provide a broader view of the world than the classical male thinkers could produce. Irigaray wants not only to open up language in order to give women a real voice, but also to recognize the uniqueness of men and women and to respect these differences. In this sense she calls for a *culture of two.*

Much in Irigaray's work has been regarded as essentialism. She has been viewed by some as promoting the notion that crucial differences between the sexes rest in biological structures. Some defend her against such accusations, challenging her critics for failure to understand her complexity as a theorist and her unique use of language. Others have embraced her as both a realist and an essentialist (Fermon 1998; Stone 2003). It is beyond the scope of this text to examine this debate. But Irigaray's challenge to male hegemony stands. It has been broadly applied to social and political analyses aimed at fostering radical social change characterized by intersubjectivity.

For many sociologists the value of any theory is in its intent and application. For Irigaray, her project to challenge the psychic structure and language supporting phallocentric domination has won her numerous supporters. In her more recent work she has attempted to link her feminist theory to the multicultural arena and generally to the politics of identity and resistance. She has often suggested that the political underdevelopment of women has forced them to become a passive medium of exchange. Thus women are always objects to men, never subjects. They are always commodities. The only way to free themselves from this oppression is through separation and the creation of alternative structures. She calls for a more radicalized agenda and a rejection of the liberal state. She does not view the struggle for equality as ever achieving an acceptable place for women. And she applies this idea to others who have been marginalized.

Another important poststructural feminist is Julia Kristeva. Although she does not identify herself as a feminist, Kristeva's work on the body and on marginality and oppression has contributed greatly to modern feminist thought. Trained in philosophy, linguistics, and later in psychoanalysis, Kristeva migrated from Bulgaria to Paris at the age of twenty-five. There she became a student of Roland Barthes and immediately immersed herself in French structuralism in the early 1970s. Kristeva joined the editorial board of one of the leading leftist journals in France, *Tel quel.* This journal published the works of Althusser, Barthes, Derrida, and Foucault. Kristeva's uniqueness rests in her deep familiarity with Hegelian and Marxist theories and in her personal transformation from a structuralist perspective to a poststructuralist one. While influenced by the work of Levi-Strauss, she came to France just as structuralism was coming into disrepute.

Kristeva (1982) borrows as much from structuralism as she does from psycho-analysis. Yet she manages to move further away from the defining orthodoxy of these disciplines. For instance, she breaks new linguistic ground in developing a distinction between the semiotic (which she borrows from structuralism) and the Lacanian Symbolic. She draws from structuralism to create new poststructuralist pathways. Semiotics becomes not an analysis of the signifier and signified as advanced by Saussurian structuralism, but rather represents an emotional or instinctual force that precedes language and that is guided by innate biological rhythm, not cognitive abstraction. This can be heard in the infant's babbling or in the poet's musicality. She sees this developing at the pre-oedipal stage or, to use a Lacanian notion, the premirror stage. It is vitally connected to the feminine or maternal.

Like Lacan, Kristeva privileges both the body and the language that defines it. Meaning can be found in the meter of language itself, in its tonality—not chiefly in abstract word definitions or its semantics. This subverbal (or vocal) focus becomes the essential basis of her feminism.

In Kristeva's division of discourse between the semiotic and the symbolic, the semiotic has come to represent women's place—one that is marginalized as inferior and excluded from access to male power. It relates more to the primal maternal body than to the intellect. It is somatic, emotional. Through semiotics, drives are discharged into signification. However, all signification requires both the semiotic and the symbolic—the somatic discharge of drives and the structural manifestation of this discharge.

For many social theorists, Kristeva's focus on oppression and domination of women speaks to a sociological dimension as Kristeva develops the notion of *abjection*, which literally means to become an outcast or to be seen as worthless. Abjection is viewed psychodynamically by Kristeva as an attempt to maintain boundaries in order to protect the integrity of group or individual identity. It is a rejection of anything or anyone who might threaten this identity. The Symbolic constitutes a hegemonic dominance of men through discourse, through law. The semiotic is seen as inferior—as affective and subjective. The Symbolic represents, in a Lacanian sense, accepting the Law of the Father or resolving the oedipal dilemma.

Kristeva sees the dependence on the maternal body as a threat to male autonomy. Like Nancy Chodorow (whose work we will consider in Chapter 6), she believes that abjection is related to womanhood in the form of the maternal body. To develop into independent subjects as opposed to objects, one must eliminate the maternal—reject it and all that it represents. She goes as far as to say that matricide is articulated as the foundation of one's emergence as a subject in male-dominated discourse. Women are stuck in a dilemma in which, if they identify with their mothers, they are securing for themselves a type of marginality and an exclusion from patriarchal power. On the other hand, if a woman rejects her mother and identifies with her father, she is promoting the patriarchal order that oppresses women. Because women cannot easily reject their own bodies, their own womanhood, they eventually develop what she refers to as depressive sexuality, which has often led to madness or suicide. Women need to transcend this dilemma by rejecting the imposition of male discourse and seeking the development of a new discourse that is less oppressive to women. To do this she must, like Derrida, undermine the privileged place of the symbolic.

While much of this might appear to be quite structuralist, Kristeva rejects the notion that language has a specific meaning conveyed from the speaker or writer to the listener or reader. Intertextuality is where she finds the key to liberation from *logocentric* oppression. For Kristeva, every text is informed by another; therefore, meaning is a dynamic construction. Beyond this, each text releases the unconscious drives, or the semiotic. It liberates one from the phallocentric discourse and control of the Symbolic order.

Kristeva focuses attention on the role of transgression in giving rise to new discourse, or what she calls *discursive innovations*. Such innovations in discourse and in practice that emerge from the semiotic have the potential of becoming themselves normalized and changing the Symbolic order. Through the arts and poetic language, we have the greatest potential for such liberation.

Kristeva's work has general applicability to the study of marginalization, yet her work has never been thoroughly mined by sociologists who deal more generally with the issues of social oppression. Her overriding focus on literature has not made her work significantly appealing to social scientists. Inherent in her work, however, is the study of alienation, oppression, and liberation.

Like Kristeva, Hélène Cixous (whose work will also be explored in Chapter 6) helped to construct a feminist poststructural perspective that recognizes language as a mean of oppression. Having started out as a structuralist, she found a need to reassess political and libidinal economies in terms of the structures originally suggested by thinkers such as Marx, Freud, and Althusser. She borrowed the term *libidinal economies* from Lyotard's book of the same name, in which the term meant the ways in which a society directs, controls, and modifies sexual desire and activity. Cixous deconstructed these elements in texts.

She agrees with Lacan, Kristeva, and Irigaray that the female body has not been represented in the use of language and has no place in the Symbolic order. But from here she makes a leap to female sexuality and how it has not been allowed to be fully recognized in this male-centered order. The so-called sexual maturation of women is viewed as necessitating the abandonment of personal agency, becoming an object and being denied the position of subject. Thus, women become both the linguistic and sexual objects in a phallocentric society. For her, all sexuality is therefore defined by men, thus negating any authentic form of female sexuality.

Cixous (1976) recognizes that women writing from their bodies most threatens patriarchy and its rigidity. It is only in this new language—a language that emerges from the female body and feminine forms of eroticism, a language that is soft, slippery, and fluid—that true liberation and authentic female creativity can be achieved.

SLAVOJ ŽIŽEK: A POSTSTRUCTURAL READING
OF POPULAR CULTURE

Born in Ljubljana, Slovenia (the former Yugoslavia) in 1949, Slavoj Žižek is a renowned sociologist, psychoanalyst, and critical theorist. The breadth of his work ranges from issues of globalization to contemporary film criticism. It was not until 1989 and the publication of his book *The Sublime Object of Ideology* (written in English) that he became one of the most celebrated post-Lacanian thinkers of our time. While Žižek works in the Hegelian tradition of critical theory, it is difficult to characterize his contributions because his topics and his approaches to them are very broad. His work has become quite popular in the social sciences, and within the past twenty years he has become one of the most celebrated thinkers in Europe.

The Sublime Object of Ideology (1989) offers Žižek's impressions of Marx's fetish of commodities and Freud's theory of the unconscious through a Lacanian lens. Just like the Frankfurt school founders, his attempt to synthesize psychoanalysis and Marxism produces interesting results aimed at destabilizing the very foundation of capitalistic society. In this book, he reformulates Lacan in an attempt to make him more defensible against the attacks on his murky poststructuralism, and at the same time recasts and reinvigorates Althusserian Marxism. Overall, his project seems intended to make the ideas of these men more humane and more accessible.

The nexus of the Lacanian Real with the Althusserian notion of ***ideology*** becomes his field of creative exploration and refinement. While the book is not a flowing, comprehensive treatise, it is filled with bits and pieces that can give the reader new insights into Marx, Lacan, and Althusser. More accessible than Hegel, Lacan, and Althusseur, Žižek has a habit of playing loose with ideas. He provides the reader with an imaginative understanding of the works he explores. Above all Žižek is entertaining and intends to be so. His critical questioning of everyday phenomena coupled with his comedic approach to the material could easily make him the Seinfeld of the popular theory set.

More than anything else, Žižek is closely identified with the work of Lacan, primarily because Žižek draws on his ideas, categories, and theories. Having been analyzed by Lacan's brother-in-law, Jacques Alain-Miller, he also studied psychoanalysis with him at the *Université Paris*. In *The Sublime Object of Ideology* (1989), he provides the reader with a meaningful interpretation of Lacan's three registers.

While it is nearly impossible to capture the full range of Žižek's work here, it is important to note that his contributions are much in the vein of Roland Barthes or Georg Simmel, but only on amphetamines. Taking a lesson from Lacan, his writing is often abstruse. It is difficult to pin him down. But this is often intentional. In some ways it is as though we find him in the midst of constant self-contradiction.

The Sublime Object of Ideology maps out Žižek's expansive intellectual terrain: Kant, Hegel, Marx, Freud, Althusser, the Frankfurt school, and Lacan. At first blush there does not appear to be an authentic sense of critical theory here. But it is actually buried in the stream-of-consciousness, free association writing style, which at times seems insufferable. Sentences run on for seven or sometimes twelve lines; examples turn into cul-de-sac detours. Different ideas are jammed between two periods. References range from Pascal to Milos Forman. Still Žižek manages to pull off what he seemingly sets out to accomplish. He succeeds at applying Lacan to understanding the role of ideology in contemporary society for those readers who are patient enough to follow him.

While Žižek never does this plainly, he does it insightfully. For Žižek, the malaise suffered in capitalistic societies is not all that different from that suffered in feudal ones, or socialist ones. The malaise (if we can call it this) is living in a delusional world and being imprisoned by illusion, which is a reaffirmation of the poststructural project. It is an attempt to show us that things are not as they appear. In fact they are often (most often) the opposite—or at least filled with contradictions. This has been an important characteristic of poststructuralism up until now. While Žižek begins by taking us through a re-exposition of Marx's notion of commodity fetishism and false consciousness, he further evolves his discussion into the Althusserian concept of ideology minus Althusser. But his work is more a reformulation or critique of Althusser.

According to Žižek, ideology is the set of ideas individuals use to understand themselves and their relationship to society. It allows people to register the world around them as whole or complete. It substitutes itself for a disjointed hegemonic reality by becoming a mode of understanding or masking, which is more fantasy than reality. But ideology is always false, always proceeding from false consciousness. People understand that they live in a world in which reality is created by powerful interests, but they are willing to accept this as their reality rather than face the fragmented nothingness or total domination that they perceive lurks beneath it. Made powerless by the means of production, they seek a place of safety. This is where the Kantian notion of the sublime comes in. The sublime masks the fissures or cracks in the whole. Here the sublime is represented by transcendental concepts that provide the individual with the impression that there are exceptional forces at work keeping the world operating, forces such as God or King, Freedom or Nationhood, Truth or Certainty.

Ideology has led to self-domination, self-delusion, inordinate alienation, and cynicism among most classes. For instance, Žižek views the entire market economy as a mirage based on behaving as though people are part of the market system. Money, which is a total abstraction, becomes the basis of all human relations and modern consumer culture. And as Marx suggested early on, the form of commodity exchange comes to characterize all human relationships. People must believe in the market. Although he does not reference Levi-Strauss, Žižek recognizes the importance of commodity exchange in producing the structures, which in turn constitute the basis for most interpersonal relations and provide the foundation for nonreflexive capitalistic ideology. Žižek's sociology is a recognition of the powers of domination inherent in those symbolic forces working to maintain the economic and social order.

He is careful to assure us that some element or kernel of the Real exists even within the fantasy that has been created. Thus, ideology is merely a partial dream, not a full one. He refers to the real element in ideology as a surplus-object. But here Žižek is referring to the Lacanian Real—that which is not corrupted by language and lives outside the system of segmentalization created through hegemonic language.

In bringing in Lacan to illuminate Marx, Žižek uses the Lacanian notion of *objet petit-a,* a term that represents the unobtainable object of desire, or an unspecific, unarticulated lack. This is what Lacan himself referred to as *excess **jouissance**,* defined as pleasure beyond that which is pleasurable, or surplus pleasure—an idea Lacan derived from Marx's notion of surplus value. This object of desire is never really specific. Therefore, it can neither be satisfied nor contained; it is open-ended.

While capitalism poses as a closed system, a self-perpetuating engine of desires and satisfactions, there is, in reality, no such thing. What puts the brakes on capitalism is supposedly the boundaries of capital itself. But there are no boundaries. Capitalism becomes a revolutionary force that, instead of being impeded by the boundaries of available capital, is challenged to change because of these boundaries—constantly revolutionizing its own material conditions. Thus, it is the lack or the *objet petit-a,* the surplus-pleasure, that drives the engine. *Enjoy* becomes the edict of unrestrained neoliberalism—the adage of capitalistic one-dimensionality. *Eat until you can eat no more. Consume until all is consumed. It is okay.* It is the *divine* order of things. It is *natural.* It is *God's will.*

One merely needs to turn to the Frankfurt school of Marcuse, Horkheimer, and Adorno to trace the historical elements of Žižek's capitalistic critique (Sharpe, 2004). Certainly, the nexus of Marx, the Frankfurt school, Lacan, and Žižek is the total sense of alienation suffered in capitalistic societies—the fragmentation and commodification of everything in capital's path. It is also the sense of hegemonic domination and totalizing ideology from which there is no escape and the mass consumer culture that accompanies it.

Inherent in Žižek is an attempt to expose and undermine all ideology. He uses Lacanian analysis to do just this, as in the example of the *objet petit-a.* Sometimes it is done successfully, other times not so much. But it is always interesting; or perhaps cynically amusing is a better descriptor. Žižek's sociological project is to expose the weaknesses inherent with the Symbolic order and to do so with humor and incisiveness.

Žižek confronts all subject matter he addresses dialectically. He challenges, pulls things apart, and negates. He also confronts what he sees as the ideology that surrounds capitalistic consumption, which is where we find his uniqueness as a poststructuralist. His obvious interest in the vicissitudes of Real life, Real politics, and his sociological orientation to subject matter give him a special place among contemporary theorists.

More than any other Lacanian, he wants to apply Lacan, not just ruminate about his value as a theorist. Thus, in his book *Looking Awry: An Introduction to Jacques Lacan Through Popular Culture* (2000) he takes the hand of the unindoctrinated and leads the neophyte through the dizzying world of his mentor. He hooks the reader with images of popular culture—films, products, and the like, and uses Lacanian thought.

The world of Žižek is an upside-down world wherein the rational is irrational; the cultural contradiction holds sway. It is a world in which the tyranny of words and, as Milan Kundera would say, a world of lightness of being Žižek's world is one in which facts are fictions and movies speak misinterpreted truths. It is a place in which critical thought is suspended and dead things come to life.

POSTSTRUCTURALISM IN THE NEW MILLENNIUM

As a perspective, poststructuralism gained considerably more currency in literary and film criticism than in the social sciences. There seem to be several reasons for this. The first is obviously the intense focus on language and symbolism in these areas. Another is that social science has taken a skeptical stance on the linguistic turn and subjective interpretations. Social scientists need to be able to communicate their findings clearly to various policy makers who reside outside the academy. The nomenclature of poststructuralist theory is relatively new and unfamiliar to most people. It is highly abstract and written in an inaccessible manner.

On the other hand the seeming resistance to poststructuralism on the part of social science might say something about the nature of criticism itself and the conflicting ways people attempt to understand human behavior and creative work. Poststructuralism has promoted a new discussion of culture and a questioning of assumptions at every level. It can be no surprise that it has slowly made its way into every corner of the academy, into nearly every nook and cranny of research. Still it remains generally esoteric.

In the United States particularly but also in France, many intellectuals have challenged poststructuralism's value as an authoritative perspective. In *Z Magazine*'s online bulletin board, Noam Chomsky once described Lacan as "an amusing and perfectly self-conscious charlatan" and once described poststructuralism as "cult-like." Two theoretical physicists, Alan Sokal and Jean Bricmont (1997) called poststructuralism a hoax and condemned Lacan as nothing more than a misguided and unsophisticated thinker borrowing terms from science and math and using them improperly. But those sympathetic with poststructuralism fired back, claiming that people who attempted to understand these ideas by the standards of positivist science were misguided (Plotniski 2002; Fink 2004). It was obvious that as the twenty-first century emerged, paradigms were shifting.

Sociologist Charles Lemert (1990) suggests that sociologists have much to learn from poststructuralism. First and foremost was that all social action is discursive activity, as is the theory that describes it. One cannot enter into an understanding of the social world without a text, and theory formation is essentially a textual process. While this does not negate the need for quantitative study, quantitative measures are primarily used to illustrate and support textual assertions and expostulations. And Ben Agger (1991), a contemporary social theorists, proposes that deconstructionism, in particular, provides the social scientist with a new means of assessing quantitative methodology—reading it as a text, which it is after all. "Deconstruction refuses to view methodology simply as a set of technical procedures with which to manipulate data. Rather methodology can be opened up to readers intrigued by its deep assumptions and its empirical findings but otherwise daunted by its densely technical and figural nature" (Ben Agger 1991, p. 114). Thus, the poststructural paradigm provides another way by which the material of sociological study can be approached. As has been noted before, it does not eliminate the need for other perspectives, but it does enrich the field of social exploration.

It seems logical that the impact of *poststructuralism* would be felt first in those areas of sociology frequently associated with feminist theorists—studies in sexuality and gender. Both feminism and poststructuralism brought the body back into focus in the social sciences and set a new course for the exploration of race and ethnicity. And while social constructionism was gaining prominence in social theory, it was deconstruction that gave it new life and helped to articulate it more adequately.

POSTSTRUCTURALISM AND THE END OF THEORY

Rumors of the death of theory have been circulating throughout the past decade, and poststructuralism is implicated quite frequently in its homicide (Eagleton 2003; Davis 2004). But there is no corpse to be found, and theory continues to live and breathe. The fragmentation of theory into a superfluity of micro-order speculations is another matter. Certainly the advent of structuralism and post-structuralism have splintered the grand narrative form and let into the academy the running dogs of postmodernism with new inventions such as poststructuralist anarchism. But many subtler categories of speculative thought have appeared, ranging from innovative feminist theory to postcolonial thought, from cultural studies to consumer semiotics. Some of it subscribes to the label of postmodern, some not so much. While much of this discourse is still wedded to the past, a lot of it is constituted by a new and creative synthesis of old and new ideas. The development of new categories and the reorganization of the old have transformed the appearance and vitality of social thought. Theory has never been more popular, more alive!

Many have viewed what is frequently referred to as postmodern theory as the newest developmental plateau of critical social thought. But in this text (see Chapter 5), it is examined not as the newest type of theory but as a broad category that takes on characteristics of the time and place in which it is found. Thus, post-modern thought exists in contrast to that deemed to be modern. Its concerns, its tools, and its structures are all quite different from that which has been catego-rized as modern.

Just as structuralism continues in the work of Žižek, poststructuralism is also carried on in his work. Structuralism and poststructuralism have often tended to morph into one another (probably having something to do with the collapse of time and space). Frequently, both are seen as postmodern perspectives. But often the authors of such theory shy away from such classifications. Very few of the

French theorists would refer to their work as poststructural or postmodern. These are critical categories carved out by critics, teachers, the academic industry, and consumers. But by whatever name theory continues.

KEY TERMS

deconstruction The skeptical and critical poststructural approach created by Jacques Derrida that undermines the meaning of structural linguistics by exposing the inherent flaws of language. A deconstructionist reading of a text subverts its "objective" meaning by unveiling the inherent contradictions within it, allowing for endless reinterpretation. There are no determinate meanings, only the infinite play of signifiers.

différance Jacques Derrida's term used to combine the idea of defer, or being somehow present while having been omitted (such as a trace), and differ, or being distinct or discernibly different.

discursive innovations Term used by Kristeva to explain the role of transgression that gives rise to new discourse. Such innovations in discourse and in practice that emerge from the semiotic have the potential of becoming themselves normalized and changing the symbolic order. Through the arts and poetic language, we have the greatest potential for such liberation.

epistemes As used by Foucault, a term for things taken as axiomatic, taken for granted at face value, such as sexuality.

Foucault's notion of power Foucault locates all power in discourse. It is his position that power rests not within people, but within institutional arrangements that have been defined by language. Power is not contained within the individual but within the structure of language.

Foucault's notion of truth For Foucault all truth is entrenched in power. One cannot achieve truth without it. Power is truth's articulation.

ideology A set of ideas that individuals use to understand themselves and their relationship to society. It allows people to register the world around them as whole, or complete. It substitutes itself for a disjointed hegemonic reality by becoming a mode of understanding or masking, which is more fantasy than reality.

labial lips An idea developed by Irigaray to challenge Lacan's phallocentrism and to explain the interdependence of the material body and discourse. The vaginal "lips" represent the complexity and dynamics of feminine signification. Irigaray posits that the discursive body precedes the physical one.

jouissance (literally: enjoyment) A French word used by Lacan to imply the desire to abolish the condition of lack.

logocentric A term used in poststructural discourse to refer to a type of thought born out of the Enlightenment wherein truth is singular and can be found only in nature.

phallocentrism The privileging of the masculine in understanding meaning or social relations.

poststructuralism A philosophical and sociological rejection of structuralism; it is marked by the decentering of the subject, the rejection of binary oppositions, a radical turn toward intersubjectivity, and an emphasis on the relativity of truth and value.

the-Name-of-the-Father The notion developed by Jacques Lacan that language is the powerful tool of male domination, and to accept the language is to resolve one's oedipal complex in his sense of the term. Not only does the child take on the language in order to be connected, but she or he also takes on the laws and assumes the imposed restrictions on desire as posited by patriarchal authority.

tracer A term originally developed by Augustine and later adopted by deconstruction to mean the clue (or trace) of a hidden original meaning behind a sign.

tyrannical reason Michel Foucault's view of bounded rationality, imbued with power that makes people into subjects.

virtual world Žižek uses this term to describe the "unreal reality" that characterizes the postmodern life-world. Constructed by the elaborate mechanisms of neocapitalist society, the virtual world is a hyper-real, exaggerated delusion created by fantastical ideology with some kernel of the "real" existing within it.

SOURCES

Agger, Ben. 1991. "Critical Theory, Poststructuralism, Postmodernism: Their Sociological Relevance," *American Review of Sociology*, Vol. 17, pp. 105–131.

Agger, Ben. 1994. "Derrida for Sociology? A Comment on Fuchs and Ward," *American Sociological Review*, Vol. 59, No. 4, pp. 481–500.

Bedggood, David. 1999. "Saint Jacques: Derrida and the Ghost of Marxism," *Critical Logic*, Vol. 2, No. 2. Electronic journal.

Cixous, Hélène. 1976. "The Laugh of Medusa," *Signs*, Vol. 1, No. 4, pp. 875–893.

Clark, Robert. 2004. "The Imaginary," *The Literary Encyclopeadia*. 10 January.

Davis, Colin. 2004. *After Poststructuralism, Reading Stories and Theories*. New York: Routledge.

Dean, Carolyn. 1994. "The Productive Hypothesis: Foucault, Gender, and the History of Sexuality," *History and Theory*, Vol. 33, No. 3, pp. 271–296.

Derrida, Jacques. 1974. *Of Grammatology*. Baltimore, MD: Johns Hopkins University Press.

Derrida, Jacques. 1994. *Specters of Marx, the State of Debt, the Work of Mourning, and the New International*. New York: Routledge.

Eagleton, Terry. 2003. *After Theory*. New York: Basic Books.

Fermon, Nicole. 1998. "Irigaray and the Political Future of Sexual Difference," *Diacritics*, Vol. 28. No. 1. Electronic journal.

Fink, Bruce. 2004. *Lacan to the Letter*. Minneapolis, MN: University of Minnesota Press.

Foucault, Michel. 1990. *The History of Sexuality, Vol. I*. New York: Vintage Books.

Foucault, Michel. 1982. "The Subject and Power," *Critical Inquiry*, Vol. 8, No. 4, pp. 777–795.

Foucault, Michel. 1975. *The Birth of the Clinic*. New York: Vintage.

Foucault, Michel. 1970. *The Order of Things*. New York: Pantheon Books.

Hall, Stuart. 1996. "The Question of Cultural Identity," in Stuart Hall, David Held, Don Hubert, Kenneth Thompson, eds., Modernity. Oxford: Blackwell.

Hartmann, John. 2003. "Power and Resistance in the Later Foucault." Paper presented at the Third Annual Meeting of the Foucault Circle, John Carol University, Cleveland, Ohio.

Irigaray, Luce. 1985. *The Speculum of Other Women*, (French edition, 1974). Trans. by G. C.,Gill. New York: Cornell University Press.

Irigaray, Luce. 1977. Ce Sexe qui n'en est pas un Editions de Minuit. Published as The Sex Which Is Not One (1985). Ithaca, NY: Cornell University Press.

Kristeva, Julia. 1982. *Powers of Horror: An Essay on Abjection.* New York: Columbia University Press.

Lemert, Charles. 1990. "The Use of French Structuralism in Sociology," in G. Ritzer, ed., *Frontiers of Social Theory: New Syntheses.* New York: Columbia University Press.

Minahen, Charles. 1997. *Situating Sartre in Twentieth Century Thought and Culture.* New York: St. Martin's Press.

Plonitsky, Arkady. 2002. *The Knowable and the Unknowable.* Ann Arbor, MI: University of Michigan Press.

Reynolds, Jack. 2004. *Merleau-Ponty and Derrida.* Athens, OH: Ohio University Press.

Sharpe Matthew. 2004. *Slavoj Žižek: A Little Piece of the Real.* London: Ashgate.

Smith, Peter Michael. 1992. "Postmodernism, Urban Ethnography, and the New Space of Ethnic Identity," *Theory and Society,* Vol. 21, pp. 493–531.

Sokal, Alan and Jean Bricmont. 1998. *Fashionable Nonsense: Postmodern Intellectuals' Abuse of Science.* New York: Picador.

Stone, Alison. 2003. "The Sex of Nature: A Reinterpretation of Irigaray's Metaphysics and Political Thought," *Hypatia.*Vol. 18, No. 3, pp. 60–84.

Žižek, Slavjo. 2000. *Looking Awry: An Introduction to Jacques Lacan Through Popular Culture.* Cambridge, MA: MIT Press.

Žižek, Slavjo. 1989. *The Sublime Object of Ideology.* London: Verso.

CHAPTER 5

Exploding the Boundaries
of Reason: Postmodernity

N o one can say for sure what postmodernity is—or what modernity is, for
that matter. Although there have been many opinions offered, both remain
rather contentious concepts. As theory goes, postmodernity is frequently
characterized as a rupture from the past and a challenge to reason. It commonly
privileges the subjective over the objective and calls into question the values of the
European Enlightenment.

Debate continues about the origins of the term *postmodernity*. The arts are
seen as the progenitors of postmodern sensibilities and aesthetics—beating out
philosophy, literature, history, and the social sciences. Some who speak of the
postmodern talk of an epoch; others see it as a reaction to the spirit of modernity,
whatever that was or is. But social theorists have frequently embraced it as a new
perspective—a way of examining the phenomenological world in which we live.
Those who never recognized its significance have seen it as a passing intellectual
fad—one that has already come and gone.

However, an important epistemological challenge in the routine of social theory is how to distinguish postmodern thought from poststructuralism. Sociologist
Ben Agger (1991, pp. 111–114) has suggested that there is no real consensus on this
matter. He sees primers on contemporary theory distinguishing the two in a vast
assortment of ways:

> Although most agree that Derrida is a poststructuralist (even though he does not
> identify himself as such), Foucault, Barthes, and Lyotard can be claimed by either
> camp and often are. And the French Feminists (Kristeva 1980; Irigaray 1985; Cixous
> 1980) are sometimes viewed as proponents of poststructuralism (e.g., Weedon 1987).
> The lack of a clear definition reflects the purposeful elusiveness of work that can be
> variously classified as poststructural and/or postmodern.

Agger goes on to suggest, "Perhaps the most important hallmark of all of
this work is its aversion to clean positivist definitions and categories" (p. 112).

Sara Ahmed (1998, p. 4), a professor of race and cultural studies at Goldsmith College at the University of London, makes the point that by attempting to define postmodernism, one must assume that it has a referent, "that there is something (out there or in here) that we can adequately call postmodern." But with deconstruction, the whole notion of a clear referent is challenged. As feminist theorist Rita Felski (2000, p. 101) has suggested: "Postmodernism is the ultimate example of a floating signifier, a term whose meaning fluctuates dramatically according to context."

While both poststructuralism and postmodernism break with modernity and all that it envisions, postmodernism appears at times to be most reckless, most radical, and most unsystematic in its critique. But again, one is at a disadvantage when conflating these two seemingly unique theoretical perspectives into a logical categorical system they both supposedly reject.

Agger (1991) proposes that postmodern theory is much more a critique of society than poststructuralism. Unlike modernism or postmodernism, poststructuralism is a form of analytic thought; it is neither a description of society at a particular period in time nor a collection of aesthetic characteristics. However, to better articulate postmodern theory, which is the primary subject of this chapter, an examination of what constitutes the modern is necessary.

MODERNITY AND ITS DISCONTENTS

Generally speaking, modernism and postmodernism are viewed as aesthetic categories. They reflect particular cultural values and outlooks distinguishing themselves from (but also associated with) particular epochs or eras, such as the *modern age* or the *postmodern era*. Modernism is seen as a reaction to the modern age, while simultaneously being a reflection of it. For Henri Lefebvre (1995), modernism and modernity are viewed as antithetical. In art and literature, modernism is an aesthetic movement that emphasizes self-consciousness, individualism, and a rejection of traditional forms of art, literature, and architecture associated with preindustrial society. This is similarly true for postmodernism and postmodernity. Modernity and postmodernity are most often used as categories that distinguish particular cultures or ways of life associated with these periods of time from the aesthetics of those eras.

To map out this territory of postmodernity accurately, one must start at modernity, which postmodernity supposedly rejects, including its notion of the importance of empirical science, and its concept of universal truth and all that goes along with it. Yet modernity is the place that calls into question traditional life; it is the anteroom of postmodernity. Very often it is difficult to distinguish the exact boundaries of the modern from the postmodern. But there have been many attempts to do so—some more fruitful than others. It must be said from the start, however, that there are strong arguments asserting that postmodernity is merely a late stage of modernity (Giddens 1990) and that there is nothing particularly revolutionary about it at all. In a sense, the modern/postmodern binary underlies all postmodern theory, which rejects all binaries. But if we accept a social constructionist view of the world, it would be difficult to deny postmodernity's existence. What is certain is that not everyone lives in a postmodern world, or even a modern one, for that matter. And even those who recognize the validity of such descriptors (or can distinguish between them) are in the minority. But to really understand these concepts as theory, we must start with an exploration of the modern. To do this, it is important to see how it has been theoretically constructed.

JÜRGEN HABERMAS: MODERNITY AS A PROJECT

The word *modern* cannot be translated accurately into all languages. Its meaning always appears to be culturally bound. Often words like *modern*, **modernity**, *modernism*, and *modernization* are used to mean the same thing. The first definition of the word *modern* in the Oxford English Dictionary indicates that it is something contemporary or current. Thus, what one person might perceive to be *obsolete* is another person's *modern*. Over the years, the word has taken on particular cultural aspects, primarily European, and has come to represent a way of life that is associated with protocol as opposed to ritual, coolness as opposed to warmth, intellect as opposed to emotion, urban as opposed to rural, atomistic as opposed to communal, and so on. The modern is associated with a particular type of architecture, art, and literature. It represents a decline of traditional and religious life and the rise of a more impersonal, secularized one. Often it is equated with industrialization; it is frequently associated with a rapidly changing order of things to the point of near disorder and chaos. At the same time, it celebrates control—particularly control over nature. It is strong on science. From the vantage point of European and American historians, modernity occupies a time in the West spanning the centuries following the decline of feudalism and marked by the rise of market capitalism. The word *modernity*, as used in the social sciences, describes this so-called modern condition. It conveys what it is to be modern.

Jürgen Habermas is one of sociology's best known contemporary social theorists and is seen by many as the successor of Max Weber and other classical sociologists who discussed social change and modernization. Like Marx, he sees modernity as having within it the seeds for human progress and liberation. Unlike most contemporary theorists, he is comfortable in articulating utopian value-laden visions based on reason in grand and all-encompassing theoretical discourse. While Habermas was educated in the Frankfurt school tradition (in fact he was a student of Adorno), he is viewed by many scholars of theory as very far removed from their critical theories, which radically challenged the European Enlightenment. Although he is not completely comfortable with all aspects of the European Enlightenment himself, he believes that it helped set the stage for a modern ethos, which he attempts to articulate and defend in his work. He subscribes to the notions of totality and wholeness, which set him apart from other contemporary theorists.

Best known for his project of establishing a theory of communicative action to help build consensus and bring about democratic order and universal understanding through a rational use of language, Habermas (1981, 1990) sees such an undertaking deeply indebted to what he has called "the project of modernity." While he recognizes the powerful aesthetics inherent in European modernism, the project of modernity of which he speaks also focuses on those ideas formulated in the eighteenth century by the European Enlightenment philosophers who wished to develop an objective science, universal morality and law, and autonomous art based on an inner logic. He sees modernism as expressed in this new consciousness, distinct from that of antiquity.

For Habermas (1997), modern thinkers and philosophers want to see society rationally organized through the use of specialized cultures and to use these specializations for the enhancement of everyday life. Beyond this, they hope that the arts and sciences will promote not only control of the natural world but also a better understanding of the inner world of the self, while at the same time encouraging justice and enabling the development of morality based on reason leading to universal human happiness.

Like Weber, Habermas sees the development of modern society driven by an underlying notion of reason, which is multidimensional but chiefly operates at two levels: instrumental reasoning (a term used by Max Weber to describe closed-ended, institutionally bounded rationality) and what he terms communicative, or moral reasoning. While these operate at different levels (the first at the structural, the second at the life-world or subjective order), both are connected and need to be preserved because each serves a particular purpose. The life-world is the source of true, noninstrumental reason, which emerges from tradition and history. From it evolves structures or social institutions that promote instrumental reason. Modernity has been attacking the subjective life-world. It has invaded and colonized this world. Habermas finds this to be something that must be overcome through communicative action. But modernity holds out the chance for a universal truth that can pierce parochialism, so all can share in a more generalized set of values and truths and all can reap its liberating benefits. Modernity splits faith from knowledge and wants to replace idiosyncratic religious myth with a transcendental moral order based on reason.

Inherent in Habermas's defense of modernity is not so much a defense of modern aesthetics, but rather a defense of Enlightenment thought, which he views as represented in that aesthetic. However, he sometimes fails to distinguish Enlightenment values from modern ones, which sometimes are at odds with each other. He frequently conflates Enlightenment thought with modernist thinking, particularly in the area of aesthetics. And there is little recognition that modern art is very often a rejection of Enlightenment notions of objectivity and reason, as much as are postmodern aesthetics. He thus posits his own particular brand of modernism, which he constructs from his reading of philosophy, particularly Kant, wherein universal truths still exist. It is a modernism at odds with Nietzsche's sense of modern disorder and cultural relativism.

While Habermas sees modernity failing in its intellectual mission as a force of human liberation and enlightenment, he believes that it has produced much good. His own work is oriented toward developing a theory of communicative action that will enable its redemption. He wants to see both the Enlightenment and modernity live up to what he views as their enormous potential.

ANTHONY GIDDENS AND THE CONSEQUENCES OF MODERNITY

Anthony Giddens's approach to modernity is somewhat different. He has taken on the task of attempting to describe it and how it works rather than coming to its philosophic defense. For many contemporary social theorists, including Giddens (1991), modernity has produced distinct social forms of social organizations, the most prominent of which is the nation-state (Giddens 1991, p. 15).

For Giddens (1990, pp. 17–18) modern social organization means "the regularized control of social relations across indefinite time-space distances." In examining what he sees as the "discontinuities" of modern life that separate the modern from the more traditional social order, he posits that a number of distinct features emerge. These features include a rapid change of pace enhanced by modern technology, and an ever-broadening scope of such change—the extent of which has greatly affected the world in which we all now live. He introduces the concept of what he calls the *time-space distanciation*. By this, he means that space and time are no longer connected through place as they have been in more traditional societies. In other words, in premodern societies, one could understand time only as a function of the place where it occurred. The advent of portable time or the mechanical clock "emptied space" of much of its meaning.

Modernity requires and uses time for coordinating activities around the globe. One of the more consequential outcomes of this distanciation is what Giddens describes as the "disembedding of social institutions," by which he means lifting out social relations from local contexts. Here human interaction is less face-to-face and more remote. Modern forms of human interaction and exchange become more impersonal and abstract. The money economy exemplifies how social relations are depersonalized, how they are disembedded. Now one must rely on experts and pay them for their advice. Here, Giddens emphasizes what he sees as an essential pillar of modernity—its reliance on trust. Given the highly abstract and impersonal nature of relationships in the money economy, modern society needs a high level of trust to function adequately.

With modern life comes intense urbanization and its various manifestations for good and for ill: commodification of products, commodification of people, and dependence on inanimate sources of power—all of which reflect the powerful influence of global capitalism. He proposes that the modern individual constantly confronts key dilemmas: fragmentation of the self versus self-unification, powerlessness versus appropriation, authority versus uncertainty, the personalized versus the commodified experience. Also, in modern societies individuals, networks, and institutions begin to move to develop new courses of action. He views this as the basis of contemporary theory. "It is impossible," he notes "to have a modern sovereign state that does not incorporate a discursively articulated theory of the modern sovereign state. The marked tendency towards an expansion of political 'self-monitoring' on the part of the state is characteristic of modernity in the West in general, creating the social and intellectual climate from which specialized, 'professional' discourses of social sciences have developed but also both express and foster" (Giddens 1984, p. xxxiii). He sees this phenomenon as affecting all modern social institutions and individuals. There is always feedback and a course of change based on new information.

Not only does he look at the broader structural aspects that have evolved to give modernity order and shape but he also takes his analysis to the level of self-identity and social interaction (Giddens 1991, 1992). In doing so, Giddens believes modern societies are characterized by a high degree of what he terms *constitutive reflexivity*. (This part of his analysis is obviously influenced by George Mead's work). Here, he means that self-identity moves further and further away from proscriptions of the traditional order of social life and becomes a product of interactions with those quite different from the more one-dimensional tradition-based self.

Giddens's theory is in the grand narrative tradition of most other modernist social theories. Like Habermas, his work is classically sociological. Over the years and in several volumes he has mapped out and refined a set of interconnected propositions that attempt to give modernity character and meaning. Unlike Habermas, who has attacked postmodernism as a rejection of Enlightenment thought and an embrace of nihilism, Giddens sees important insights within this area of theoretical development. He finds Habermas's embrace of a universal truth unfounded and disconcerting (Giddens 1987).

POSTMODERNITY WITHOUT MODERNITY: IHAB HASSAN

Not having captured any universal meaning of modernity at this juncture, we are required to move speedily into the intellectual thicket of postmodern theory. This makes perfect sense if we come to understand that there are no universal definitions in the postmodern world either. Ihab Hassan will help us with this venture.

Ihab Hassan is an Egyptian-born American literary and cultural theorist. Much of his work has focused on what he viewed as the emergence of the postmodern and what has been used to distinguish it from the modern. Well ahead of others on this subject, he spoke of postmodern sensibilities in art and literature as long ago as the 1960s. Others are just catching up to him. But Hassan himself makes no claim to truly understand what the postmodern is exactly, nor does he claim it actually exists. To serve us with some sort of roadmap in this regard, he has created lists and an array of descriptors, which have been generally used to liberate the term *postmodern* from *modern*. Of course, Hassan warns us that his lists of characteristics are overlapping, too general, too constricting, conflicting, conflating, and unstable. But all of these are indeed features of the so-called postmodern world. Perhaps Hassan is best known for a list of stylistic oppositions, which appears in dozens of essays and texts, and which attempts to articulate the

TABLE 5-1   Schematic differences between modernism and postmodernism

Modernism	Postmodernism
purpose	play
design	chance
hierarchy	anarchy
presence	absence
centering	dispersal
signified	signifier
metaphysics	irony

Source: Part of a list provided by Hassan (1985, p. 123).

essential difference between modern and postmodern. Table 5.1 constitutes a fraction of his original list.

Hassan also offers what he calls a cantena of postmodern features that, for him, "[stakes] out a cultural field" (1986, p. 504). These features include *indeterminacies*, which encompasses all manner of ambiguities, ruptures, and displacements affecting knowledge and society; *fragmentation*, or opposition to totalization because of the trust only of fragments; *decanonization*—representing the destabilization of the historical place of authoritative works and their displacement by more minor ones from the margins that challenge them; *selfless states*, representing the loss of the modern notion of the stable self in which there exists both a subject and an object; *the unrepresentable*, which signifies a rejection of a division between the real and the artificial, or the imagined from the perceived—something formless and perhaps amorphous; *irony*, representing the rejection of seriousness, wherein both humor and playfulness take the place of rationalistic, comprehensive paradigms; *hybridization*, meaning an embrace of parody, pastiche, and kitsch in place of a romance with pure holistic types; **carnivalization**, which he derives from Bakhtin's "embrace of the celebratory" or continued renewal a feast of becoming that rejects authority and seriousness (Bakhtin 1941); *performance,* wherein the stage represents society and all life is a show directed to an audience and where the actor works to construct some form of role; *constructionism*, where thought constructs reality and fiction is as vital as fact; and, finally, Hassan speaks of *immanence*. By this he means that each person is extended through time and space, through media and reflexivity, into a dimension that places one's being at the center of the universe. This has to do with the power of language, which trumps all other power.

Hassan is not so naïve to believe that postmodernity will ever be truly defined. He plays with the notion as he feels it plays with us. Certainly, there is no consensus on what it is. Neither is there a consensus on what constitutes modernity. And all Hassan can say about postmodernity is that it is constituted by a "shifting matrix of ideas" that might never find consensus and might never harden from its intrinsic "softness" into a term like *baroque*. Yet the lack of definitions has never stopped scholars from developing social theory—certainly not the postmodern kind.

DAVID HARVEY AND THE POSTMODERN CONDITION

But to understand postmodernity and postmodern theory, one needs to develop some sense of the alleged distinctions between the modern and the postmodern. In doing this, it is important *not* to assume a binary or dichotomous relationship between the two categories. Accordingly, various things long considered modern might well be considered postmodern by some, and some things that are postmodern are nearly indistinguishable from things that are modern. So where do we start?

In many ways, postmodern social theory is a serious attempt to come to terms with radical changes that undermine modern societies and disturb order and a sense of stability. While elements of postmodern theory can be found in the work of Immanuel Kant, this theory is more immediately an outgrowth of poststructuralism and postexistential phenomenology. Habermas (1981) suggests that, in philosophy, the break with modernity and the European Enlightenment came with Nietzsche. Nietzsche attacked the notion of universal truth and viewed it as the imposition of colonial power to create order and regimentation in the western world.

David Harvey, a professor of geography and anthropology at the Graduate Center of the City University of New York, has presented an important comparative discussion of the modern/postmodern condition without delving deeply into philosophical discourse. In his brilliant book, *The Condition of Postmodernity* (1989), Harvey recognizes the historic, aesthetic, cultural, and social significance of these labels, and presents us with the dramatic motifs running through both modernism and postmodernism.

Drawing on architectural literature, where postmodernism was first clearly articulated and defined, Harvey presents a description of postmodernism as a legitimate reaction to the monotony of universal modernism's vision of the world: "Generally perceived as positivistic, technocratic, and rationalistic, universal modernism has been identified with the belief in linear progress, absolute truths, the rational planning of ideal social orders, and the standardization of knowledge and production." This is contrasted with postmodernism, which privileges "heterogeneity and difference as liberative forces in the redefinition of cultural discourse" (PRECIS 6, Cited in Harvey 1989, p. 9). Part of this postmodern condition is the rediscovery of pragmatic philosophy and an emphasis on discontinuity. Like Hassan, Harvey goes on: "Fragmentation, indeterminacy, and intense distrust of all universal or `totalizing' discourses (to use the favored phrase) are the hallmark of postmodernist thought" (Harvey 1989, p. 9). In attempting to define postmodernity as a condition, Harvey borrows descriptions from a variety of observers, such as Andreas Huyssens (1984), Terry Eagleton (1987), Fredric Jameson (1984), and Jean-François Lyotard (1979), none of whom are social scientists, and all of whom make extensive use of literary theory.

For Andreas Huyssens, who is a professor of comparative literature at Columbia University, the postmodern condition is primarily an aesthetic one that involves cultural and political changes resting outside the conceptual framework of both modernism and *avant-gardism*. It is not that postmodernity is an extension of the modern aesthetic condition; rather, it is a reaction to that condition—what Huyssen calls a great divide, or division between what he views as high culture and mass culture. For him, postmodernism is a cultural and social phenomenon that transcends the division.

Huyssens sees postmodernism as embracing much of what modernism attempted to overcome—that which did not sit well with modernism. At the same time, much like modernity, postmodernity is an historical and cultural condition that houses within itself oppositional cultural practices and strategies. He views it as distinct from modernism in that it raises new questions of cultural tradition and conservation both as aesthetic and political issues operating within a field of tension between tradition and innovation, conservation and renewal, mass culture and high art—a field of tensions but wherein there is no true opposition, no binary. Postmodernity is a place that no longer offers a privileged position such as opposition between reaction and progress, present and past, modernism and realism. While such oppositions were vital to modernism, they are not important under the postmodern condition.

Terry Eagleton, a British literary critic and influential theorist, views postmodernism simply as a style of thought that is suspicious of classical notions of reason, truth, identity, and objectivity. It is suspect of the drive for universal progress and emancipation, of single frameworks and grand narratives. It positions itself as opposed to these and other Enlightenment norms, and views the world as contingent, ungrounded, unstable, diverse, and indeterminate. In this place the body becomes the site of struggle and resistance. It is well in keeping with rampant consumerism.

Eagleton (1987) sees a cultural leveling associated with postmodernism. Culture, not science, becomes the central way of knowing. And science becomes merely one among many diverse avenues to knowledge or to truth that is viewed as relativistic anyway. Despite its many shortcomings, postmodernism does seem to have had some powerful positive implications for gender and race, in that it seems to have challenged structured notions of human sexuality and identity.

Fredric Jameson, a renowned Marxist literary critic, views postmodernism as the culture of late capitalism. He also sees it as associated with mass culture, which emerged after World War II. While modernism promoted the concept of an authentic self, postmodernity denies its existence considers it as ideological, much as Althusser had proposed. Postmodernism retains many of the features of what was once defined in the arts as high modernism, but it is fully integrated into the system of commodity production. For this, like Huyssen, Jameson draws on Adorno's critical critique of the culture industry. However, Jameson's postmodernism represents an historical periodization—a condition that emerges over time but is relegated to a period. This one rests beyond industrial capitalism, beyond the 1950s and 1960s. He also uses the term *a cultural dominant* to define it.

By this he means that which allows for both the presence and the coexistence of a range of diverse features—some old and some new. He also sees postmodernism as a "force field" through which different sorts of cultural impulses must push their way into the realm of cultural production (Jameson, 1984).

Based on what he views as a logic associated with late capitalism, postmodernism is characterized by its fragmentation, depthlessness, ahistoricity, pastiche, and a schizophrenic structure that was described by Lacan and Deleuze. Jameson always speaks of postmodernity in cultural or aesthetic terms, as an hysterical sublime, a *derealization* of the surrounding world and every day reality.

Unlike many analysts of postmodernity, Harvey's emphasis is on changes taking place in the social structure as related to or symbolic of this postmodern *condition*. Therefore, he is highly critical of the aesthetic eclipse of ethics and reason that appears to come along with this condition, as he locates its emergence in post-fordist capitalism—a contemporary condition under which mechanisms of production and assembly become more flexible and are dispersed globally. And while he is critical of what he views as the dismissal by some postmodernists of the most important theoretical perspectives to have emerged in the last century (including Marxism), he also finds in some of their narratives room for contemplating postcapitalist development.

GILLES DELEUZE AND FELIX GUATTARI

Two of the most prominent postmodern thinkers who established the path for Lyotard and other postmodernists to follow were the radical psychoanalyst Felix Guattari (1930–1992) and the academic philosopher Gilles Deleuze (1925–1995). Guattari was a practicing French psychoanalyst who had been psychoanalyzed himself by Jacques Lacan but came to reject psychoanalysis because of its collaboration with capitalism in an attempt to maintain order. Deluze was a radical thinker who offered an unconventional reinterpretation of Nietzsche in an effort to understand the modern social condition. Their first collaborative work, *Anti-Oedipus* (originally published in 1972), was an outgrowth of their disillusionment with the failure of the French student and worker strikes of 1968. The book was a call for a new kind of revolution and an attack on capitalism, traditional Marxism, and classical psychoanalysis. It became a popular book in the intellectual circles of France and helped influence the work of Foucault, with whom they were friends.

In *Anti-Oedipus* (1983), Deleuze and Guattari launch into an assault against what they call **aborescence**—a type of knowledge structure that dominated western culture and that emphasized taxonomies as well as hierarchical ways of knowing and understanding things. Like a tree, knowledge was seen as spreading out from a main trunk into various branches. In its place, they suggested that knowledge emerges like a **rhizome**—a type of vegetation or weed that grows horizontally instead of vertically and often grows underground. This represents knowledge that does not spread from one root upward into branches, but rather represents a type of understanding that spreads out along the ground like so many interconnected roots—none of which is central to the plant. Rhizomes are always rearranging their formation through a vast network of such interconnections. Knowledge, in this way, is viewed as proletarian as opposed to hierarchical and autocratic.

Deleuze and Guattari attack Freudian psychoanalysis for its metatheoretical pretentions, its conservative reductionism, as well as for its hierarchical attributes. Like Wilhelm Reich, who wrote *The Mass Psychology of Fascism* in 1933, they contend that the unconscious is a political force and that it houses ideologies such as fascism. They accuse Freud of romanticizing the patriarchal family that is an outgrowth of capitalism. They view the family as a force of repression. The oedipus complex represents the false narrative based on capitalistic familialism and its inherent triangulation (mommy–daddy–me) that justifies the repression of desire. Like Reich they also see no separation among the political, the economic, the social, and the psychological. The psyche comes about through the same processes as society. It is a product of an inordinate number of interactions and "energy flows."

The fascism that dwells within the psyche is a product of capitalism just as is the fascism that dwells within society as a whole. It is connected to the oedipal family wherein children must learn to accept the authority of the father and learn to become obedient citizens and tools of capitalistic production. Then psychoanalysis is used for those neurotics who have not resolved the complex accordingly.

It is desire that becomes central to their understanding of human development. They locate desire in a time prior to creation itself—prior to knowledge, culture, and law. Desire is a transcendental force that drives all human action, yet it is not free from the influence of power. Its flow is constantly restricted. They view it as having been hijacked by capitalism, converted into a "lack," and channeled into the service of the consumer economy. In fact, they view desire as the site of all power struggles. For them, desire can take many forms but can generally be classified into two: a *reactive desire*, which is associated with personal repression, fascism, and capitalism, and a *productive desire*, which is an expression of creative potential. They refer to this first type of desire as paranoid and the second type as schizophrenic.

For them, schizophrenia describes those who are not fully controlled and manipulated by the forces of production and consumption—those who have not surrendered to these forces and who do not approach the world through the established oedipal order. Deleuze and Guattari are not discussing schizophrenia in the sense of mental illness; however, it does represent a resistance to an imposed capitalistic order that rests outside narrow individuation. Here schizophrenia is a liberating ideal.

Deleuze and Guattari make extensive use of Neitzsche's notion of the will to power to explain the way this operates. Like Nietzsche, they want to see productive desire liberated from the forces that attempt to repress, control, and manipulate it. For Deleuez and Guattari, all people need to strive to realize their desire. They see productive desire as a force with revolutionary potential that emanates from the primal social unconscious—the primary instrument of that production. This is not the Freudian unconscious containing individualized fantasies and characterized by guilt and lack; rather, it is the *raw flow* from which all other flows are channeled. This ubiquitous desire and its flows produce reality.

For Deleuze and Guattari, *flows* of all sorts constitute the energy in the world. For them, everything is comprised of flows: desires, books, ideas, people, air, water—everything. Flows constitute energy that is ubiquitous in the universe. What allows one to distinguish among specific flows is a point that restricts, stops, or cuts off a flow. Such points are what distinguish elements in the universe from one another—these they refer to as machines. Thus, the anus machine controls the flow of excrement, the breast machine the flow of milk, *desiring machines* the flow of desire. Yet all machines are interconnected. And while being restrictors of flows, all machines are also flows themselves.

Deleuze and Guattari use the metaphor of machine to complement the Marxist critique of capitalist production and to emphasize the nonhumanistic orientation of their work. For both of them, the human and the machine are simultaneously natural and unnatural. Actually they see no distinction between the natural and the unnatural—the human and the machine.

They charge capitalism with an attempt to manipulate these flows and to privatize desire through an array of desiring machines. Capitalism deterritorializes and decodes that which was previously territorialized and coded. In the process, it undermines everything that is social. And while it once had the potential as an instrument of liberation, it now has recoded and reterritorialized to the point of imposing a new oppressive order not all that different from the one it had confronted. Capitalism attempts to split the personal and the political (one's self from the machinery that has produced the self for exploitation), and it is assisted in this effort by psychoanalysis. In psychoanalysis, the political is isolated from one's psyche as family becomes a closed-system generating the psychic disorder.

Deleuze and Guattari see revolutionary desire flowing through small groups that are capable of producing collective action. Such groups can grasp the artificial polarities established by hegemonic order. Deleuze and Guattari aim to see people freed from the repressive chains of language and codes, and able to recapture what Lacan referred to as the *Imaginary*, a presymbolic stage wherein rests spontaneity, passion, and unmediated desire. This is in tune with Nietzsche's notion of an abandonment of societal consciousness. Furthermore, they see the body as a machine housing and reflecting the culture. To this end, they call for a **Body without Organs** *(BwO)*that can transcend the proscriptions of capitalistic society. The BwO is the virtual body of enormous potentiality. To make oneself a Body without Organs is to actively experiment with oneself to draw out and actualize these potentials by connection to other bodies. In a sense, it is a nonrestrictive machine—one that is constantly becoming.

JEAN-FRANÇOIS LYOTARD

Jean Lyotard (1924–1998) was an important figure in the burgeoning of postmodern thought in the 1970s. Like the work of Deleuze and Guattari, Lyotard's work emerged from the seeds of the poststructural turn a decade earlier. As a young man, he had been an active Marxist and a radical socialist. Eventually, he was influenced by the poststructuralism of Jacques Lacan, studying psychoanalysis and attending Lacan's seminars in Paris in the 1960s. Early in his career Lyotard taught philosophy in secondary schools and in the 1970s occupied a chair in philosophy at the University of Paris.

Lyotard had been an early advocate of the uses of phenomenology in the social sciences, and although he believed that phenomenology could help define the meaning of the "social" and address some of the epistemological challenges that existed in sociology, he took it to task for its lack of materialist connection—its failure to effectively critique capitalism and class struggle. Still he used the phenomenology of Merleau-Ponty to attack structuralism as antithetical to sensuality and sensual understanding.

Lyotard was interested in positioning the body as central to all knowledge and feeling central to truth. His work takes a page from Nietzsche's *On the Genealogy of Morals* (1967) and Gilles Deleuze and Guattari's *Anti-Oedipus* (1972). Accordingly, without the body there can be no thought. Bodies become systems for regulating the flow of feelings and desires. Centering the body as the primary mode of experience was a notion that was profoundly influenced by the work of the phenomenologist Maurice Merleau-Ponty (see Chapter 4).

Lyotard's notion of the libidinal economy, one drawn from Deleuze and Guattari, became key to his understanding of the postmodern condition. Here, Lyotard uses both Freud and Marx to better comprehend the flows of energy that help to instigate social change. In other words, how does desire animate action? The libidinal economy transcends capital. Unlike the mechanistic revolutionary struggle of the oppressed against the oppressor inherent in Marx's materialistic struggle, these flows of desire are viewed as setting the world into motion. Desire is inherently more primal—it is felt rather than represented. It is lived rather than enacted.

In his *Libidinal Economy* (1993), Lyotard challenges the historic construction of social theory. In fact, he views theory as detached and often unrealistic. In its place he calls for a libidinal philosophy that signifies the liberation of desire, which much of social theory has coldly repressed. Thus, the libidinal economy is human society itself and libidinal philosophy is an attempt to understand it.

In the work of Lyotard, we have one of the most comprehensive insights into postmodernity as both a social and cultural condition. While Lyotard is often seen as a poststructuralist, his later work takes exception to much of poststructuralism. His 1979 study, *The Postmodern Condition*, surveyed the role of science and computer technology, and concluded that there had been a radical shift in science toward a concern with language and narrative. It further contended that this was having a considerable impact on the production and retention of knowledge. He predicted that anything in the constituted realm of knowledge would disappear if it did not translate into quantities of information that could easily lend themselves to computer languages. Thus, the social and cultural legitimation of knowledge was seen as the basis of postmodern language. In his work, Lyotard suggests that increased knowledge can no longer be connected to the training of minds. Instead, it will become the basis of institutional power, particularly at the nation-state level where the gap between developed and underdeveloped countries will grow wider. He asserted that nation-states will eventually lose power to the commerce of information dominated by multinational corporations, whose information will dominate discourse. Knowledge itself seemed to be losing its use value and becoming a mere commodity competing with others. Scientific knowledge was emerging as only one particular type of discourse in a competing field of others. He asserts that scientific knowledge is only as valuable as the culture and market decide. In his work, he contrasts postmodernity with modernity—wherein there was a belief in what he called **grands récits**, grand narratives or metanarratives, that projected the present into the future. For Lyotard, such metanarratives become useless in the postmodern age.

Lyotard advocates the demise of such metanarratives. He contends that such grand narratives associated with the Enlightenment or Marxism had to give way to smaller narratives that would compete with each other. He borrows heavily from Wittgenstein's work on language games to show that various categories of utterance (i.e. denotations, prescriptions, evaluations, performances) needed to be defined by their own unique set of rules, which would specify language use. Therefore, rules were not inherent in language itself—as some insisted—but rather were devised in a negotiated fashion as one speaker yielded to the next within a discourse category. Each utterance was seen as a move in the game. This attack on metanarratives becomes essential to postmodern criticism. Losing the comprehensive proscription of a grand narrative or metanarrative allows room for diversity. In fact, it encourages diversity. Lyotard had no qualms about letting his position on this be known. He viewed the decline of grand narratives as liberating. Nevertheless, these grand visions or grand narratives appeared to have held societies together in the past. Their demise certainly led to a major change in social bonding.

Many view the disintegration of social bonds based on these modernist notions as leading to further and further fragmentation and individuation. But Lyotard rejected this idea. For him, the grand narratives were never based in reality, nor were the social bonds they supposedly created. This was an illusion of a totality that was the object of modern romanticism. The quest for totalism (which was not only connected to Marxism but also to fascism and Stalinism) would have to give way to new modes of connectedness and not be forced on others by powerful elites. For Lyotard, postmodernism represents an escape from an oppressive oneness.

Here science, art, and philosophy can serve various interests and come to reflect the fragmentation inherent in language games. In the postmodern world, of Lyotard one can never have a full understanding of the workings of society because it doesn't exist.

ZYGMUNT BAUMAN

Prior to becoming a significant theorist of the postmodern social world, Zygmunt Bauman had been a career Marxist. He turned away—disillusioned with state socialism—but did not embrace capitalism as an alternative. For him, these are two sides of the same modernist coin. He, too, recognizes the powerful and oppressive role of totality in the modern era inherent in both these systems. Like Lyotard, he rejects it, sees it as fascistic, and favors the pluralism he finds inherent in postmodernity. Still his embrace of postmodernity is bound up in his rejection of a particular type of modernity.

Unlike most postmodernists, or those who have been assigned this label, Bauman's academic career began in Soviet Poland. He came to teach in London after an anti-Semitic purge of the academy in 1968, where he lost his chair at the University of Warsaw. In his work, Bauman links modernity to the European Enlightenment with its quest for absolute truth wedded to absolute power. He views it as a quest to impose structure on the unstructured, order on the disorderly. Like the Holocaust, modernity represents a nightmare of total unified order at any cost. He views it as a dead end. Total control, as he sees it, is an inherent quality of modernity, reflecting its moral indifference and personal ambivalence.

On the other hand Bauman envisions the postmodern world as a place of enchantment, or at least *reenchantment*. Postmodernity is open to a plurality of otherness—an end to hierarchies and the rigidity of place. At the same time, it is characterized by products and their associated fantasies. Reality, as proposed by the Enlightenment philosophers, has no place here. For Bauman, postmodernity is a social condition that evolved at the end of the twentieth century in affluent consumerist countries of Europe and Asia, and, of course, in the United States. It is characterized by pluralism, variety, contingency, and ambivalence. It is also a condition that warrants its own sociological theory. And this is Bauman's project.

In the early 1990s, Bauman (1992) set out to identify those characteristics most common to a postmodern sociological perspective. However, he first identified what such a new perspective would have to leave behind. Essential to postmodern theory is the abandonment of the metaphor of progress associated with modernity. It must discard social totality that was previously associated with the work of Talcott Parsons and other functional structuralists and, in effect, dismiss the holistic notions of systems and equilibrium.

Bauman also proposed that a sociological theory of postmodernity needs to focus on agency rather than structure. But more specifically, he suggested that this focus be considerate of the habitat in which agency operates (1992, p. 190). Habitat offers agency the "sum total of resources for all possible action" as well as the field in which such action takes place. This notion is reminiscent of Bourdieu's model of *habitus* and field. But for Bauman, habitat neither determines nor defines the agent's conduct. It is only a place of potentialities and possibilities—a place wherein action and meaning assignment are possible but not dictated. It is a place from which one must draw for self-construction or self-assembly. In a sense, it is a place or a space of chronic indeterminacy where nothing is certain.

While orthodox sociology resonates with the theoretical world of modernity in which identity was relatively stable, postmodern sociology and, in particular, postmodern social theory deal with the potential for self-reinvention. In the postmodern world, individual identity is a source of great uncertainty. People no longer gain their identities from the communities from which they emerged, or even from their families. Communities and the state lose their power to the marketplace. Identity emerges more from the market exchange (particularly consumerism) in postmodern societies than from nation, employment, or residence.

Bauman, like Baudrillard, throws into question the entire notion of the social. For Bauman, our concept of the social is a modernist one, which emerges from some degree of order in the world. It is here that stability of self seems to exist. It is the modernist notion of social order that makes identity possible. But in postmodern society, one's identity is intricately connected to consumption and the market. Consumerism is the postmodern order. All strive to be integrated into the consumerist world. Flawed consumers are those who are marginalized—those who are unemployed or incapable of fully participating in the consumerist life style. All legitimation that once flowed from social elites and intellectuals now emerges from product and service advertising.

Bauman sees postmodern social theory as predicated on the work of Schutz and Garfinkel. It is a type of social phenomenology rooted in the interpretive arts. Postmodernity is characterized by an excess of meanings, as is art. In the postmodern world, no meanings stand the test of time. None are determined by a preordained structure. Postmodern sociology must recognize the "fragility and brittleness of social reality" (Bauman 1992a, p. 40).

Bauman rejects the pessimism that colors the typical assessment of the postmodern condition. He suggests that, although there needed to be a rejection of universalism, moral and otherwise, there never was a need to reject the notion of postmodern human connectedness by whatever name—both personal and political. Thus, one needs to see oneself as the *other* in order to connect to the *other*. For him, human connection is as essential to postmodern life as it is to a moral life, which is possible in the postmodern world.

What Bauman most obviously rejects is the Rousseauian notion of community—a community predicated on a permanent central force holding people together through coercive power and manipulation. He views this as a totalism that has no place in the postmodern world. In his book *Liquid Modernity* (Bauman 2000), we get a sense of what Bauman means by this. Bauman sees the world as having evolved from a state of "solid" modernity to a state of "liquid" modernity wherein nothing keeps its shape. This is a place where social forms and human experiences are changing at increasingly accelerated rates, replacing what was thought to be more definitive in terms of structure. What seemed well fitted to a relatively stable world can no longer guide us. The map must be displaced by a GPS, which is an antimap, recognizing no permanent boundaries and no fixed streets. This is a world guided by subjective action. Knowledge for knowing's sake is devalued since it has little currency in liquid modernity. Relying on knowledge from the past will not sustain the world today. In the world of liquid modernity, there are many competing authorities, never one. It is the individual's choice to select the authority with which to align oneself. This liquid-modern world is most fragile where the cohesiveness of nation-states erodes. Business becomes independent from the state, and the reach of corporations becomes even greater.

Like many critical theorists who came before him, Bauman sees the world of liquid modernity, or the postmodern world, as the one in which consumerism defines one's relationship to society—where a synthetic individuality defines the marketplace. Individuals become little more than promoters of commodities—and commodities themselves (Bauman 2007). Harking back to Marx, Verben, Simmel, and Marcuse, Bauman sees all this as an essential aspect of the postmodern world. Unlike his critical predecessors, however he views a potential for liberation as hidden away in the order of consumption and consumables—a world in which one can individualistically construct one's own narrative.

JEAN BAUDRILLARD AND RADICAL POSTMODERNISM

Jean Baudrillard (1929–2007) has been an extremely important representative of postmodern social theory. Like Bauman, Lyotard, and Deleuze, Baudrillard's early roots were in Marxism. As a sociologist, however, his work is representative of a type of theory that does not curry support from leftist sociologists.

Unlike Bauman, who emerges from the Soviet system and brings to his work a detachment from French social theory of the 1960s and 1970s, Baudrillard personally experienced the worker and student uprisings in France in 1968. He was influenced by Levi-Strauss, Barthes, Lacan, Deleuze, and the whole era of structuralism and poststructuralism that attempted to reassess Marxism in the mid-twentieth century. His mentor was Henri Lefebvre. As a French postmodernist, he had been much closer to Lyotard than Bauman, who straddles the line between being a sincere postmodernist and using postmodernism as a category to house some of his more eccentric thoughts.

Baudrillard's earlier work was an attempt to reformulate Marx using semiotics and structuralist methodologies. Most impressive of his earlier works were *System of Objects* (1968), *The Mirror of Production* (1975), and *For a Critique of the Political Economy of the Sign* (1981). In these works, Baudrillard connects Marx's notion of commodity fetishism to structuralism, semiotics, and to Thorstein Veblen's notion of consumerism.

Baudrillard contended that consumption, and not production, served as the driving force in the world. Where Marx only toyed with the notion of commodity fetishism, Baudrillard made it central to his understanding of the postmodern, postcapitalist world. For Baudrillard (like Deleuze), all needs were socially constructed rather than inherent in nature. Thus, Karl Marx and Adam Smith had it wrong.

Drawing on the work of semiotics (referred to by some as semiology), and particularly the theoretical marriage of Roland Barthes to Thorstein Veblen, Baudrillard asserted that objects say something important about their users. Starting with the classical notions of *use value* (the practical value of the object in use) and *exchange value* (the value of an object determined by the flow of supply and demand), Baudrillard adds two more distinct object values: symbolic value and sign value. *Symbolic value* is what an object can signify in terms of meaning; *sign value* is the object's value within a system of other objects—its prestige, and status position. All objects (all commodities) are signs. This is something Marx missed in his analysis. These signs constitute a coded means of communication about who we are and what we want. They constitute a language with its own rules.

While much of Baudrillard's important work centered around consumerism and the language of consumption, he became particularly important in the 1990s and in the early 2000s for his postmodern critique of society. Borrowing much from Lyotard, Baudrillard suggests that authenticity is a myth of the modern era and that there is only *simulacra*. Western societies have particularly witnessed an evolution in experiencing things. Originals have been replaced by copies and copies of those until we no longer have originals. This is what he refers to as the third order of simulacra. The real has been superseded by the hyperreal. For Baudrillard, this means that the real no longer exists. We live a virtual existence in a virtual world: Fisherman's Wharf in San Francisco, South Street in New York, Quincy Market in Boston, Harbor Place in Baltimore are reformulations of history. The artificial world created by market institutions eclipses anything that might have claimed historic authenticity. In the postmodern world of Baudrillard, there is no authenticity.

For Baudrillard, people in postmodern societies have become zombie-like hypercomformists obsessed with spectacle. They would much rather be watching television or playing video games than engaging in social or even sexual inter-course. While this is particularly true in the United States and Britain, it is becoming universal. He refers to this as *the death of the social*.

Like other postmodernists, Baudrillard tolls the end of modernity, an era characterized by industrial capitalism and a political economy governed by the powerful bourgeoisie or, as it's now called, the top "1%". In its place he describes an era of simulations governed by signs, codes, and communication technology. Here illusion, not reality, dominates. While modernity was characterized by rigid distinctions, postmodernity is more associated with the collapse of such distinctions. Where modernity was characterized by a subject/object binary in which the subject controlled the object, the tables have turned and objects in postmodern societies reign supreme. All are objects. He refers to this as the "death of the subject". No longer do individuals have strong and clear personal identities. In the postmodern world, the self is decentered. All identity is fragmented to meet the needs of a fragmented world.

Baudrillard uses the concept of implosion to describe the simultaneous proliferation of signs and the collapse of meaning associated with them. For Baudrillard, we have entered a world without truth and meaning, where meaning and truth can change at a moment's notice. He views the resultant meaninglessness as liberating. His work calls on people to accept and enjoy the meaninglessness of the world and to feel free to play with forms, appearances, and impulses. He celebrates the contradictions in the world and in his own work.

Toward the end of his life, Baudrillard had become a pop icon in the West—particularly in English-speaking countries. His celebrity status as a public intellectual required him to engage in cultural commentary and to publish more than what was necessary. However, his controversial remarks on the Iraq War (which he opposed) and the terrorist attack on the World Trade Center (which he viewed as a real challenge to hegemonic authority) along with his criticism of globalization collided with his seemingly noncaring attitude.

Social theorist Robert Antonio (2007), in a piece he wrote after Baudrillard's death, quotes an interview wherein Baudrillard was asked about postmodern. theory. He replied: "I have nothing to do with it. I don't know who came up with the term ... But I have no faith in 'postmodernism' as an analytical term. When people say: 'you are a postmodernist,' I answer: "Well *why not?*' The term simply avoids the issue itself ... [I'm a] nihilist," he declared, "not a postmodernist." Baudrillard's cynicism was world-renowned, but this cynicism never took away from his keen insights as a theorist writing at the edges of acceptability.

THE LEGACY OF POSTMODERNISM

What has postmodernism left behind, aside from the writings of some of the most imaginative thinkers of the twentieth century? Even those who violently disagree with this perspective will have to admit that these theorists contributed some of the most creative insights into the human social condition without ever taking a single sociological survey.

Despite its strangeness and incongruity, postmodern theory has helped to predict the fragmentation of theory itself into commodified domains. It has revealed a world where shallowness is rewarded and superficiality is considered a virtue, a world where image and spectacle are used to manipulate and control. For some, the world these theorists describe is a Weberian nightmare where hyper-rationality competes with hyperirrationality for commercial air time. At the same time, postmodern discourse celebrates cultural relativism, diversity, and the power of performativity. However, in the end it was a creative and bold venture into a theoretical cul-de-sac.

KEY TERMS

aborescence In the work of Deleuze and Gattari, this is a type of knowledge dominated by western taxonomies.

Body without Organs (BwO) For Deleuze and Guattari, a body without the mechanisms or organs of desire; bodies that can transcend capitalism.

carnivalization A term taken from Bakhtin to represent the carnival-like pushing away of the seriousness of hierarchy and authority and an undermining of this authority through play and celebrations of otherness.

constitutive reflexivity How one develops a narrative about one's life through self-reflection and social feedback. This idea is connected to Gidden's notion of modern life.

desiring machines Used by Deleuze and Guattari to describe people's bodies as comprised of various mechanisms or machines that require food, sex, comfort, etc. People themselves in capitalistic societies are viewed as desiring machines.

disembedding social institutions Social institutions that are "lifted" out of particular social contexts (such as usefulness, time, and culture) and placed in another. Giddens sees this as a characteristic of globalization.

exchange value A term used in classical economic theory (Marx) that signals the value of a product as determined by its level of demand in the marketplace.

flows A concept used by Deleuze and Guattari to represent the movement of energy in the world comprised of ubiquitous desire. This energy is used to produce reality in capitalistic societies.

grands récits For Lyotard, a term meaning grand narratives or metanarratives that are widely accepted accounts espousing a universal truth and set of value assumptions, which can no longer be viable in the heterogeneous, changing postmodern world.

modernity A condition associated with post-feudal, post-traditional society characterized by a strong emphasis on secularization, reason, order, industry, and progress.

productive desire A term used by Deleuze and Guattari to mean a type of desire that produces real human connections, personal investments, and intense states between bodies.

postmodernity A cultural condition that transcends modern life and is characterized by a break with Enlightenment thought and its strong belief in scientific rationality and a unitary theory of progress. It emphasizes, in its place, cultural fragmentation and the relativity of truth.

reactive desire According to the work of Deleuze and Guattari, this is a dead ended desire, which promotes difference and enslaves the body and retards further development.

rhizome A type of vegetation or weed that grows in various directions underground. Deleuze and Guattari use this image to explain the flow of energy.

simulacra A term used by postmodernists to represent the notion that there is no original, only copies.

sign value According to Baudrillard this is the value of an object within a system of other objects.

symbolic value A term used by Baudrillard to represent the nonmonetary value of something, for instance, the prestige associated with an object.

time-place distanciation A term used by Giddens to refer to the disembedding of human relations from space and the rise of more abstract forms of communication where face-to-face contact is no longer the norm and wherein distinct social systems become more highly integrated.

SOURCES

Agger, Ben. 1991. "Critical Theory, Poststructuralism, Postmodernism: The Sociological Relevance," *Annual Review of Sociology*, Vol. 17, pp. 105–131.

Ahmed, Sara. 1998. *Differences That Matter: Feminist Theory and Postmodernism.* Cambridge, UK: Cambridge University Press.

Antonio, Robert. 2007. "The Passing of Jean Baudrillard," *Fast Capitalism*, Vol. 4, No.1. Electronic format.

Bakhtin, Mikhail. 1941. *Rabelais and His World.* Bloomington, IN: Indiana University Press

Baudrillard, Jean. 1968. *System of Objects.* London: Verso Press.

Baudrillard, Jean. 1975. *The Mirror of Production*. St. Louis, MO: Telos Press.

Baudrillard, Jean. 1981. *For a Critique of the Political Economy of the Sign*. St. Louis, MO: Telos Press.

Bauman, Zygmunt.1992. *Mortality, Immortality and Other Life Strategies*, Stanford, CA: Stanford University Press.

Bauman, Zygmunt. 1992a. *Intimations of Postmodernity*. London: Routledge.

Bauman, Zygmunt. 2000. *Liquid Modernity*. Cambridge: Polity Press.

Bauman, Zygmunt. 2007. *Consuming Life*. Cambridge: Polity Press.

Best, Shaun. 1998, June. "Zygmunt Bauman: Personal Reflections Within the Mainstream of Modernity," *British Journal of Sociology*, Vol. 49, No. 2, pp. 184–201.

Cixous, Helene. 1980. *The Laugh of Medusa*. Trans.by K. Cohen and P. Cohen. Manchester: University of Manchester Press.

Deleuze, Gilles, and Felix Guattari. 1983. *Anti-Oedipus: Capitalism and Schizophrenia*. Minneapolis, MN: University of Minnesota Press.

Eagleton, Terry. 1987. "Awakening from Modernity," *Times Literary Supplement*, No. 4377, February 20, p. 194.

Felski, Rita. 2000. *Doing Time: Feminist Theory and Postmodern Culture*. New York: New York University Press.

Giddens, Anthony. 1984. *The Constitution of Society: Outline of the Theory of Structuration*, Berkeley: University of California Press.

Giddens, Anthony. 1987. "Reason Without Revolution? The Critical Theory of Jürgen Habermas" in A. Giddens, ed., *Social Theory and Modern Sociology*. Stanford: Stanford University Press, pp. 225–252.

Giddens, Anthony. 1990. *The Consequences of Modernity*. Stanford, CA: Stanford University Press.

Giddens, Anthony. 1991. *Modernity and Self-Identity*. Stanford, CA: Stanford University Press.

Giddens, Anthony. 1992. *The Transformation of Intimacy*. Stanford, CA: Stanford University Press.

Habermas, Jürgen. 1981. "Modernity Versus Postmodernity," *New German Critique*, No. 22 (Special Issue on Modernism), pp. 3–14.

Habermas, Jürgen. 1990. *The Philosophical Discourse of Modernity*. Cambridge, MA: MIT Press.

Habermas, Jürgen. 1997. "Modernity, An Unfinished Project," in M. P. d'Entrèves, ed., *Habermas and the Unfinished Project of Modernity*. Cambridge, MA: MIT Press.

Harvey, David. 1989. *The Condition of Postmodernity*. Cambridge, MA: Basil Blackwell.

Hassan, Ihab. 1985. "The Culture of Post Modernism," *Theory, Culture and Society*, Vol. 2, No. 3, pp. 119–131.

Hassan, Ihab. 1986. "Pluralism in Postmodern Perspective," *Critical Inquiry*, Vol. 12, No. 3, pp. 503–520.

Huyssens, Andreas. 1984. "Mapping the Post-Modern," *New German Critique*, Vol. 33, pp. 5–52.

Irigaray, Luce. 1985. *This Sex Which Is Not One*. Ithaca, NY: Cornell University Press.

Jameson, Fredric. 1984. "Postmodernism or the Logic of Late Capitalism," *New Left Review*, Vol. 146, pp. 53–92.

Kristeva, Julia. 1980. *Desire in Language: Semiotic Approach to Literature and Art*, L. Roudiez, ed. New York: Columbia University Press.

hooks, bell. 1990. "Postmodern Blackness," *Postmodern Culture*, Vol. 1, No. 1. Electronic format.

Lefebvre, Henri. 1995. *Introduction to Modernity: Twelve Preludes September 1959 to May, 1961.* Trans. by John Moore. London: Verso.

Lyotard, Jean-François. 1979. *The Postmodern Condition.* Minneapolis, MN: University of Minnesota Press.

Lyotard, Jean-François, 1993. *Libidinal Economy* (originally published in 1974). Trans. by I.H. Grant. London: Continuum.

Nietzsche, Friedrich. 1967. *On The Genealogy of Morals* (originally published in 1887). Trans. by W. Kaufmann. New York: Vintage.

Weedon, Chris. 1987. *Feminist Practice and Poststructuralist Theory.* London: Blackwell.

CHAPTER 6

Feminist Social Theory

The social and political unrest of the late 1960s produced a wave of cultural transformations. A new women's movement, often referred to as the second wave of feminism, was emerging. Not only did women around the world protest the suppression of their voices in matters of the body and the state, but they also rebelled against the patriarchal dominance of political, economic, and cultural life. All of this appeared to come together just as a shift was taking place in social theory.

While the existentialist thinker Simone de Beauvoir is often credited with providing the first social constructionist explanation of womanhood as early as 1949, her theoretical combination of psychoanalytic and Marxist critique was also supported by women influenced by theories of structuralism and poststructuralism emerging in Europe. There was some immediate affinity between feminist social philosophy and the battles for equal rights for women in the far corners of the globe. In the 1970s, feminist theorists began making sense of what was happening through the use of newly emerging paradigms. Thus, much contemporary feminist theory has its roots in structuralism and poststructuralism as well as in the politics and social movements of this era. A substantial amount of this theory was also influenced by psychoanalysis, particularly the work of Jacques Lacan (Grosz 1990; Brennan 1993).

This chapter begins with an assessment of some of the most creative feminist thinkers who found their voices in social theory through the emerging ideas of that era. It reviews various approaches to feminist social theory and provides a history of the development of many of these influences.

STRUCTURALISM AND EARLY FEMINIST THOUGHT

During the late 1960s and early 1970s, women gained a heightened awareness of the structural features of patriarchal oppression. Much of the contemporary feminism of that time dealt with struggles for autonomy and liberation in patriarchal societies. For many, gender inequality was believed to be a system of exploitation and oppression, wherein women were objects of social, economic, and sexual abuse aimed at maintaining male dominance and centrality. Called *radical feminism*, this perspective was less critical of capitalism than it was of male oppression. In later feminist theory, however, an attack on capitalism commanded a more central role.

Marxian and neo-Marxian feminist theory, as well as more structurally oriented psychoanalytic and cultural theories, characterized much of early contemporary feminist thought. While the union between Marxism and psychoanalysis was frequently central to continental European thought, it took a while before it found greater acceptance among feminist scholars and thinkers in the United States. Feminist Marxists in Great Britain, such as Juliet Mitchell, worked to promote a critical feminism aimed at emancipatory social change.

Mitchell was somewhat suspicious of radical feminism, which attributed women's inequality primarily to male chauvinism and patriarchy, and took a dim view of Marxism. On the other hand, she was highly critical of socialists who wrote off women's liberation as a "lesser than" movement because it rejected the need for revolution and failed to see capitalism as the primary target. She also challenged those on the left who refused to see the structural conditions that women *alone* had to face.

Mitchell (1966) promoted accommodation between the two opposing camps. While most feminists viewed men at the center of women's oppression and exploitation, Mitchell insisted that this could not be viewed as separate and apart from the structural role that capitalism played. She called for both the full development of feminist consciousness and the sociological application of Marxist analysis. She believed that to do only the first was to engage in a directionless female chauvinism. However, when this is combined with scientific socialist analysis, there could be an emergence of a political consciousness that would lead inevitably to change.

In her most important work, *Psychoanalysis and Feminism* (1974), Mitchell reaches into psychoanalytic theory, from which she constructs a feminist interpretation of sigmund Freud, Wilhelm Reich, and R. D. Laing. And just as she saw women overlooking the importance of Marx's work and dismissing it for it phallocentrism, Mitchell called attention to finding value in Freud by placing psychoanalytic thought into the service of women. She found the opposition to Freud and psychoanalysis particularly strong in the English-speaking world—especially among radical feminists in the United States such as Andrea Dworkin (1987, pp. 188–189) who called Freud "a pornographer" in "real life" and asserted that in Freudian theory "men use the penis to deliver death to women who are, literally, in their genitals, dirt to the men."

Freud, Mitchell asserts, enables one to better understand the origins and dynamics of patriarchy. It is through his work that one might best come to terms with the important forces shaping the modern forms of authority and power. Mitchell contends that, by focusing primarily on Freud's *biologism*, feminists miss his critical articulation of how culture is itself constructed. She sees in the work of Reich and Laing not the misogyny that *radical feminists* have seen, but rather the seeds of revolutionary change that helped to usher in the activism of the 1960s and the rise of feminism itself. Both Reich and Laing emphasized the patriarchal family and the sexual and social repression that it constituted. As they attempted to move psychoanalysis further away from the psychological importance of the unconscious, their work laid the foundation for more sociologically oriented feminist theorists who were to follow, particularly Nancy Chodorow and Jessica Benjamin. Mitchell is one of the first English-speaking theorists to bring the work of Lacan to feminists. She recognizes his importance to a small group of feminists in France who were influenced by his work. She stresses the significant contribution made by Lacan to understanding language and its role in the development of gender. While Mitchell was not part of the linguistic revolution sweeping France, she was able to translate the concerns of the French structuralists into the needs of the English-speaking world.

The impact of the linguistic turn and deconstruction on French feminist thought was significant by the mid-1970s. Not only did its male proponents celebrate *subjective knowledge* or understanding of the world, both women and men were rejecting much of the patriarchal elements of Enlightenment thought, including positivism itself. However, not all feminism was of this poststructural variety. Clair Moses (1998), in her study of the differences between American and French feminisms, found that in the early 1970s there were substantial areas of agreement. However, in France, there was a much greater influence on feminist theory by the writings of Marx and Freud, that most American feminists tended to ignore or dismiss.

As we already noted in Chapter 4, the work of Luce Irigaray, Julia Kristeva, and Hélène Cixous had been considerably influenced by structuralism and later by poststructuralism the latter of which they helped to develop in France. The work of all three women owe a certain intellectual debt not only to Derrida's deconstructionism but also, and most importantly, to the psychoanalytic theory of Jacques Lacan. Irigaray, Kristeva, and Cixous attempt to explain how language and patriarchal order construct meaning through hierarchically organized binaries. However, their work often entails the centering of women and a decentering of men in order for women to find their own voice. Such work emerged at a time when women were just beginning to recognize the power of language to oppress.

As Nancy Fraser (1992) said, the failure of poststructural French feminism to reach a wider audience in the English-speaking world was not its irrelevance, but rather its lack of relevance for the political situation in which women in Britain and the United States found themselves in the 1980s, when these French texts made their way into English-language feminist discourse. Many women viewed this brand of feminist language as too abstract and inaccessible. Just as the male language these theorists condemned was phallocentric, the language of these French feminist theorists seemed gynecocentric. Also, there was a tendency to lump all

French feminist theorists together, and for academic feminism to recognize only certain people who helped lead the poststructuralist revolution in France.

While poststructural theory (particularly French feminist theory) had a tremendous impact on new directions of theory in the English-speaking world, it appeared far less pragmatic than some of the theory that was being produced in Britain and the United States. Additionally, it failed to resonate with the Third World experience.

DOROTHY E. SMITH AND INSTITUTIONAL ETHNOGRAPHY

Dorothy Edith Smith was among the pioneers in shaping the course of a more contemporary feminist social theory. Both an activist and a scholar, Smith was instrumental in articulating a vision of feminism that was both pragmatic and theoretically sophisticated.

She was born and raised in Britain and attended the London School of Economics, where she received her undergraduate degree in cultural anthropology in 1955. She continued her studies at the University of California at Berkeley, where she completed her doctorate in 1963. Smith taught at Berkeley during the height of the free speech movement and moved to the University of British Columbia in Vancouver in 1967, as a single mother, where she was instrumental in helping to found the women's studies program.

The major influences on Smith's work have been Karl Marx, phenomenology, and the ethnomethodology of Harold Garfinkle. Her early work focuses on how men and women experience things differently. This does not stem from any sort of biological determinism, but rather is associated with structural and ascribed statuses that produce different life ways and therefore different conceptualizations and understandings of the same phenomena. One's gender is critical to how one experiences the social world—and how one makes sense of it. While Smith doesn't deny the centrality of class and race, gender is more privileged in her approach as she attempts to help construct feminist theory. She takes up much of the same theme in her work as Hegel did in his construct of the master/slave parable, as pursued by Marx in his notion of proletarian false consciousness, and by W. E. B. DuBois in his concept of *double consciousness*. Smith contends that women dwell within a "line of fault" in their daily lives whereby they develop a "bifurcated consciousness." There is official knowledge on one hand—a generalized knowledge, extralocal in nature—presented to them as though it were objective and separate from that which they themselves experience as women. Such an objective reality is the propaganda of the male ruling element of society, which denies or excludes the validity of women's experiences. On the other hand, there is the truth in their shared personal experiences as women that unites them both emotionally and epistemologically.

Smith is not interested in grand theoretical approaches to sociological subject matter. Like her thesis supervisor, Erving Goffman, her work also reflects a concern with the creation of understanding not of formal institutionalized behaviors, but of the most informal of human actions. That is, she is most interested in attempting to understand the experiences of everyday life (Smith 2005). This leaves her operating primarily at the micro-order level. However, she is fully aware of the macro-structural bases of interaction here as well. Much of her earlier work was an attempt to show the relevance of Marxist theory to the feminist movement. Despite her training and skill in ethnographic research, she draws on Marx to better understand the organization of power arrangements affecting women's lives and shaping their interpersonal relations with others. Also, she seeks to find a place for Marx among feminists and to open up Marxists to feminist thought. Like Mitchell, Smith finds a commonality between Marx's concern with the exploitation of the working class and her own concern with the oppression of women. Smith sees the same institutional apparatus attempting to direct the lives of both.

Smith (2006) was particularly influenced by the phenomenology of Alfred Schutz and Maurice Merleau-Ponty. Her focus is often on the everyday world, which could best be understood through an emphasis on a negation of dualities, both body/ mind as well as subject/object. For her, the phenomenological perspective has had an enormous advantage over positivism in better explaining the subjective nature of women's struggles. She develops what she refers to as *institutional ethnography* aimed at demystifying ruling relations. The everyday lives of people constitute the starting point for this type of research. But rather than focusing on the people we directly identify as controlling our lives, she gives special consideration to how individual lives are ruled and directed by the activities of those who occupy positions of influence and control in the companies, agencies, and organizations that both are empowered by us and eventually come to produce us.

These bureaucratic actors operate in schools, hospitals, governmental agencies and private corporations and derive their capacities to act from the organizations for which they work and from the social relations they both help to produce and by whom they themselves are produced (Smith 2005, p. 18). Smith asserts that ruling relations are embedded not only in these organizations but also in the knowledge and judgment of those who constitute these organizational relationships, as well as in the texts that are central to their operation. Such texts "are essential to the production of the generalizability, generalization, and objectivity of institutional regimes" (Smith 2005, p. 44).

While one might assume Smith to have fully embraced the linguistic turn, this was far from the case. Although she agrees with many elements in the work of both postmodernists and poststructuralists, she does not accept the contention that discourse alone can define who we are as people. Nor does she accept the pessimistic notion that agency is a fiction embedded in the text, an idea the French feminist Helene Cixous has been charged with embracing. This notion flies in the face of her strong Marxist and feminist positions. Despite her tough critique of sociology and the social sciences and their overriding emphasis on discovery of some sort of objective truth, Smith believes that peoples' realities extend beyond the limits of any science. Social relations transcend beyond what is immediately known to the actors. For her, the knowing actor or subject is a real flesh-and-blood person situated both bodily and in time and space. Discourse does not "speak through them," as some poststructuralists contend. Rather, it is Smith's contention, like Goffman's and others, that people make meaning together (Smith 1999).

SANDRA HARDING AND FEMINIST STANDPOINT THEORY

Sandra Harding is a feminist philosopher of science. Former director of UCLA's Center for the Study of Women, she has been instrumental in articulating a critique of unwarranted claims of scientific objectivity in contemporary science that has led to the oppression of people around the world. Harding contends that western science has attempted to maximize scientific objectivity through excluding social factors from the production of knowledge. It has long been held by the male-dominated scientific community that the personal biases distort findings and therefore must be excluded from scientific understanding. But in turning this position on its head, Harding contends that the process of scientific inquiry itself is valid only if it begins from a specific social location—often the lived experience of those who have been excluded from the production of scientific knowledge in the first place (Harding 1998). Drawing on the work of Marxist philosopher Georg Lukács, Harding develops what she refers to as *feminist standpoint theory*.

For Lukács, workers were in a unique cognitive position because of their subordination in the labor process. Under capitalism, workers have an understanding of the world and their position in it that is quite different from that of the capitalists. Where the generation of profit is seen by the capitalists as a result of superior management and greater efficiency, workers perceive it as masking the exploitation of labor—the true source of profit (Lukács 1971, p. 166). These two groups obviously see things from different standpoints. Harding asserts that such subjugated knowledge (a term she borrows from Foucault) needs to be brought into scientific understanding to improve the quality of scientific objectivity. This applies equally to all whose knowledge has been subordinated to that of the more powerful. *Standpoint theory*, for Harding, attempts to enhance the usefulness of scientific knowledge without resorting to naïve subjectivism.

Harding recognizes that women and men occupy different positions in the natural and social worlds and share some perspectives and positions, but not all. Women and men also stand in different relations to discursive and material resources: "they will tend to produce and sustain different patterns of knowledge and ignorance" (Harding 1998, p. 107). These respective standpoints result in different consciousnesses. But to make sense of the natural world, it must be perceived from a particular social standpoint. And while one standpoint might provide great insight and understanding, it necessarily closes off another perception that is no less important, no less real. Harding insists that no one perspective is in complete harmony with the "natural" state of things.

Harding sees the relevance of standpoint theory not only to the assessment of women's contributions to science, but she also extends this idea to other types of subjugated knowledge, including standpoints based on race, ethnicity, disability, sexual orientation and class. Each standpoint opens new and important perspectives. Modern science itself is a perspective that dominates both the western and, increasingly, the non-western worlds. And although western science is a powerful perspective, all perspectives have something to offer in helping us to better understand the natural world.

Still, all contain systemic errors. However, the marginality of women and others of the postcolonial world speaks to the bias inherent in this dominant knowledge-producing system that attempts to present itself as both universal and neutral. Its work is tied up with corporatism and military production. All knowledge, asserts Harding, is both local and political. The claim of neutrality in science is just that—a claim. It is nothing more than an acceptance of an established hegemonic and patriarchal consensus. Modern technoscience reflects the masculine culture of universal truth through detachment and withdrawal (Harding 1998, p. 181).

In some sense, Harding's ideas are in keeping with the theories of Max Weber, Heidegger, and the Frankfurt school theorists who are critical of instrumental reasoning. Her attack is not against the value of science; rather, it is a challenge to technocratic liberalism and the epistemological injustice that flows from it. Her primary target has often been the Eurocentric distortion of objectivity.

Harding recognizes the ways in which feminist theory can make good use of perspectives that have been developed by white European males to better understand the extent of the oppression of women. She warns other feminist thinkers of the dangers in dismissing perspectives such as Marxism, psychoanalysis, and poststructuralism because they are essentially male models of the world. She is adamant in her assertion that quality theory is a necessary requisite to true liberation. She believes that all women will not share all the theories or categories developed by other feminist thinkers. And this is a good thing. Theory cannot afford to be applied universally; and, if it could be, it would not be a valuable theory.

RACE AND BLACK FEMINIST THOUGHT: Bell Hooks AND PATRICIA HILL COLLINS

bell hooks has been steeped in feminist thought since her undergraduate days at Stanford University in the 1970s. Her first book, *Ain't I a Woman: Black Women and Feminism*, published in 1981, was written when she was just nineteen years old. The book examines the effects of sexism and racism on black women in the United States. In it, hooks argues that, because of racism and sexism black women have been ascribed the lowest status of all groups. She was among the first to find difficulties with a feminist movement that was comprised primarily of middle- and upper-class white women who had little knowledge of, or concern with, the dire condition of most black women.

hooks objects to the tendency of white middle-class women in academic life to construct feminist theory with no regard to issues of race, and class, and she was often marginalized for her position. She believes that the founders of the feminist movement in the United States, such as Betty Friedan, ignored the plight of women of color and the poor. hooks has asserted that "[r]acism abounds in the writings of white feminists . . ." (hooks 1995, p. 272). She contends that white women who write feminist theory frequently have had little or no understanding of white bias and class assumptions. Liberal, white, middle-class ideology underlies most feminist thought. She views much of feminist social theory as "Eurocentric, linguistically convoluted and rooted in Western male sexist and racially biased philosophical frameworks" (hooks 1989, p. 36). Too often accepted in such work is the competitive, atomistic individualism, which characterizes capitalistic society. She sees this as undermining the feminist struggle.

hooks posits that for the most part, white middle class women who dominate feminist discourse erect exclusionary barriers that prevent new ideas from entering their journals and other informational outlets. And to a great extent, white feminist theorists and hooks are not speaking the same language. She makes this point about postmodern theory, too. Such theory stresses otherness, but it is very far removed from the lives of poor people and people of color. While hooks does appreciate the nonessentialistic paradigm characteristic of the postmodern perspective, she finds problems with the narrowness of such discourse. For her, the feminist movement needs accessible liberatory theory. And such feminist theory needs both to integrate the most visionary methods of feminist analysis and to connect this analysis to models of social action and change aimed at eradicating male domination (hooks 1989, p. 35).

Although hooks realizes that most theory will emanate from academia, she takes issue with its lack of accessibility and the academy's stranglehold on feminist thought. Believing that theory must appeal to the whole collectivity of women and men, including those in the working classes and those living in poverty, she sees much of contemporary feminist thought as undermining its revolutionary potential. For example, she sees the French feminist theories of Julia Kristeva and Luce Irigaray as particularly obtuse. She does not see how this theory can be relevant to the black experience. hooks quotes black poet and activist Audre Lorde's warning that "the master's tools will never dismantle the master's house." (cited by hooks in 2000a).

One of her main sociological concerns is the value many black Americans place on familial patriarchy. She sees this as a holdover from slavery. Because black males have been denied full participation in the economic and social life of society, many African Americans see the patriarchal family as a means of addressing the hurt inflicted by racism. It is far easier to cling to this myth, she contends, because patriarchy is viewed by mainstream white society as the bedrock of American life. And it is much easier to accept benevolent black male domination of family life than to support the type of revolutionary change that would end race, gender, and class exploitation (hooks 1999). At the same time, many members of the black community view feminism as a threat to the "traditional" family. In her book, *We Real Cool: Black Men and Masculinity* (hooks 2004), hooks contends that it is patriarchal masculinity that most threatens authentic black maleness and undermines the revolutionary potential of the black community. She calls for a new radical male consciousness that rejects this stereotype.

While many white families have been positively affected by feminist thought in the way they live their lives, this is not true for many black families. Progressive black feminists have not had an equal impact on communities of color as have some of their white counterparts on their communities. Outspoken black women confront a culture where most want them "to stay in their place." Too many black women are fearful of being portrayed as vicious and domineering, or worse. This often translates into less action on their part because they are reluctant to take actions deemed non-conformist. It is much more likely that they will take a conservative position relative to domestic life—more so than their white feminist counterparts. hooks states "Anti-feminist backlash, coupled with narrow forms of black nationalism which whole-heartedly embrace patriarchal thinking, has had a major impact on black females" (hooks 1999). hooks believes that only through undermining black patriarchy and an emphasis on greater diversity in feminist thought can feminism ever be successful.

Patricia Hill Collins, who served as the president of the American Sociological Association in 2008 and who teaches at the University of Maryland, is a radical social theorist who has been able to identify the important intersections between feminist thought and scholarship and issues of racial, class, and sexual oppression. As one of the most important black feminist social thinkers today, Collins contends that race is but one factor in a matrix of interlocking objects of oppression and domination, and that black women often find it difficult to identify with many of the middle-class white feminist thinkers who embrace a Eurocentric view of the world.

Often the life experiences of black women are quite different from those of their white counterparts. In some respects, women separated by race, live in different worlds, and the same can be said about those occupying different social strata or sexual orientations. But Collins rejects what she refers to as an *additive approach* to understanding oppression that begins with gender, or even race and adds age, sexual orientation, disabilities, social class, and ethnicity. Rather, she views these variables as interlocking systems of oppression. She proposes that Afrocentric feminist theory has much to teach the feminist movement by privileging the role of women of color by examining the form that oppression takes for these women (Collins 1990, pp. 221–225). One specific outcome of such an examination is a deeper understanding of the role of black women in their communities and their unique struggles with patriarchy.

For Collins, the feminist Afrocentric view of community stands in opposition to other feminist models and to the concept of community that prevails throughout white culture. Unlike the market-driven notion of community that prevails in white dominant societies (which emphasizes competition), the Afrocentric feminist notion of community stresses connection, caring, and mutual responsibility. This comes out of the experiences and struggles of black women. She contends that the communities *created* by black women are aimed at empowering their members. Within this vision of community can be found a reconceptualization of power.

What she means by this is that the prevailing notion of power (in white com-munities) is married to domination, which is not the case in the lives of black women. Here, Collins refers to the important leadership roles occupied by women of color in church organizations, charities, labor unions, schools, and the like. Within these organizations, community and power take on new meaning. Black communities often represent sanctuaries wherein black women and men are nur-tured in order to confront oppressive social institutions external to them. Where communities exist in this form, they serve as places of true empowerment. But here power is a tool of creative change and adjustment and not a hammer of domi-nation. The stronger the community, the greater the potential for one's personal empowerment.

Eurocentric masculine models of organization require a ranking in terms of power. They fail to recognize that strong, egalitarian communities produce health-ier, more powerful people who can more intelligently resist domination. Collins contends that much can be learned from the experiences of black women who have been nurtured by these communities.

She identifies six features that are characteristic of black feminist thought, especially in the United States (Collins 1990, p. 22). First, she views black feminist thought as emerging from an experience of oppression. And while such oppres-sion is not unique to African American women, it does take a particular form of resistance to oppression. Second, Collins contends that the experiences of black women are linked to their theory construction. Theory responds to particular chal-lenges experienced by this group. Third, she emphasizes the standpoint of such women as individuals who experience oppression based on their social and self-defined positions. Thus, black feminist knowledge and theory originates in the standpoint of the group. Looking at black feminist thought as dynamic products of black feminist intellectuals constitutes a fourth distinguishing feature. Here scholarship is joined to activism, and black feminist intellectuals help to provide these links between knowledge and action. Thus the fifth feature is the struggle for social change. Finally, Collins insists that black feminist thought promotes new projects focusing on solidarity and justice.

Collins attacks the positivist approach to knowledge. She contends that women of color must struggle against the norms of white, male-dominated social science to let their true condition be recognized. Black feminist theorists and scholars risk rejection of their positions by prevailing scholarly norms. Positivism often creates descriptions of reality based on empirical generalizations. Positivists follow strict methodological processes, distancing themselves from values, emo-tions, and interests—often distancing themselves from matters of race, class, age, gender, and sexual orientation. Social scientists too frequently believe that they must step outside the realm of their own subjective experience and become detached observers, which is impossible to do. Thus, Collins rejects such subject/object dichotomies.

All black feminist theories begin with the position of the outsider group. While she recognizes the specific role of black feminist theorists as outsiders *within*, serving *within* the white-dominated academic institutions of society, she nevertheless believes that there can never be one unitary black feminist perspective given the *matrix of oppression*. Collins' most recent work deals with this diversity of standpoints within this matrix. She contends that such complexity constitutes the future and that all theorists need to be more aware of the intersections of demographic attributes that constitute the modern world (Collins 2004).

NANCY FRASER: REDISTRIBUTION AND RECOGNITION IN FEMINISM

Working out of the New School for Social Research in New York City, Nancy Fraser is a contemporary critical theorist, very much in the tradition of the Frankfurt school. She is also a noted feminist thinker who attempts to connect feminist thought, Marxism, and poststructuralism (Fraser 1989). As a social theorist, she also addresses the growing chasm between what she sees as a "politics of redistribution" (or, simply put, the socialist ethos) from a "politics of recognition," which frequently takes the form of *identity politics*.

According to Fraser (2009), second wave feminist theory of the 1960s and 1970s took aim not only at patriarchy, but also at the capitalist system which fostered and institutionalized it. These feminists were initially part of the New Left and attacked both capitalism and the social injustices it tended to produce economically, politically, and culturally. Feminist theorists saw post World War II capitalism as promoting a class-centered society along with an unfair economic distribution of resources. State protected capitalism valued economic relations while it marginalized communal ones. It was *androcentric*, privileging the male position in society. State capitalism promoted and protected white males at the expense of women and people of color. It obscured or marginalized the value of domestic labor as "women's work" and naturalized the injustice of gender discrimination in the workplace. These were the things feminists fought against. They also fought the bureaucratic and administrative ethos associated with this fordist form of capitalism, which depoliticized culture and substituted technical questions for value questions. Feminists of the 1960s and 1970s challenged the validity of the nation-state that distributed justice on the basis of affiliation and the interests of state capitalism. They fought against imperialism promoted by this system. They also operated on the grass-roots level and believed that change to the entire system could grow from such action.

By the 1980s, however, much of the feminist critique in the United States moved steadily away from its earlier criticism of capitalism; it rejected what it viewed as androcentric Marxism and instead focused on the other, more culturally charged issues, especially issues of identity. Fraser contends that *second wave feminism* unintentionally supported and was co-opted by neoliberalism as it emerged in the Reagan era. The fragmentation of feminist interests into separate or splintered areas of concern diminished the impact of feminism as a powerful force for social change. That is, black feminists, radical feminists, socialist feminists, lesbian feminists, and ecofeminists vied for a voice. By the late 1970s, there was a greater move toward liberal reform and accommodation rather than one toward radical change. And such reform was seen as capable of taking place under a new kind of capitalism that had seemingly embraced many elements associated with a more begin form of feminism. Capitalism in the 1980s and 1990s was different from the postwar variety. Women were welcomed into the job market. This is what hooks called a "life-based" feminism (hooks 2000, p. 11). A diversity of feminist ideas thrived under this system. No longer was it one set of values directed at state capitalism; now feminism was many things to many people.

Neoliberalism and the new feminism played down issues of redistributive justice. The new feminism focused instead on the rights of women and minorities to exert greater responsibility in this system. Its focus was more on cultural and group concerns. Nancy Fraser (1989) calls this a turn from redistribution to recognition. While the feminization of poverty was a concern, more immediate was the glass ceiling.—a term used to indicate the limited access women had to top-paying jobs. While there was still criticism of the system, the focus was on attempting to reform it. Many new feminists shared with neoliberals a disdain for the state apparatus that attempted to restrict their freedom in the market place. In fact, a large number embraced the market place and their enhanced role in it by becoming what some refer to as "lipstick feminist"(Hollow and Moseley 2006). Here, is where women can be powerful by wearing high heels and makeup.

Where there had been a concern with women's domestic work not being recognized, women were now brought into the payroll economy in greater numbers as real wages of men dropped. Now two-worker and three-worker households (where children joined the work force) became the norm. There were double shifts as wages were lowered and production increased. At the same time, corporations attempted to be less hierarchical and more inclusive. Fraser sees many intersections between neoliberalism and late twentieth-century feminism. While highly critical of identity politics, Fraser still believes that recognition and redistributive justice for the whole of society is a possibility through some form of transformative politics.

Unlike feminists who have embraced Lacanian theory, Fraser remains dubious about its relevance. She particularly sees Lacan's structuralism as a dead end in helping to uncover issues of identity for women (Fraser 1990). However, she is not averse to feminist discursive theory based on what she calls the pragmatic model of social discourse inherent in some of the work of Michel Foucault, Pierre Bourdieu, and others. She views Lacan's work as essentialistic and phallocentric, and claims that "Lacan falls prey to psychologism when he claims that the phallocentricity of the *symbolic order* is required by the demands of an enculturation process that is itself independent of culture" (Fraser 1998, p. 129). She views his particular brand of psychologism and symbolism as deterministic and of little use to feminist theory and politics. His male/female identity binary, based on having a penis or not having one, is inadequate for understanding both women and men.

For Fraser, structuralism, unlike the pragmatic approach in discourse theory, fails to focus on the social context and social practice of communication. It also fails to be pluralistic and is for the most part formulaic. She concludes that in more pragmatic forms of poststructural analyses contribute the most to our understanding of meaning..

FEMINIST THOUGHT AND THE POSTSTRUCTURAL BODIES

As the poststructural ideas of Lacan and Foucault became absorbed into feminist thought, so too was there a heightened emphasis on the centrality of the body. As we saw in Chapter 4, much was made of somatic perception by the French post-structural feminists. Thus, the body became the locus of power distinction between men and women. It was viewed as intensely symbolic text. French theorists like Kristeva, Irigaray, and Cixous, who were part of the poststructural movement, recognized the critical connection between the body and gendered language. They focused on the importance of women coming into their own by establishing a new language that was reflective of who they were.

Hélène Cixous, who shares the same intellectual roots as Foucault, Barthes, Derrida, and Deleuze, (and who taught alongside some of them at the experimental *Université de Paris VIII* at Vincennes shortly after the student riots of 1968), sees language, but particularly writing from the body, as a revolutionary means toward social change. She hopes that feminist writing will undermine or subvert phallocentric narrative myths that seem to underlie western patriarchal culture. Such texts must be written not to wrestle power from men but to find a new space. But to accomplish this, the female body must first be written. This is her goal. It means liberation from the mastery of a language constructed by men for men that comes from a reference to their own bodies. Cixous (1994), like Irigaray and Kristeva, believes that sexuality is directly connected to how we communicate in society.

Cixous believes that women who write and speak are forced to do so from the Symbolic, male, position because women have long been denied an authentic voice in the West. For women to *write from their own bodies* is to escape from hierarchical bonds and false binaries into a realm of *joissance*, which Cixous defines as the metaphysical fulfillment of desire that transcends mere satisfaction; it is a realm that allows a fusion of the erotic, the mystical, and the political (Gilbert 1986, p. xvii). Women need to write themselves for themselves—to tell their own stories. They must not write like men, denying who and what they are.

On the other hand, while men do write from their bodies, they also are seen as alienated from them. While privileged, they are consigned to the Symbolic Order, which separates them from their erotic power and potential to be more than just a *phallus*. Thus, Cixous views men as equally challenged by the false binaries that constitute western culture. This same binary system is what produces racism and imperialism, which ultimately established apartheid in the South in the United States and in South Africa. Such a position has sociological significance.

It is her firm belief that what she refers to as *l'ecriture feminine*, or feminine writing, can destabilize this entrenched structure of the binary and create a rupture in the entrenched system. This is where, as Derrida has suggested in his work, the totalizing and concrete qualities of the system break down and reveal its emptiness. Only at this point can a new type of nonlanguage reconnect us to the body and to the erotic. It is only here, she asserts, that definitions lose their usefulness. And it is here that sexuality can no longer be divided between homosexual and heterosexual, or between male and female. These divisions will no longer stand. Only when this occurs will bodies no longer be divided into binary categories and be assigned binary genders. All binaries will fall apart and a more egalitarian system will replace it.

In the United States, Susan Bordo has been instrumental in articulating this importance in feminist theory by emphasizing the impact of culture on both women's and men's bodies. Bordo, whose training was mostly in literature, gained renown as a social theorist when she published her first book, *The Flight to Objectivity*, in 1987. In it, Bordo critiques Descartes's notion of objectivity. This work was the initial inspiration for her later study of the body. Here, she explores the cultural pressures that gave rise to the Cartesian notion that the body is a "prison the mind must escape to achieve knowledge" and the underlying notion that the separation of intellect from the body is necessary to achieve any rational understanding. She calls into question Descartes' culturally grounded notion that men tend to represent the intellect and women the body.

In *Unbearable Weight: Feminism, Western Culture and the Body* (1993), Bordo presents the reader with a cultural analysis of bodies. Her poststructural analysis eschews both a left/right political binary and an intensely focused psychoanalytic critique. Instead, she explores how history and culture have helped to construct the body over time. Drawing on the work of Foucault and Bourdieu, the body is viewed as a medium of culture. She views eating disorders, specifically, not as personal pathology but rather as social formations, and she contextualizes them historically. The body in the West is seen as constructed by an ideology that depicts it as a source of conflicting needs, hungers, and vulnerabilities—a site surrounded by cultural demands and anxieties. While consumer culture encourages indulgence and "giving in to desire," western cultures also glamorize self-discipline.

Bordo recognizes vast contradictions on the particular demands imposed on women in this contemporary culture. The slender, toned female body becomes a cultural fetish. It is associated with assertiveness, self-discipline, and independence. Men view it as less sexually threatening, and women see it as a rebellion against rigid nurturing demands imposed by society. The slender female body often represents resistance. Bordo also views the male body as an equally important cultural signifier, one that she sees as becoming more important with time.

But it would be an error to promote the notion that the body is primarily the feminist domain. In general, the body has become an essential aspect of social theory. In fact, in 1995 a journal devoted to the sociology of the body, *Body and Society*, was launched, suggesting that the body could itself serve as an organizing principle for the discipline (Shilling 2004, p. 1). Thus, more and more the body is becoming an important signifier of gender and theories of sex.

In *Bodies That Matter* (1993), Judith Butler attempts to see the body as a pure construction of discourse, not a material entity that precedes discourse. Influenced

by poststructuralism, she proposes that we have no knowledge of a body without discourse. It is invented through language. And while she does not hold that
the body can be reduced to discourse, she does believe that matter (which is also
the body) can be *materialized* only through discourse. Although she believes matter exists without discourse, it can only become manifested through it. Therefore,
Butler refutes the notion of some of the French feminists cited earlier in this chapter by arguing that the body can never ground feminist theory because it can never
serve as an ontological foundation for theory.

Donna Haraway, an important postmodern feminist theorist, has made her
reputation to a large degree by explaining how all humans, women and men,
are constituted not so much by biology as, increasingly, by technology. Haraway
proposes that the postmodern individual is no longer human but rather *cyborg*—
part human, part machine. In a sense, technology has come to replace traditional bodies. In 1985, Haraway published her important essay, "The Cyborg
Manifesto." It is often difficult, she insists, to tell where the person ends and the
machine begins. The cyborg is postgender—neither male nor female—a creature
of both social reality and fiction. Unlike some feminists who retreat from technology as a realm of patriarchal domination, she views it as a source of liberation for
all, but especially for women. Women and men are both socially and culturally
constructed, and fewer things are biologically determined. It is her expectation
that as humans merge with their technology gender will become increasingly
insignificant.

She embraces the cyborg as a means of liberation from classical essentialist
models. She claims that there is nothing about being female that naturally binds
women together into a unified category. She argues against radical feminism as
being guided by identity politics, which she dismisses. She instead embraces this
connection to machines. As a socialist, she calls for an oppositional consciousness
that will undermine patriarchy. The cyborg identity can lead to radical political
action and liberate women from the quest for similarity based on body imagery.

NANCY CHODOROW AND JESSICA BENJAMIN: PSYCHOANALYTIC FEMINISM

In contrast to Haraway's cyborg feminism, both Nancy Chodorow and Jessica
Benjamin promote a feminist view grounded in psychoanalytic concepts. Each of
these writers is an analyst-clinician as well as an important feminist theorist.

Nancy Chodorow (1989) sees the psychoanalytic framework as more suited
to understanding the current condition of women than the models offered by
Marxist theorists such as Mitchell. She views Karen Horney and Melanie Klein
as having laid the groundwork for more contemporary psychoanalytic feminism.
Horney's interpersonal psychology appears to offer a clearer understanding of the
role of women in society, and Klein's object relations approach adds significantly
to our understanding of gendering.

Chodorow's most important work, *The Reproduction of Mothering* (1979), drew significantly from the work of Melanie Klein and other object relations theorists. Her central concern here was the process of socialization that both girls and boys undergo, and how they come to take on gender identities and roles. For Chodorow, psychoanalytic theory, particularly ***object relations theory***, provides us with the best understanding of how we develop a self-concept in childhood, and how early patterns of connection and separation are formed and then affect our worldview and relationships with others throughout our lives. *The Reproduction of Motherhood* focuses closely on how the role of mother has been enacted in the West. Rejecting essentialist arguments that privilege biology and so-called mothering instincts, Chodorow sees mothering better defined as the social, emotional, and physical care of children. In this sense, the birthing process has little to do with how this care is given or who actually gives it. Why, she asks, are women selected for this role when men are just as capable?

Chodorow sees nurturing and caring for others to be characteristics that are assigned to baby girls at birth, which then develop into a woman's role in society. Not only are women assigned to the nurturing and caring of children, but also they are often assigned to mothering their husbands. In older age they are expected to mother their own mothers. She sees a man's role in this regard as minimal. Men and boys are rarely called upon to parent. And this is where she sees a problem. To be a male, a boy is required to reject the "femininity" within him and identify primarily with men, while girls are required to identify with their mothers. Boys must reject the emotional dependence and intimacy girls are encouraged to have. Boys tend to be "overseparated" from their mothers, and girls are "underseparated." This, she finds, is the root of much adult pathology. It also promotes male domination and devaluation of women. The only way out of this bind is to integrate boys and men more fully into the mothering/parenting system. Chodorow's basic premise, then, is that one's early relationship with one's mother sets up interpersonal patterns for the rest of one's life.

Jessica Benjamin's ideas are rather different, although these are also grounded in western psychoanalytic discourse. Her most famous work, *The Bonds of Love* (1988), likewise deals with male domination but draws on the intimate complexities of domination and submission in love relationships in contemporary society. Rather than accepting Freud's contention that women are unable to dominate, she examines how women have been prevented from doing so and are relegated too often to submissive positions in love relationships by the dominant culture. The woman loves that person she cannot be but wishes to be.

For Benjamin, men in contemporary societies are empowered as dynamic agents and women are viewed as unchangeable objects. The reason for this division is the quest for power and the decline of mutuality in patriarchal society. Like Hegel's master/slave parable, women are forced into a social position of subordination and are expected to gain pleasure from this position by connecting to a powerful male. This sadomasochism often becomes the very basis for love relations.

Like Chodorow, Benjamin sees the only solution to this practice in reciprocity gained through early socialization and mutuality developed among mothering figures, infants, and paternal figures. This is what enables both attunement and healthy adaptation to seperation. Benjamin recognizes that both sameness and personal sovereignty must be part of an ongoing dialectical process, especially in early childhood development as these patterns will become translated into mature adult relationships. This issue is later taken up in Benjamin's work on the importance of intersubjectivity.

Benjamin sees much Lacanian theory as problematic. The oedipal triangulation inherent in Lacan's theory does not prove to be a valid way of understanding patriarchy. Despite his critique of patriarchy, Lacan's work seems to be predicated on a classical male/female binary taken from Freud. Benjamin takes issue with Freud's view of the active male versus the passive female, and challenges his classical oedipal notion. She calls for a reconfiguration of this seminal psychoanalytic notion based on a theory of pluralities of gender.

In *The Shadow of the Other* (1998), Benjamin argues that people of both genders are intersubjective. The challenge here is for each subject to contain different attributes, including his or her contradictions and contrary positions, which come from this social conditioning. Only by appreciating these differences and finding a space for mutual understanding can there be personal growth.

LESBIAN FEMINISM AND FEMINIST THEORY

A cultural and theoretical perspective that was extremely influential in the 1970s and 1980s was lesbian feminism. This branch of feminism was an offshoot of both the second wave feminist movement and the gay liberation struggles of the early 1970s. Second wave feminism was sometimes driven by women's reactions to the patriarchal domination of the antiwar and civil rights movements of the 1960s, in which women who struggled alongside men were denied access to decision making. In a similar way, *lesbian feminism* was frequently a reaction to the heterosexism inherent in the feminist movement and the male sexism present in the gay liberation struggle. Organizations like the National Organization of Women, to become more inclusive of conservative middle-class white women, marginalized the more vocal lesbians who were an essential part of the struggle for women's rights (Seidman 2008, p. 237). Lesbian feminists worked to fight against not only male oppression of women, but also the oppression lesbians experienced both as women and as non-heterosexuals. Out of this struggle emerged important theorists who helped to formulate ideas that were to influence feminist, gay, and queer theory.

Adrienne Rich, an activist, poet, and scholar, is one of the most important theorists of lesbian feminism. In her work, she proposes that patriarchy is institutionalized and supported through a system of compulsory heterosexuality. According to Rich, such a system is neither natural nor normal. Male societal dominance is predicated on what she views as a gynophobic splitting of thought from feeling, which underlies compulsory heterosexuality. Her work is a generous integration of her own personal experiences with a more scholarly understanding of human relations.

Rich did not embrace political lesbianism because of a hatred of men. She embraced it out of a love and compassion for women, whom she felt had been denied the ability to develop as full individuals in a male-dominated culture. Like Chodorow, she saw the construction of motherhood as a mechanism used for female exploitation and economic disenfranchisement. In her work, *Of a Woman Born* (1976), she contends that men appropriated motherhood to serve their own interests. Where traditional societies revered the ability of women to give birth, modern patriarchal societies deny women control over their own bodies and substitute science and medicine for nurturance and care.

Audre Lorde (1934–1992), another important contributor to lesbian feminist theory, criticized the public dominance of middle-class white heterosexual women of second wave feminism. Born to Caribbean immigrants who settled in Harlem in New York City, Lorde was educated at Columbia University and the National University of Mexico, and eventually taught at the City University of New York and Howard University. Like Rich, she was not only an activist-intellectual, but an important American poet.

Lorde contended that there could never be a general category of women because the issues of race and class directly affected each person's experience. She also contended that racism and homophobia were inherent in the feminist movement, and that much of this movement unintentionally worked in the service of patriarchy. She argued that all intolerance was linked and that racism, sexism, and homophobia emanated from patriarchy. She contended that homophobia was as much a crucial life issue for the black community as racism was for the gay and lesbian community. She spoke out clearly against categorical binaries—male/female, black/white, citizen/immigrant, gay/straight—as tools of oppression. Like Rich, her definition of lesbianism was not a narrow one. It was not confined to homosexual relations among women but encompassed care and love for all women. For Lorde as well as for Rich, *any* dedicated feminist was also a lesbian (i.e. a woman of lesbian consciousness).

As a self-proclaimed socialist and critic of capitalism, Lorde noted, "Institutionalized rejection of difference is an absolute necessity in a profit economy which needs outsiders as surplus people. As members of such an economy, we have all been programmed to respond to the human differences between us with fear and loathing and to handle that difference in one of three ways: ignore it, and if that is not possible, copy it if we think it is dominant, or destroy it if we think it is subordinate" (1984, p. 115).

While lesbian feminism has not been extinguished, it has been struggling over the years to reinvent itself, especially in the light of queer theory—a topic that will be covered more thoroughly in Chapter 9. Arlene Stein (1992, p. 51), a sociologist who serves in the women and gender studies department at University, has written about the struggle of lesbian feminism to come to terms with issues of identity as lesbianism began to recognize its own enormous diversity in the late 1980s and 1990s. With the advent of queer theory, lesbian feminism lost ground as a political force because the emphasis on queer was very broad and encompassing. Now lesbianism became a provisional identity—meaning that it is now situated within a network of multiple identities and oppressions. In fact, Sheila Jeffreys, a lesbian feminist scholar and political activist, went as far as to claim, "The appearance of queer theory and queer studies threatens to mean the disappearance of lesbians" (1994, p. 459).

With the advent of postcolonial feminist theory, lesbian feminism was not able to preserve the notion of a universal lesbianism on which the movement was originally founded. The acceptance of flexibility of sexual orientation and sexual identity challenge the tradition of identity politics on which the movement was founded.

POSTCOLONIAL FEMINIST THEORY

While theories of postcolonialism will be discussed more fully in Chapter 8, it is important that this approach to feminist theory be introduced here. *Postcolonialism* is a contentious term, but it is taken to mean the social, economic, political, and cultural conditions wrought by the Euro-American colonialization of nonwestern societies. Thus, postcolonial feminism has been a reaction to western feminist discourse, which ignores the position of women living in postcolonial societies or, worse, attempts to speak for these women. Postcolonial feminism, sometimes referred to as Third World feminism, tends to be highly critical of a radical feminism that sees gender as more essential to analysis than class and ethnicity. It also rejects the attempts of second wave feminists to universalize the experiences of women. While gender is crucial, these theorists suggests that much of the ordeal of women in postcolonial societies is related to that residue of patriarchy that is associated with the colonial experience and is essentially an outcome of capitalist imperialism. Many see a direct parallel between patriarchy and colonialism and the marginalization and exploitation that animate both. Every culture has its own unique history of oppression based on gender.

These feminist thinkers neither romanticize the precolonial past, nor attribute all oppression against women as emanating from the West. Each culture has its own form of sexism. Chandra Talpade Mohanty (1991), originally from Mumbai, India but now living in the United States, makes it clear that women in postcolonial societies do not speak with one voice. However, they are thought of in this way far too frequently by many of their sister feminists in the West. For Mohanty, this type of assessment appears quite common, and she sees it as part of an ethnocentric universality, wherein familial, economic, and religious practices and social structures are judged by western standards. The "average Third World woman" is based on a misguided attempt to translate western values into nonwestern ones. The issues of oppressed women of the First World are transformed into the struggles of oppressed women of the Third World. There is a diminishment of the importance of local culture as every group of women around the world has had a unique history that has shaped their current condition.

While Mohanty's groundbreaking essay "Under Western Eyes: Feminist Scholarship and Colonial Discourses" (1988) dealt with some of these struggles, she has gone on to analyze globalized capitalist relations, particularly in terms of the marginalization of the work performed by women. She explores how women are literally forced into both domestic and low level factory work. While not a classical Marxist, she attempts to understand the condition of women in the global marketplace drawing upon a Marxian critique.

This issue has been taken up by cultural anthropologists and African feminists such as Ifi Amadiume at Dartmouth College. Amadiume takes issue with western feminists' imposition of Euro-American cultural values on women in nonwestern areas. She takes particular exception to the theories of American feminists who see motherhood as disempowering for women. For Nigerian women, it is just the opposite. She notes, "In my research I have found that the traditional power of African women had an economic and ideological basis, and derived from the sacred and almost divine importance accorded to motherhood. This has led me to argue that the issue of the structural status of motherhood is the main difference between the historical experiences of African women and those of European women" (Amadiume 1997, p. 146). It is clear that secularism and capitalism are primary to motherhood being seen as unproductive work in the West. But as cultures are leveled by the forces of globalization, the values of the so-called developed world are imposed on nonwestern societies.

Mohanty (2003) also looks critically at the impact of globalization, particularly the impact of global capital, on the lives of women, both in postcolonial societies and in the West. It is her contention that capitalism opposes feminism on many different levels. And feminist scholars need to confront this head on. Her work illuminates the significance of international racism in capitalist development around the world. At the same time, she argues for women to negotiate the conceptual differences that divide them. Most important, Mohanty urges women to unite to oppose the abuses of global capitalism through global feminist solidarity. This united force, she contends, can confront and resist the racist, colonialist influence of hegemonic power. She rejects a cultural relativism that imbues culture with essentialism and romanticizes cultural differences. Mohanty views such identity politics as getting in the way of seeing commonalities, especially the commonalities of exploitation. The rise of queer theory, which recognizes the diverse sexualities that exist throughout the world, has found considerable favor among postcolonial feminist theorists, such as Mohanty, who reject universally structured notions of sexual identity and sexuality.

POSTMODERNISM AND POST-FEMINIST FEMINIST THEORY

It is important to point out that there is no consensus among feminist social theorists about the value of postmodern theory. Judith Butler (1992), who is often branded a postmodern theorist, confesses that she has no real sense of what this actually means. She sees the term as often confused with poststructuralism and deconstruction. However, it is significant that postmodern discourse shapes much of her feminist critique. Many feminists do appreciate that the postmodern does not take as its starting point the western, heterosexual, male-centered experience but instead offers new paradigms of social criticism that do not rely on traditional philosophical underpinnings (Fraser and Nicholson 1990).

Feminist theorists who have embraced postmodern thought and have developed postmodern theory find justification for doing so in their feminism. Postmodernism opens up new spaces for discussion in that it seemingly rejects essentialism and those aspects of western grandiosity that have long been connected to validating patriarchal oppression. Postmodern theory challenges logocentrism. It contests Eurocentric classification systems predicated on historic development and questions the methods of classical positivism. It challenges the subject/object binary. Feminist theorist Jane Flax (1986, p. 3) has noted that feminism and postmodernism both share "a profound skepticism regarding universal (or universalizing) claims about the existence, nature and powers of reason, progress, science, language and the 'subject/self.'" Flax has suggested an almost natural affinity between feminist thought and postmodern theory.

Some of the most impressive critiques of modernity have come from postmodern feminists. Susan Bordo's articulate attack against the Cartesian masculinization of thought stands as an essential postmodern feminist dissection of a major product of the European Enlightenment (Bordo 1987). The escape from feeling into objectivity, she contends, has defined western intellectual discourse, and it displaces the value of subjective understanding with the imposition of a hyperrationalist empiricism.

But there are also strong feminist suspicions of postmodern theory. Christine Di Stefano (1990) has suggested several reasons for such wariness. Primary among these is that it often appears to express the needs and sensibilities of a white, Eurocentric, and male privileged class that has experienced "the Enlightenment" and would like to move on to assess it critically. Also, the philosophical roots of this intellectual perspective are western, with a strong masculine bias, that can be traced back to Plato and Aristotle. At the same time, many of the central currents of this perspective as promoted by Lyotard, Foucault, and others often appear to be insensitive to issues of gender in their reading of the past. And finally, if the postmodern project was to be seriously adopted by feminists, this "would make the semblance of a feminist politics impossible" (p. 76). In a sense, it moves beyond the notion of womanhood by denying its very existence except as a social construction. It provides in its place a sort of utopian, gender-free paradigm.

Most feminists who engage in the construction of postmodern theory are ambivalent about its potential usefulness. Rita Felski, a professor of literature at the University of Virginia, has made the point that postmodernism has no historical memory in that it disrupts the modern notion of linear time: "Women, people of color and other disenfranchised groups are portrayed as suddenly bursting on to the historical stage, as if they had no prior experience as social subjects and human agents. Otherness is recognized only in the context of the present and subsumed within a familiar story of evolution from sameness to difference, from the one to the many" (Felski 2000, p. 3). Sara Ahmed (1998) makes the point that postmodernism is a continual *denial* or movement away from the political, which is the actual basis for most feminist thought. She contends that women need to interrogate the role of postmodern theory in denying women a tool for acquiring rights.

Other postmodern feminists such as Toril Moi (1988) and Alison Jagger (1983), have expressed concern that there has been an abandonment of political struggles in order to embrace what Julia Kristeva and some of her postmodern followers refer to as a "third space"—a space free from battles for equality and political reform—for a place that rejects all identity, all binary oppositions, all *phallocentric logic*, and is open to hybridity. The danger Moi sees in giving up on resistance is not that the battles still must be fought and won (which they must), but by accepting this third position without operating simultaneously in that space created by men and for men, feminist theorists will be working against their own interests.

Teresa Ebert (1991), who teaches postmodern and feminist theory at the State University of New York at Albany, contends that not all postmodern feminist theories are equal. While some of them contribute significantly to the advancement of social thought and a better understanding of the experience of women in society, many of them are significantly narcissistic and narrow. She divides postmodern thought into two areas. The first she refers to as *ludic postmodernism*, which deals primarily with an articulation of ideas involving rhetoric, textual play, and meaning. The second she calls *resistance postmodernism*, wherein signs become the arena of class and group struggle. It is this type of theory she finds lacking and in need of reinforcement in postmodern feminist thought.

Moi warns of some of the dangers inherent is what others refer to as postfeminism. Although postfeminism has multiple levels of meaning, it signifies for some that the ultimate goal of feminism is its own outmodedness—the need for it to outlive its usefulness by destroying patriarchy. Postfeminism involves a wide range of discourses related to the end of feminism.

Some of this has been taken up in the area of cultural theory. While some of this is a conservative and reactionary belief that second wave feminism has done its job and there is no longer a need for a feminist movement; that women are free to be women and can now "have it all." Sometimes postfeminism is used to represent the *third wave* of the movement that challenges the notion of gender. Here Judith Butler, Ann Fausto-Sterling and Donna Haraway are sometimes included. But even if acting "womanly" is a performance, a social construction, is it any less real in its consequences to the individual? This notion will be examined more closely in the next chapter.

However one conceives of postfeminism, it is clear that feminism, as it once was articulated in the first and second wave movements, is no longer the same feminism that exists today. While feminist theory might assimilate into the study of gender and sexuality, feminism will continue to generate rich discourse.

KEY TERMS

additive approach A type of identity theory wherein one's unique identity is a product of a multiple set of social characteristics, such as: female, black, lesbian, wealthy, educated.

androcentric The character of having the male or the masculine point of view as being central to a culture.

biologism A form of biological determinism in which all human behavior is viewed as stemming from biology.

cyborg An individual whose body comprises both biological and technological or mechanical parts.

double consciousness A term coined by W. E. B. DuBois to mean understanding oneself as a black person in a racist society and seeing oneself through the eyes of the dominant white race. But it has similar application to members of any other oppressed groups. For example, an individual who lives in a group where she or he is not accepted as a member but must share that group's consciousness as well as their own consciousness of an outsider.

feminist standpoint theory The assertion that women do not see the world in the same way that men do. Their biology, life experiences, and social conditions have given them a different perspective or way of seeing the world.

identity politics This is civic organization and engagement based on personal affiliation and group identity, particularly with a disenfranchised group identity such as race, ethnicity, gender, able-bodiness, or sexual orientation.

institutional ethnography A sociological method of inquiry that explores the social relations that structure people's everyday lives.

lesbian feminism Emerging as a response to the homophobia of the second wave women's movement, lesbian feminism was both a political movement, centering on identity, and a theoretical critique of homophobia, patriarchy, and sexism.

matrix of oppression Sometimes referred to as a "matrix of domination. Race, class, and gender constitute axes of oppression that often determine the intensity of discrimination, or lack of opportunity, experience by a person who falls into a certain place in the matrix.

object relations theory A theory in psychoanalysis that describes the developmental impact of an infant's relationships with others, particularly focusing on mother–child relations in the early years of the child's socialization.

phallocentric logic A system of logical understanding devised and utilized by men to control and organize society so that men are central to it.

phallus A key element in Lacanian thought. The phallus is not to be confused with the penis in that it is not part of the body but rather part of the social order. For Lacan, the phallus helps to construct our understanding of the very nature of the social structure; it is the center of all things.

radical feminism A category of feminist theory holding that the oppression of women is the key to understanding other forms of oppression, including class oppression. It targets patriarchy, not capitalism, as the center of all oppression.

second wave feminism Exemplified by the feminist movement in the United States in the 1970s wherein women fought for control over their own bodies, equality in the workplace, and greater representation in positions of power in business and government. This movement began to focus on the notion of womanhood and identity shared by women everywhere.

standpoint theory Feminist thought holding that the standpoint of women in society as objects of oppression is key to their clear understanding of how the society operates. Nancy Hartstock derived this idea from Marxist theory.

subjective knowledge An understanding of the world based on one's own experience and position in it.

symbolic order For Lacan, an order imposed on society through language and its rules.

third wave feminism Feminist thought that came from the feminist movement in the 1970s and focuses on women's gender oppression rather than on the fight for voting and political rights.

SOURCES

Agger, Ben. 1991. "Critical Theory, Poststructuralism, Postmodernism: The Sociological Relevance," *Annual Review of Sociology*, Vol. 17, pp. 105–131.

Ahmed, Sara. 1998. *Differences That Matter: Feminist Theory and Postmodernism*. Cambridge, UK: Cambridge University Press.

Amadiume, Ifi. 1997. *Reinventing Africa. Matriarchy, Religion and Culture*. New York: Zed Books.

Benjamin, Jessica.1988. *The Bonds of Love*. New York: Pantheon Books.

Benjamin, Jessica. 1998. *The Shadow of the Other*. New York: Routledge.

Bordo, Susan. 1987. *Flight to Objectivity*. Albany, NY: SUNY Press.

Bordo, Susan, 1993. *Unbearable Weight: Feminism, Western Culture and the Body*. Berkeley: University of California Press.

Brennan, Teresa. 1993. *History After Lacan*. New York: Routledge.

Butler, Judith. 1992. "Contingent Foundations: Feminism and the Question of 'Postmodernism,'" in J. Butler and J. Scott, eds., *Feminists Theorize the Political*. New York: Routledge.

Butler, Judith. 1993. *Bodies That Matter*. New York: Routledge.

Chodorow, Nancy. 1978. *The Reproduction of Motherhood*. Berkeley: University of California Press.

Chodorow, Nancy. 1989. *Feminism and Psychoanalytic Theory*. New Haven, CT: Yale University Press.

Cixous, Hélène. 1994. *Three Steps on the Ladder of Writing*. New York: Columbia University Press.

Collins, Patricia Hills. 1990. *Black Feminist Thought: Knowledge, Consciousness and the Politics of Empowerment*. Boston: Unwin Hyman.

Collins, Patricia Hills. 2004. *Black Sexual Politics: African Americans, Gender, and the New Racism*. New York: Routledge.

Di Stefano, Christine. 1990. "Dilemmas of Difference: Feminism, Modernity, and Postmodernism," in Linda Nicholson, ed., *Feminism/Modernism*. New York: Routledge.

Dworkin, Andrea. 1987. *Intercourse*. New York: The Free Press.

Ebert, Teresa. 1991. "The Difference of Postmodern Feminism," *Teaching English*, Vol. 53, No. 8, pp. 886–904.

Felski, Rita. 2000. *Doing Time: Feminist Theory and Postmodern Culture*. New York: New York University Press.

Flax, Jane. 1986. "Postmodern and Gender Relations in Feminist Theory," in Linda Nicholson, ed., *Feminism/Modernism*. New York: Routledge.

Fraser, Nancy. 1989. *Unruly Practices: Power, Discourse and Gender in Contemporary Social Theory*. Minneapolis, MN: University of Minnesota Press.

Fraser, Nancy. 1998. "The Uses and Abuses of French Discourse Theories for Feminist Politics," in S. Mariniello and P. Bové, eds., *Gendered Agents*. Durham, NC: Duke University Press.

Fraser, Nancy. 1992. "Introduction," in N. Fraser and S. Bartky, eds., *Revaluing French Feminism*. Bloomington, IN: University of Indiana Press.

Fraser, Nancy. 2009. "Feminism, Capitalism, and the Cunning of History," *The New Left Review*, Vol. 56, pp. 97–118.

Fraser, Nancy, and Linda Nicholson. 1990. "Social Criticism without Philosophy: An Encounter between Feminism and Postmodernism," in Linda Nicholson, ed., *Feminism/ Modernism*. New York: Routledge.

Gilbert, Sandra M. 1986. "Introduction" in *The Newly Born Woman*, in Hélène Cixous and Catherine Clement, eds. Trans. By Betsy Wing. Minneapolis, MN: University of Minnesota Press.

Grosz, Elizabeth. 1990. *Jacques Lacan: A Feminist Introduction*. New York: Routledge. *Solidarity*, Durham, NC: Duke University Press.

Haraway, Nancy. 1985. "A Cyborg Manifesto: Science, Technology, and Socialist-Feminism in the Late Twentieth Century," *Socialist Review*, No. 80, pp. 65–108.

Harding, Sandra. 1986. "The Instability of Analytical Categories in Feminist Theory," *Signs*, Vol. 11, No. 4, pp. 645–664.

Hollows, Joanne and R. Moseley. 2006. *Feminism in Popular Culture*. Oxford. Berg Publishers.

Harding, Sandra. 1998. *Is Science Multicultural?* Bloomington, IN: Indiana University Press.

hooks, bell. 1981. *Ain't I A Woman: Black Women and Feminism*. Cambridge, MA: South End Press.

hooks, bell. 1989. *Talking Black: Thinking Feminist, Thinking Black*. Cambridge, MA: South End Press.

hooks, bell. 1995."Black Women: Shaping Feminist Theory" in B. Guy-Sheftal, ed., *Words of Fire: An Anthology of African-American Feminist Thought*. New York: The New Press.

hooks, bell. 1999. "Ain't I Still a Woman," *Shambhala Sun*, January Halifax, CAN Electronic format.

hooks, bell. 2000. *Feminist Theory: From Margin to Center*. Originally published in 1988. London: Pluto Press.

hooks, bell. 2000a. *Feminism Is for Everybody*. Cambridge, MA: South End Press.

hooks, bell. 2004. *We Real Cool: Black Men and Masculinity*. Cambridge, MA: Routledge.

Jagger, Alison. 1983. *Feminist Politics and Human Nature*. Totowa, NJ: Rowman and Littlefield.

Jeffreys, Sheila. 1994. "The Queer Disappearance of Lesbian Sexuality in the Academy." *Women's Studies International Forum*, Vol. 17, No. 5, pp. 459–472.

Lorde, Audre. 1984. *Sister Outsider: Essays and Speeches*. Freedom, CA: Ten Speed Press.

Lukács, Georg. 1971. *History of Class Consciousness: Studies in Marxist Dialectics*. Cambridge, MA: MIT Press.

Mitchell, Juliet. 1966. "The Longest Revolution," *The New Left Review*, Vol. 1, No. 40, pp. 11–37.

Mitchell, Juliet. 1974. *Psychoanalysis and Feminism*. New York: Basic Books.

Mohanty, Chandra Talpade. 1988. "Under Western Eyes: Feminist Scholarship and Colonial Discourse," *Feminist Review*, No. 30. pp. 61–88.

Mohanty, Chandra Talpade. 1991. "Introduction" and "Under Western Eyes," in C. Mohanty, A. Russo and L. Torres, eds., *Third World Women and the Politics of Feminism*. Bloomington and Indianapolis: Indiana University Press.

Mohanty, Chandra Talpade. 2003. *Feminism Without Borders: Decolonizing Theory, Practicing Solidarity*. Durham, NC: Duke University Press.

Moi, Toril. 1988. "Feminism, Postmodernism, and Style: Recent Feminist Criticism in the United States." *Cultural Critique*, No. 9, pp. 3–23.

Moses, Clair. 1998, Summer. "Made in America: French Feminism in Academe," *Feminist Studies*, Vol. 24, No. 2, pp. 241–274.

Rich, Adrienne. 1980. "Compulsory Heterosexuality and Lesbian Existence," *Signs,* Vol. 5. No. 4, pp. 631–660.

Shilling, Chris. 2004. *The Body and Social Theory*. London: Sage.

Smith, Dorothy E. 1999. *Telling the Truth After Postmodernism, Writing the Social: Critique, Theory and Investigations*. Toronto: University of Toronto Press.

Smith, Dorothy E. 2005. *Institutional Ethnography: A Sociology for People*. Lanham, MD: Rowman & Littlefield.

Smith, Dorothy E. 2006. *Institutional Ethnography as Practice*. Lanham, MD: Rowman & Littlefield.

Seidman, Steven. 2008. *Contested Knowledge: Social Theory Today*, Oxford: Blackwell.

Stein, Arlene. 1992. "Sisters and Queers: The Decentering of Lesbian Feminism," *Socialist Review,* Vol. 22, No. 1, pp. 33–55.

Wharton, Amy S. 1991. "Structure and Agency in Socialist Feminist Theory," *Gender and Society*. Vol 5, No. 3, pp. 373–389.

CHAPTER **7**

Cultural Studies and Cultural Theory

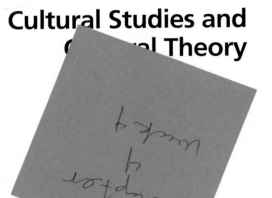

ultural Studies has been part of an effort to ~~refine~~ the boundaries that
have been erected between disciplines, particularly between the social sciences and the humanities. As an eclectic academic field, its aim is the study
of cultural phenomena in society by means of various interdisciplinary strategies
and approaches. Its theory flows from this eclectic approach. While sociology is
part of this mix, so too are literary theory, media studies, cultural anthropology,
geography, history, philosophy, art history, and a host of others.

Walter Benjamin (1892–1940), an associate of the *Frankfurt school* and a
close friend of Bertolt Brecht, wrote amazing cultural critiques in the 1920s and
1930s He is one of the twentieth century's quintessential cultural theorist. Like
Theodor Adorno (another affiliate of the Frankfurt school), he was a Marxist and
developed an aesthetic based on *dialectical materialism*. Like the French structuralist Roland Barthes (see Chapter 2), Benjamin became an important interpreter
of cultural iconography and was among the first critics to apply semiotics to the
analysis of popular culture—something rarely taken seriously.

The history of more contemporary cultural studies as a field of theoretical
inquiry is associated with the work of Richard Hoggart, a professor of literature
at Birmingham University in Great Britain. Hoggart was instrumental in direct-
ing scholarly attention to the products of popular culture. He was the founder of
the *Center for Contemporary Cultural Studies (CCCS)* at Birmingham in 1964,
which became an important center of early cultural theory and cultural studies
research (Turner 1990). However, it was Stuart Hall, his successor to the director-
ship at CCCS in 1968, who began giving the field a greater sociological depth
and global breadth. Hall drew significantly from the work of Marx in his cultural
critique and began developing a critical assessment of media and consumption.
While the field of cultural studies has had a mixed record of successes and fail-
ures, it survives as an important interdisciplinary area of study. Unlike any discrete area of the social sciences, it does not seek social intervention or political

132

remediation; rather, it is exploratory in its orientation. Perhaps this emanates from its literary origins.

STEWART HALL AND CULTURAL CRITIQUE

Stewart Hall grew up in a working-class family in Jamaica in the 1930s and 1940s before becoming a Rhodes Scholar at Merton College at Oxford University in 1951, where he eventually stayed to do postgraduate work in literature. While he had been sympathetic to the Jamaican independent movement while growing up, it was not until his student years at Oxford that he became radically politicized (Rojek 2003, pp. 57–59). As a young Jamaican man of color living at Oxford, Hall experienced a sense of marginalization as well as overt racism and condescension from those around him.

Like other intellectuals of this era, Hall was swept up in the enthusiasm associated with *New Left* politics; in 1960, he helped to found the *New Left Review.* While he and other young progressives protested the British takeover of the Suez Canal and the Soviet invasion of Hungary, much of their theoretical work was directed toward critiquing capitalist culture. The *New Left Review* became a primary instrument for organizing radical intellectuals of this era. Its contributors included the renowned socialist, activist, and author Edward P. Thompson; notable Marxist theorists Ralph Milibrand, Perry Anderson (a sociologist and historian who took over the journal's editorship when Hall left), and Raymond Williams (a Marxist literary critic who we will discuss later). The *New Left Review* continues to publish the works of most prominent social theorists today.

Eclecticism characterizes Hall's scholarship. His keen interest is in power relations and how they are played out in contemporary culture. He views culture, particularly popular culture, as a way of better understanding societal power dynamics. Within his work is a strong sense of anti-imperialism and anticapitalism. Consumerism of the postwar era becomes an important focus of his critique and a gateway into his analysis of popular culture.

Rejecting what he views as a "vulgar" Marxian model of culture characterized by structural determinism, Hall wants to explore culture's complexities as well as its own internal and external structural dynamics. For this purpose, he embraces the work of Antonio Gramsci to provide a theoretical foundation for his own work. Gramsci was an Italian Marxist thinker and activist living and imprisoned in Italy after the rise of fascism. In his famed *Prison Notebooks* (originally published between 1929 and 1935), he promoted the salience of culture and its role in political change. Like Gramsci, Hall also views culture as a tool for liberation. It was Gramsci's idea that capitalism imposed control over the working people by what he called *hegemonic culture*. Gramsci felt that, despite the cultural variations in any one society, societal diversity is often dominated by one social class imposing its values and way of life on the others. These values appear to all as "just common sense," but in reality the status quo is achieved through a complex process of manipulation and coercion. For Gramsci, the working class needs its own culture and the ability to see through the "natural order" imposed by cultural elites. Whereas the Frankfurt school theorists recognized a culture imposed on the working class by an elite, they gave little heed to culture developing "from below" and having a significant impact on society.

Hall also is attracted to the work of Mikhail Bakhtin in this regard. Bakhtin, whose concept of *carnival* was taken up briefly in Chapter 4 was a Russian linguist and philosopher whose work did not gain prominence until after his death in 1975. His notion of **heteroglossia** had particular appeal to Hall and other cultural theorists who were looking at culture as an avenue to promote liberation. Bakhtin (1941) used this term in his work to suggest that culture and its related narratives—even those that appear monolithic—contain many opposing voices. Culture is never monolithic. For Bakhtin, culture is inherently responsive and interactive, which he refers to as dialogism, meaning that all culture is a dialogue.

Also, Bakhtin introduced the notion of the **carnivalesque** to underscore the importance of culture and play as ways for people to confront what might appear to be intractable cultural elitism. He traces back the notion of carnival to the medieval festival of the Feast of Fools, where lower-order church officiates in France poked fun at the solemn, sacred ceremonies performed by the high priests and upper-ranking church clergy. For Bakhtin, the *carnivalesque* is the challenge of the cultural elitism from below. It is an attack on the seriousness of the established cultural hegemony, often with an attempt to bring it down. It is an insurgency wherein the kings become beggars and their power is diminished.

Hall's early work also recognizes the importance of consumerism and popular culture. While the old left appeared to be threatened by and dismissive of consumer culture, Hall and his New Left colleagues (working out of the CCCS) saw popular culture as a challenge, and something that could perhaps contain the seeds of political liberation. Like the cultural critics of the Frankfurt school, they analyzed it seriously and viewed it as politically salient. Unlike the Frankfurt school theorists, they saw no stark binary between producer and consumer. The consumer was empowered to give meaning to the products of consumption. They saw the arena of popular culture as providing real opportunities for radical change.

While Marx viewed culture as a secondary outcome of capitalism and not an active ingredient that helped to produce and support it, Hall saw popular culture as a potential generator of power and resistance. He took this idea from his reading of Gramsci. In 1964, Hall and Paddy Whannel, a leader in the field of British film studies, co-authored *The Popular Arts*. This was a reaction to the condemnation of the charges leveled against popular culture by established voices of cultural criticism in the late 1950s and early 1960s. There they rejected the binary notion of high culture of the established elites and low culture associated with the working classes. Hall and Whannel dismissed the accusation that there was a debasement of cultural standards taking place in the world. For them, *popular culture* was a third term—one that recognized its internal complexities and important diversity inherent in culture. This idea also distinguished them from theorists like Theodor Adorno, who viewed popular culture as inferior to high culture associated with elites.

The early approach to cultural studies emphasized what is referred to as *culturalism* (Barker 2003, p. 14), an historically informed perspective that suggests common people are capable of actively and creatively constructing meaningful common practices that could constitute a popular culture. In this sense, culture was the ordinary lived experience and could be explored empirically along with the context of its material conditions. This position stood in contrast to the notion of culture as elitist (Procter 2004, p. 38).

By the early 1970s, this culturalism was nearly eclipsed by structuralism (see Chapter 2). Theorists, including Hall himself, insisted that there were profound inadequacies inherent in culturalism's approach. The work of Claude Levi-Strauss, Roland Barthes, and others heavily influenced the work at the CCCS in the late 1960s and early 1970s. Culture as a language became an attractive point of view. The Marxian structuralism of Louis Althusser also affected British Cultural Studies at Birmingham. Some theorists, such as Hall, initially saw in Althusser's work a way of reuniting cultural studies with Marx through a structuralist rereading of his writings.

Although we discussed Althusser briefly in Chapter 2, it's important to reiterate his rejection of *Marxian humanism*. Althusser fully developed his notion of the structuralist Marx in his book, *For Marx* (1965). In this book, he rejected most of *early* Marx, including the notion of false consciousness emanating from capitalist ideology. Instead, Althusser proposed ideology as an empirical system of representations, including images, myths, and concepts by which people lived their lives and made sense of their world. Ideology is the *imaginary* relationship of individuals to the real material conditions of their own existences played out within the social structures of which they are part. As such, ideology is the true source of subjection—that which makes us into subjects, that which dictates that we yield to those we perceive as more powerful. In this way, we turn ourselves into subjects. Therefore, ideology becomes the site of struggle—the place where one is called to serve as a subject. Althusser referred to this process as *interpellation*.

Hall and others viewed Althusser's structuralism as too deterministic. E. P. Thompson (1978) and other humanists condemned its emptiness. This was one reason for Hall's turning to Gramsci, who was neither a culturalist nor a structuralist. Gramsci offered a greater sense of human potential and agency (Rojek 2003, p. 109). In terms of his own contributions to theory, Hall's eclectic focus is the most significant aspect of his work. While he doesn't create theory, he makes use of wide array of perspectives and applies them effectively to cultural critique. Hall would like to see theory as practice, or at least set the foundation for it. In this way he is unlike Althusser and Parsons who were more involved in the task of theory construction for its own sake. For Hall, theory is useful only if it can be applied somewhere. And this is his strength. This emphasis reveals a sociological project that might have application for social change, not merely a theoretical venture (Procter 2004, p. 64). He derides what he sees as "the fashion of theory," where "you can wear new theories like t-shirts" (Hall 1996, p. 149). Just the same, he believes there can be no practical understanding of culture without theory.

Like many other cultural theorists, Hall's efforts are directed to synthesizing existing theories rather than establishing new ones. He *employs* theory and finds new applications for it. Hall is constantly attempting to link discrete theories in order to move beyond the limits of each one (Procter 2004, p. 54).

RAYMOND WILLIAMS

Without the work of Raymond Williams (1921–1988), cultural studies could not have emerged as a significant intellectual field of study. One of the most important literary and cultural historians of the twentieth century, Williams brought to his work Marxist sensibilities and a willingness to cross artistic and intellectual boundaries. Raymond Williams was Welsh born and Cambridge educated. As a working-class literary critic and novelist, he became a leading figure in the British New Left. Williams's intellectual scope and vigor, and his astonishing level of scholarly and creative productivity has been unmatched in cultural studies.

Williams established his reputation for his literary histories and cultural analyses in the late 1950s and early 1960s. His major work, *Culture and Society*, was published in 1958. In it, he deconstructed the meaning of the term *culture*. Williams contended that culture did not merely consist of a body of artistic work but rather represented a way of life (Williams 1963, p. 11). He examined the growing significance of working-class culture that came about in England with the Industrial Revolution. As a socialist, it was his position that culture was not something bestowed onto those "lesser" but rather was in part a creation of this group. Like Hall, Williams believed that, while culture was at one time the pastime of the old leisure class, it had become the inheritance of this working-class majority (Williams 1963, p. 306). *Culture and Society* was in part his attempt to wrestle the concept of culture away from conservative elites and the domain of the likes of T. S. Eliot and Matthew Arnold.

Williams' historicism underscored the importance of his work. He drew on a variety of English literary figures and categorized the themes of their work in a timeline that revealed cultural changes taking place in society. Thus, culture was not an object of study removed from the people who helped to creat it. Rather, it was a complex of lived relationships, and it constituted a field of study. As a socialist and humanist, Williams believed that culture was a democratic project. His work was a radicalization and redefinition of culture itself. Throughout the 1960s and 1970s, Williams' work became foundational to critical cultural analyses. Not only did he draw on literature for his discussion, he also integrated significant sociological explorations. He was interested in the material manifestations of culture and how sense was made of it. Among his chief concerns was the relationship between culture and ideology. Unlike Althusser's abstract notion of ideology as imaginary, Williams saw culture as emanating from lived experience. Such experience is material and, physical and experiential. For Williams, there could be no separation between culture and materialism, between culture and human action. Culture is constructed through human action.

Like the Frankfurt school theorists, who critically examined what they referred to as the *culture industry*, Williams saw culture as part of an institutionalized productive process. In defining the social significance of culture, he devised the term *cultural materialism* to distinguish material culture from idealist culture—that which was most central to literary analysis. Put simply, idealist culture was comprised of those products considered in isolation from their means and conditions of their production. Cultural materialism was an extension of Marx's notion of historical materialism into the cultural realm. Williams asserted that culture needed to be understood in terms of its underlying system of production. Art and literature were as much an extension of this system of production as anything else it produced. In this sense, culture is always political. Social processes that produce culture were always part of its essence.

For Williams, the goals of cultural analysis are to analyze material culture with respect to its given time and place, to explore its various forms of signification, and to examine the shared feelings and values that underlie it (Williams 1981, pp. 64–65). It was perhaps his emphasis on what he called structures of feeling that made his work so very human, while structuralism and poststructuralism (particularly the French varieties) were bleaching theory of this quality. Structure of feeling has to do with how we see things from the vantage point of our culture at a given place in time. Williams believed that these structures provided the basis of our aesthetic perceptions. Such structures have their own hierarchy, and their own rules. Structure of feeling articulates the individual's totality of impressions of and responses to the culture to which she or he is exposed.

In his work, Williams embraced semiotics. It was integrated into his analysis of culture. He characterized culture as a signifying system through which a social order is communicated. But he developed a type of radical semiotics that was historically grounded in material culture and recognizes the power of subjective agency. Williams saw structure as a force of liberation rather than one of control.

Much of Williams' energies were spent in his analyses of contemporary cultural media such as books, television, music, and motion pictures. While a visiting professor at Stanford University in 1972, he wrote extensively on the popular media. His work inspired generations of younger people interested in the development of contemporary cultural analysis.

ANGELA McROBBIE: FEMINISM AND CULTURAL STUDIES

Stuart Hall recognized the dominance of the male perspective in much of the early British cultural studies. He worked to open up the field to women as well as to the LGBT population. Angela McRobbie, who trained in Birmingham at the CCCS with Hall, did ground breaking work on the study of young women in contemporary culture. McRobbie was most instrumental in bringing the subject of gender into the cultural studies fold. Much of her early research and writing focused on the various subcultures and cultural practices of young women and girls. In this work, she examined the messages contained in women's magazines aimed at the youth market. Much of her research was directed toward popular dance, recycled clothing as fashion, and the culture of femininity. McRobbie's work in the cultural gendering of working-class boys and girls has been innovative. She has used a wide variety of cultural artifacts, including song lyrics, dances, and the like. But beyond this, McRobbie's work might be best described as reflexive. She not only engages her subject, she also attempts to understand the history and trajectory of cultural studies itself. As a regular contributor to the journal *Cultural Studies*, she has explored and contributed to the vitality of her own field.

McRobbie's work is set off from that of Hall and Williams not merely due to her generational and gender differences, but also due to the decentering of Marx in her work. While she does not move away from Marxist sensibilities, they are not central to informing her ideas. In fact, she sees Marxism as no longer having the relevance it once had for cultural studies primarily because of world political reforms having occured in Eastern Europe and the changes in mass popular culture. McRobbie views cultural studies as post-Marxist. In this respect, she views the work of Fredric Jameson as untenable and believes cultural studies and postmodern thought have much more in common with one another than either does with Marxism.

For McRobbie (1994), postmodern perspectives are quite useful to the analyses of contemporary culture such as her own. She finds structuralism too weighty and contrived to provide a meaningful analysis of contemporary cultures. In the 1990s, she spent a considerable amount of time examining the relevance of postmodern theory for cultural studies and contends that such a perspective appears to have enormous value because it rejects the quest for a unified and comprehensive understanding of phenomena associated with modern positivism and replaces it with a fragmented and more pluralistic set of perspectives. It shifted semiotics away from a structuralist coding and substituted more relativistic positions.

McRobbie views postmodern thought as more open and fun loving than those perspectives that often ignore issues of diversity. She believes that postmodernism respects those voices that went unheard during their heyday of modernism (p. 15). In this way, it complimented the interdisciplinarity of cultural studies. McRobbie was particularly interested in understanding the role that postmodern thought would have on better exploring and understanding culture, and particularly the cultures of women.

McRobbie's (2009) more recent work has centered upon what she describes as a postfeminist age. This is an end to a somber feminism associated with the 1970s and the struggle for equal rights. McRobbie believes that this is in part a popular media construction of a lighter, less serious consideration of femininity. This ahistorical approach is dismissive of the past achievements of women who, through social action, won these rights from a resistant patriarchal society. Demanding women are viewed as crude because they are thought to have already achieved what they need. Accordingly, the sophisticated woman supposedly enjoys her sexuality and her recently found "liberation." However, McRobbie suggests that the price she pays for this is to accept the dominant ideology.

McRobbie sees a form of retraditionalization of femininity taking place. While many factors are responsible for this trend, she sees it primarily connected to a neo-liberal consumerist ideal of personal freedom. Of course, this current perspective assumes that feminist principles of the past are already in place and that there is little to no need to stress them today. Women are seen as free to construct themselves (see reference to "lipstick feminism" in Chapter 6.).

Drawing on the work of Jacques Lacan and Judith Butler, McRobbie suggests that a women's self-identity is put into play by the Symbolic patriarchal order. Until now, the Symbolic Order (in a Lacanian sense) was one that imposed an identity on her through social and political institutions and laws. When overt patriarchal authority is threatened, it delegates power to the commercial domain such as the fashion and cosmetic industries, and standards of beauty that become the source of judgment and authority in a young woman's life. One is convinced to go along or join in by the market forces that dictate belonging as central to a woman's life. One strives for the postfeminist body, as opposed to the hideous feminist one. The covert nature of market forces go unidentified. This brings into play what McRobbie describes as a *postfeminist masquerade*, which describes a new cultural dominant for women. Here women assume the role of having attained power, so as not to offend those denying them of it. However, this only translates into their own further exploitation (McRobbie 2009, p. 69).

In combining the work of Judith Butler and Joan Riviere, McRobbie posits that such a masquerade hides what might be a closer approximation to a feminine self. She sees this masquerade as an interpellative device—a call to which a young woman is expected to respond. This is a call from the commercial domain to assume the retro mask of femininity in what might be viewed as an unthreatening or playful manner. Such a masquerade ushers in a hyperfemininity of stiletto heels and cleavage-producing bras as a matter of choice rather than a matter of obligation. Thus, in adopting this masquerade, the woman wants to signal that she is not coerced, that she is freely acting. Such a masquerade rejects and disavows the castrating figures of the lesbian and feminist with whom young women might otherwise be linked. At the same time, it shores up hegemonic masculinity "by endorsing this public femininity which appears to undermine, or at least unsettle the new power accruing to women on the basis of their economic capacity" (McRobbie 2007, p. 725).

TERRY EAGLETON

Terry Eagleton was a student of Raymond Williams at Cambridge. Although viewed primarily as a literary theorist, like Williams, Eagleton's work traverses boundaries. Like many cultural theorists, Eagleton uses a Marxist perspective in his work in keeping with the tradition of Walter Benjamin, Theodor Adorno, and, of course, his teacher Raymond Williams. For Eagleton, literary criticism is the means through which he deeply dissects the political, historical, and social elements running through western contemporary society. He has been highly critical of cultural studies as a field.

Much of Eagleton's earliest work focused on the use of Marxist analysis of important texts of literary icons such as Shakespeare and the Brontë sisters. He suggested new ways of looking at these writers in the context of the period in which they wrote. Eagleton often pulled from their work seemingly insignificant characters and events to magnify their meaning by analyzing their importance to the stories. This he often referred to as "reading against the grain" (Wroe 2002). Much of this work was in keeping with Raymond Williams's understanding of the individual's life in the context of the society in which he or she lived. Some of his earlier work drew heavily upon structuralists such as Althusser.

Like Williams, Eagleton aims to connect cultural and political discourse. To do so, he uses theory. Eagleton is not so much a fount of new theory as he is a chronicler and employer of new theory. Like Hall, he uses theory effectively in his work to examine the harsh realities of capitalism. And he is reflexive in doing so, also examining the viability of theory itself. He is ambivalent about deconstruction and other poststructural forms. He derides Derrida as a genius who had attempted to bring down not only bourgeois capitalism but every form of meaning. Eagleton proposes that such a position serves the interest of the dominant class (Eagleton 1981).

Much of Eagleton's concern focuses on ideology. He takes issue with the Marxist notion that ideology is always associated with the dominant power in society and how that power is used to control others. He does not simply see it associated with capitalism. Also, he has problems with the Althusserian use of the term ideology as a type of false consciousness or indoctrination. He points to radical groups such as Suffragettes and the Diggers and asks if they were not guided by ideologies of feminism and socialism. Can we call their value premises and utopian visions ideological? Are they nonideological when they challenge authority, but ideological when they come into power? Eagleton still believes that ideology can be associated with the oppressed as well as the oppressor. But it always appears to be defined by an intersection between values and power. And it is the values that most occupies his thinking as a humanist socialist. He refuses to accept the end of oppositional politics based on the belief that there are no longer binaries. What he takes exception to is the notion of many postmodern thinkers, such as Baudrillard, that ideology is an empty and meaningless signifier. His move to defend ideology as a powerful construct is to see its meaning evolve in history and politics.

Eagleton views the end-of-ideology as a reactionary intellectual ploy to deny the meaning and vitality of resistance and opposition. As a Marxist, he is critical of left-wing intellectuals relinquishing their values to the most conservative elements in society, including religious fundamentalist and right-wing politicians. He would like to see ideology reclaimed by the left as a tool of class struggle. For Eagleton, ideology is that which holds societies together and provides ways of understanding. It operates both at the macro and micro level. It is a form of social practice. It needs to be studied and used, not abandoned. Instead of seeing ideology as a meaningless signifier, he would like to see it applied as a tool of political, cultural, and social analysis. Thus, he calls for an understanding of ideology that helps to illuminate the processes of liberation.

Eagleton (2003) has trumpeted the end of theory—at least important theory. He views much of cultural theory to be far too apolitical and trivial and incapable of bringing about any form of constructive change, which according to him should be its purpose.

FREDRIC JAMESON

One of the most celebrated literary theorists in the United States is Frederic Jameson. Like other renowned literary critics who have crossed over into cultural theory, Jameson's intellectual roots are in Marxism. He sees Marxism as a way of understanding history and culture. Unlike Williams or Eagleton, however, he is more comfortable in making use of ideas borrowed from poststructuralism and postmodernism, though he is certainly ambivalent about these paradigms.

Born in Ohio and schooled at Yale, he seems an unlikely radical Marxist. However, he was deeply influenced by Sartre's work and that of other existentialists. Like Hall and Eagleton, he was very much inspired by the New Left and the cultural revolutions of the 1960s. Much of his early research focused on the Frankfurt school, particularly the works of Theodor Adorno and Walter Benjamin. But he was profoundly affected by the writings of Marxist-Hegelian Georg Lukács (1968), particularly the latter's critical assessment of capitalism and consciousness.

In one of his most important books, *The Political Unconscious* (1981), Jameson grapples with the Althusserian notion of ideology and the Freudian concept of the unconscious. As a literary critic, he believes that he needs to attempt to develop alternate ways of understanding texts. They appear to have within them fragments of history. He views psychoanalytic criticism as a dead end. It is too individualistically focused and cannot take a position outside bourgeois ideology. He believes the goal of criticism is to step outside the totalizing influence of capitalistic culture, or perhaps develop a Marxist hermeneutic. As a Marxist, he believes it is difficult to rescue one's political understanding of the world from the false consciousness imposed by the bourgeoisie. All conscious as well as unconscious understanding of the world is ideological. This holds true from the vaguest of thoughts to the dimmest of desires, from philosophical systems to social and political institutions. It is impossible for any individual working alone to transcend such ideological system ushered in by capitalism. As Marx suggested, false consciousness imposes a way of looking at the world that runs counter to the way the world actually exists for the working class. It's not just ingrained in the culture; it is the culture. It is in each of us. Lukács develops this idea much further in *History and Class Consciousness* (1971).

Again, the real challenge in overcoming false consciousness is its totalizing influence. One cannot easily step outside and critique it because it constitutes the individual's conscious mind as well as that person's unconscious. It is written in all history. It is ideological and conveys all meaning. It can be challenged only by a dialectical reversal, or by somehow getting outside this imposed consciousness. Because texts come to us as already read and interpreted, one must sift through the sediment to find their real historic significance. This requires unearthing history, ever mindful of bourgeois class interest. As Marx said, all history is the story of class struggle, which is why Jameson searches here for a new radical criticism based on new historical interpretations. For Jameson, a true Marxist analysis will reveal the structural limitations of other methods of interpretation.

Jameson is highly critical of structuralism as a way of reading texts, and he is highly critical of Saussure. He stresses that works of art ought not be enshrined and isolated from their own history, which structuralism, similar to formalism as a mode of critique, appears to do. On the other hand, he seems considerably more sympathetic to poststructuralism, particularly some of the elements of Lacan. He especially makes use of Lacan's three orders—the Imaginary, the Symbolic, and the Real, which he believes speaks to his own concerns about the limits of languages. And he has integrated much of Lacan into his work. However, he is ambivalent toward postmodern theory.

Jameson is true to his Marxian critique describing postmodernism as a new way of life (as well as a new aesthetic) associated with the latest stage of capitalism—*late capitalism*. He accepts many descriptions of postmodernity as a type of historic periodization. He wants to distinguish between what is valuable in the postmodern theory and what is not. While he sees value in the postmodern portrayal of a radical break from modernism, which characterizes contemporary culture, he also sees the postmodern critique as inferior to Marxist cultural analysis.

Jameson gives his readers a Marxist reading of that break between modernity and postmodernity—between the modernist aesthetic and the postmodern one. He fully understands that a close reading of postmodernism will reveal little that was not present in modernism, if only in traces. Yet he believes it is this newest stage of capitalism that has brought about an observable rupture between these two periods. Given this observable rupture, he describes what he sees as the essential characteristics of this new aesthetic form.

First, and most visible, is its depthlessness which emphasizes form over substance. Here, simulacrum is seen as a dominant form eclipsing any modernist sense of authenticity. Second, that which was once subversive in the arts becomes domesticated. What were considered radical new forms by artists like Picasso and Joyce became classical forms. Third, culture itself becomes completely commodified and increasingly fragmented. Fourth, there is little distinction here between high and low culture. Jameson sees the fifth feature in terms of a new ahistoricism, or what he refers to as a consequent weakening of historicity. Temporal distinctions fade. Sixth, the significance of space fades as new technologies that are in line with the new order of transnational capital destroy the old meaning of space. Finally, utopianism and moralisms associated with the modernist form give way to *dystopianism* and cynicism. Future visions are now dark and bleak, and nothing is to be taken seriously.

Jameson is merely describing what he views as characteristics of postmodernity; he is not advocating this or embracing it as a way of life. However, he views many of these descriptions as quite accurate and an outcome of the logic of late capitalism.

BLACK CULTURAL STUDIES: PAUL GILROY

Born to Guyanese parents in East End London, Paul Gilroy completed his doctorate at Birmingham University. He is currently a professor of sociology at Goldsmith College at the University of London. His work has focused on issues of the African diaspora, black identity, and black culture.

Gilroy contends that British and American cultural studies have frequently ignored issues of ethnocentrism, racism and nationalism in their work. He observes that few have examined the roles played by that slavery and race in the development of western cultures (Gilroy, p. 5). And fewer have explored the impact diasporas have had on black cultures in the West.

Gilroy points to the transatlantic slave trade as essential to the European and American project of modernity. For him, slaves moving from Africa to the Atlantic, particularly the Americas, the Caribbean, and Western Europe, not only defined the black experience but also underscored the brutality of western modernity. Gilroy asserts that slavery helped give rise to western hegemony. However, it also laid the foundation for the *transnational character* for black artists and intellectuals. This character is one that shares no firm allegiance to country but is free floating and quintessentially transnational. Gilroy sees the experience of black peoples as a transnational experience. There is little commonality that slaves shared, aside from their history of terror. It was neither blackness nor the national culture into which they were originally enslaved that profoundly shaped black identity.

W. E. B. DuBois' understanding of Hegel's master/slave dialectic gives Gilroy an important insight into black transnational identity. The experience of the slave, not the master's position, enabled a true consciousness. The master's consciousness was contained, or repressed in itself. The master could only understand from his position relative to the slave. He knew what he knew through his slaves and those around him only. But the slave's consciousness transcended the position of slavery. The slave's transcendental position, this escape from slavery into freedom, has now become manifest in the black aesthetic. It is an aesthetic not wedded to one's cultural or national view. For Gilroy, such double consciousness is at the core of a socially motivated literary tradition. The black artist frequently challenges the Enlightenment's focus on reason. The Euro-American attempt to pit western civilization against the unreasonable "bestial" slave is a case in point. It is predicated on a racist ideology that is part of the project of a brutalizing western modernity. Gilroy takes exception to black feminist writer Patricia Hill Collins's Afrocentrism and views it as racial essentialism (see Chapter 6). He argues against the notion of a pure culture, a position that stands out in most of his work. He sees modern identity as a messy affair, characterized by multiplicity. He stands solidly against essentialism of any sort. He is interested in the fluidity of cultural meanings.

In his book, *Against Race* (2000), Gilroy asserts that the concept of race is a tainted construct emerging from slavery and the ideology of racism that supported it. He views it as a tool of subordination and oppression. He strongly critiques the embrace of racial identities by diasporic black communities to gain some sense of pride in a culture that is not their own. Race is a tool of oppression as well as a myth, and any embrace of it is to take on the consciousness of the oppressor. He dismisses hyphenation, such as African-American, as misguided and self-defeating. He rejects the notion of racial superiority espoused by white racists and by black leaders such as Marcus Garvey, who admired Hitler for his open racial politics. He also condemns all forms of black nationalism. But he is particularly perturbed by the embrace of public multiculturalism by the black middle class. He fears that such an embrace condemns poor black people to lives of misery and relegates many to poor schools, impoverished neighborhoods, and unemployment. As a cultural theorist, Gilroy is concerned that the culture industry has co-opted many young black artists into a conformist racialism under the guise of a benign but commercial multiculturalism. He sees this as propping up race as a justified division and as endangering the inherent fluidity that has been characteristic of transnational black aesthetics.

It is not cultural diversity itself that Gilroy finds disquieting. He is not interested in the development of a homogeneous world. He sees a multiculturalism that respects historically produced differences as a healthy thing. What he has little tolerance for is racial identity embedded in multiculturalism. He calls for an end to politics of cultural identity and a greater dedication to "rootless cosmopolitanism" and "planetary humanism." He embraces cultural hybridity and welcomes a new cosmopolitan *diasporic culture*.

IEN ANG AND THE GLOBALIZATION OF POPULAR CULTURE

Ien Ang is a professor of cultural studies and director of the Center for Cultural Research at the University of Western Sidney in Australia. She was born in Indonesia and educated in the Netherlands. Broadly speaking, her work has focused on culture in the globalized world, with a particular emphasis on identity, media, nationalism, and migration.

Unlike members of the British and American cultural studies communities, Ang is an outsider. She wants to look at culture from a global vantage point rather than an Anglo American one. Thus, she has written about the movement of large nation-states from culturally homogeneous and politically sovereign territories to places of global flows. By this, she means an interconnected world wherein cultures and peoples intermingle, and the confluence of cultural diversity has become routine (Ang 2001, p. 5).

In Ang's first book, *Watching Dallas: Soap Operas and Melodramatic Imagination* (1989), she proposes that there are definite elements of television programs, particularly soaps that have universal appeal. The television show, *Dallas*, was equally popular abroad in the 1980s as it was in the United States. In fact, the show was followed avidly by millions of viewers in over ninety countries, from Turkey to the Netherlands, where over half of the television sets in the latter country would be tuned into the program at almost any one broadcast. She finds a problem with the contention that a show like this is but one more example of cultural imperialism. While she understands the concerns of some cultures that shows like this are imposed upon them, Ang observes through her own survey research that most people watched *Dallas* because it gave them pleasure—an element most overlooked by cultural researchers. The mass culture industry is not imposing ideology or aesthetic values, but rather allowing people to enjoy cultural experiences with little accounting for taste. Western media knows how to give people what they want without making them feel culturally inferior. They do not create homogeneity as much as they cater to heterogeneity. The same could be said about *Sex and the City*, a show produced years later, or *Desperate Housewives*, which premiered in 2004. For Ang, the audiences of the mass culture industry are not undifferentiated. But the need for pleasure seems to cross cultural borders. She cites David Held's observation that over 2 billion people from around the world watched each episode of *Baywatch* and millions around the world continue to watch it in reruns.

Ang also takes issue with a number of feminist writers who view such television programming as stereotyping women and at the same time demeaning of them. Here she sees something much different. For Ang the very basis of such viewing was fantasy and pleasure, something many women felt they needed. While Ang views herself as a feminist, she is mindful that there can never be one feminism that explains the predicament and needs of all women. She understands that women around the world have different needs and different priorities.

Ang has observed that audiences are likewise heterogeneous. Audiences, which include audiences of women, do not sit by passively and allow media to dictate what they take from watching television, nor what message is being conveyed. She believes that audience members must choose from a variety of media directed toward them. The audience members then actively co-construct the programming by infusing it with their own meaning. She proposes that meaning is constructed by three elements: audience, text, and context. This poststructural spin gives much more power to the audience than previously considered.

Unlike many poststructuralists, Ang does not dismiss the need for radical politics. While audiences help create what they see, this does not translate into political power, which is essential for women and others around the globe who are disenfranchised. Ang insists that culture is often created from below. It is not always constructed from the top down.

Much of Ang's more recent work has focused on issues of identity. She has problems with the cultural studies focus on diaspora, and she sees as inherent in some of this discussion a vulgar tribalism and an us versus them mentality, a false binary. As a world immigrant (she is an individual of Chinese descent who was born in Indonesia and educated in Europe, and who pursued her professional career in Australia), she is more like Paul Gilroy in that she prefers to speak of hybridity. She sees **hybridity** as an "unsettled" identity, or "inbetweenness." She discusses the problems of fixed and essential identities in the modern world. She challenges authenticity in contemporary ethnicity. In some sense, she views all identity is fractured and multiple. Thus, ethnicity is also made less significant by elements of class, gender, and sexuality.

Ang's world future is not only *multicultural* but also transcultural. She sees the world heading for a time where particularist identities all give way to hybridity. This is not assimilation but rather a world of greater diversity.

CULTURAL STUDIES AND SOCIAL THEORY

Exactly where cultural studies finds its place among disciplines in the academy today is quite contentious. For an overwhelming majority, it still is viewed as a branch of literary studies and it frequently draws on and helps to construct literary theory. But sociologists, anthropologists, political scientists, and media analysts claim at least a piece of cultural studies as their own; so do academics engaged in women's studies, gender studies, art history, queer studies, consumer studies, American studies, and postcolonial studies. It is nearly impossible to separate cultural studies from the rest, and any thorough examination of culture requires crossing disciplinary lines. Those who teach and write about culture are in various fields, and not merely in a field called cultural studies. It should be noted that cultural studies, if it can be called a discipline, draws on various theoretical perspectives as well as various methodologies. It is actually a form of hybridity.

The intellectual and theoretical roots of cultural studies is Marxist and neo-Marxian analysis. This was certainly obvious in the works of its British founders. Much of it has been an extension and refinement of critical theory, which came out of the Frankfurt school of Adorno, Horkheimer, Marcuse, Fromm, and Benjamin. This theory drew on the work not only of Marx but also of Hegel, Nietzsche, Freud, and Max Weber. Early British cultural theory had strong sociological and political overtones. Like the Frankfurt school theory, it viewed structural oppression as a central cause of concern. But cultural studies has rejected the notion of authenticity and what they frequently see as the elitist take on culture evident in some Frankfurt school works.

The current trend in cultural studies is the poststructural view that culture is not imposed from above but rather is something people participate in creating. Some of it uses Althusser's structuralism and some uses Lacan's psychoanalytic paradigm. It is much more cozy with postmodern thought than with sociology. It often seems at best antagonistic toward the social sciences, and sociology in particular, in this regard. It rejects macro-order paradigms and expresses a strong interest in human interaction and theories of social construction. It is highly critical of positivism and empiricism.

American cultural theory has eschewed the neo-Marxian orientation of its British counterpart. It tends to be somewhat more scattered and focuses more on agency than on structure. To some extent, it overly romanticizes the power of the individual in the construction of contemporary culture.

On the whole, cultural studies comes out of a political period of challenging boundaries. Its hybridity reflects diasporic inflow from a variety of disciplines that have touched on the very same issues at which it aims. It draws from the theories of various scholars who are often self-exiled from their original areas of study and live outside disciplinary boundaries. It is a reflection of the fragmentation that has been sweeping the academy for decades.

KEY TERMS

carnivalesque A term used by Bakhtin to identify celebrations to mock or attack the established culture.

Center for Contemporary Cultural Studies (CCCS) Founded at the University of Birmingham in 1964 by Richard Hoggart, a professor of literature there, its objective was to establish a new field of study focusing on popular culture.

culturalism The notion that individuals are determined by their culture.

cultural materialism A term devised by Raymond Williams to describe the production of a politicized form of culture.

culture industry A term developed by Frankfurt school theorists Adorno and Horkheimer to refer to the mass production of the products of society by the forces of capitalism to spur on a consumer economy and promote contentment and passivity.

dialectical materialism A Marxist theory that posits that everything is material and all change in the world throughout history is the product of conflict arising from internal contradictions.

diasporic culture Culture maintained in a host territory or nation by people who left or were forced to leave their native lands.

dystopianism The opposite of utopian: the dystopian society is characterized by darkness and an array of severe human problems that have no solution.

Frankfurt school A group of Marxist intellectuals who were part of the Frankfurt Institute for Social Research, which was founded in 1922. Members of this group were sociologists and philosophers who constructed critical theory that synthesized the work of Marx, Freud, Nietzsche, Weber, and others.

hegemonic culture The culture of the ruling class that is imposed on the subjugated group or accepted by them as generalized common sense. Taken from a theory developed by the Italian Marxist, Antonio Gramsci.

heteroglossia A term used by Bakhtin to mean all cultural products contain opposing ideas and voices.

hybridity The creation of new transcultural forms out of a mixture of cultures.

interpellation Althusser's notion of putting someone into a subjective position by an authority "calling out" to him or her and having that person respond accordingly as a subject.

late capitalism The modern phase of capitalism first identified by the Frankfurt school now generally thought to be typical of industrial nations from the 1950s onward.

Marxian humanism The writing and ideas of Marx primarily contained in his earlier work, such as the *Economic and Philosophic Manuscripts of 1844*, that focus more on the individual issues such as alienation as opposed to his later examination of social structures.

multicultural Acknowledging and promoting of cultural pluralism to protect various cultures comprising a society.

New Left A social movement of activists and intellectuals in the 1960s working to bring about radical social and economic changes throughout the world, including an end to racism, colonialism, and various forms of political oppression.

postfeminism A term sometimes suggesting that women have made plenty of progress because of feminism, and that feminism is now irrelevant and even undesirable. But as it relates to radical gender theory, it is often used to focus on a time when there are no longer male/female binaries.

postfeminist masquerade A concept developed by Angela McRobbie to describe how many modern women must act as though they have gained their liberation and social equality with men in order not to be seen as a threat.

retraditionalizing feminism The action of women returning to more traditional female stereotypes in a playful manner, suggesting that the work of feminism is done or passé.

transnational character A heightened interconnectivity of people and the loosening of the boundaries between nations.

SOURCES

Althusser, Louis. 1965. *For Marx*. London: Penguin Press.

Ang, Ien. 1990. "Culture and Communication: Towards an Ethnographic Critique of Media Consumption in the Transnational Media System," *European Journal of Communication*, Vol. 5, pp. 239–260.

Ang, Ien. 2001. *On Not Speaking Chinese: Living Between Asia and the West*. London: Routledge.

Bakhtin, Mikhail. 1941. *Rabelais and His World*. Bloomington, IN: Indiana University Press.

Barker, Chris. 2003. *Cultural Studies: Theories and Practice*. London: Sage.

Eagleton, Terry. 1981. "Marxism and Deconstruction," *Contemporary Literature*, Vol. 2, No. 4, pp. 477–488.

Eagleton, Terry. 2003. *After Theory*. New York: Basic Books.

Gilroy, Paul. 1993. *The Black Atlantic: Modernity and Double Consciousness*. Cambridge, MA: Harvard University Press.

Gilroy, Paul. 2000. *Against Race*. Cambridge, MA: Harvard University Press.

Hall, Stuart, and Paddy Whannel. 1964. *The Popular Arts*. London: Hutchinson Educational.

Hall, Stuart. 1992. "Cultural Studies and Its Theoretical Legacies," in L. Grossberg, C. Nelson, and P. Trichler, eds., *Cultural Studies*. New York: Routledge.

Hall, Stuart. 1996. "On Postmodernism and Articulation: An Interview with Stuart Hall," in D. Morley and K. Chen, eds., *Stuart Hall: Critical Dialogues in Cultural Studies*, London: Routledge.

Held, David .2002. "Cosmopolitanism and Globalization," *Logos*, Vol. 1, No. 3, pp. 1–17.

Jameson, Frederick. 1981. *The Political Unconscious: Narrative as a Socially Symbolic Act*. Ithaca, NY: Cornell University Press.

Jameson, Frederick. 1991. *Postmodernism, or, The Cultural Logic of Late Capitalism*. Durham, NC: Duke University Press.

Lukács, Georg. 1971. *History and Class Consciousness*. London: The Merlin Press.

McRobbie, Angela. 1994. *Postmodernism and Popular Culture*. London: Routledge.

McRobbie. Angela. 2007. "Top Girls: Young Women and Post-Feminist Sexual Contact," *Cultural Studies*, Vol. 21, No. 4, pp. 718–737.

McRobbie, Angela. 2009. *The Aftermath of Feminism*. London: Sage.

Procter, James. 2004. *Stuart Hall*. New York: Routledge Critical Thinkers.

Rojek, Chris. 2003. *Stuart Hall*. Cambridge: Polity Press.

Smith, James. 2008. *Terry Eagleton*. Cambridge: Polity Press.

Thompson, Edward 1978. *The Poverty of Theory and Other Essays*. London: Merlin Press.

Turner, Graeme.1990. *British Cultural Studies: An Introduction*. Boston: Unwin Hyman.

Williams, Raymond. 1963. *Culture and Society*. Originally published in 1958. New York: Columbia University Press.

Williams, Raymond. 1981. *The Sociology of Culture*. New York: Schoken.

Wroe, Nicholas. 2002. "High Priest of Lit Crit," *The Guardian*. February 2.

CHAPTER 8

Postcolonial Theory and Globalization

Postcolonial theory is considered a branch of postcolonial studies, which emerged in the 1980s as a result of the so-called *cultural turn*. It primarily deals with the impact and aftermath of European colonialism on subjugated peoples. Like cultural studies and feminist theory, postcolonial studies draw from a wide range of theoretical perspectives but has a strong affinity to post-structuralism. While it primarily analyzes literature, it is often grounded in the humanities, the arts, and the social sciences. The term *postcolonial* frequently gives rise to the notion that colonialism has collapsed and what is now required is an intellectual assessment of what destruction it left behind. However, some scholars take exception to the term *postcolonialism*, contending that it is prematurely celebratory, and that it acknowledges a commitment to linear time and the notion of "development" (Gandhi 1998, p. 174; McClintock 1992, p. 2). Edward Said (1994) suggests that colonialism is not a moment in history but a continuing discourse between Empire and the people it dominates.

While the spiritual inspiration for much of postcolonial study comes from the writings of Frantz Fanon, particularly his important book *The Wretched of the Earth*, which was published in 1961, more contemporary figures who have been seen as instrumental in the development of this field of study have included Edward Said, Gayatri Spivak, and Homi Bhabha. Fanon's work was instrumental, however, in bringing a modern intellectual rigor to the study of colonialization and its aftermath.

Fanon (1925–1961) himself was born in the French Caribbean colony of Martinique, where he studied with Aimé Césaire, an internationally renowned poet and leftist intellectual. Césaire's critique of the racism inherent in European colonialism, *Discours sur le colonialisme* (published in French in 1950), had a major impact on Fanon's worldview.

Fanon went on to study medicine in France, specialized in psychiatry, and was appointed as chief-of-service of a French colonial psychiatric hospital in

Algeria. During the Algerian War of Liberation, he worked to supply Algerian rebels with medical assistance. At his hospital, he aided the National Liberation Front by training Algerian nurses and treating victims of French torture at the hospital. From this point forward he dedicated his life to the Algerian cause and fighting colonialism around the world (Salerno 2004, p. 155).

The Wretched of the Earth (1961) deals with Fanon's insights into the workings of colonialism and the emergence of *decolonization* and postcolonialism. He viewed colonialism as working to destroy native cultures both physically and psychologically through the categorical use of race and class. For Fanon, colonialism not only physically disarms the colonized but also robs them of their cultural identity. He asserted that only through bloody revolution and not accepting "rights" bestowed by colonial powers, was the only true path to decolonization.

Fanon's work draws heavily on Marx and uses his ideas to assess the conditions confronted by colonized peoples in their struggles for liberation. His work also borrows from philosophy, particularly existentialism, and makes extensive use of psychoanalytic theory. In fact, his friend and fellow psychoanalyst Jean-Paul Sartre wrote the introduction to *The Wretched of the Earth*.

IMPORTANCE OF EDWARD SAID'S *ORIENTALISM*

It was perhaps Edward Said (1935–2003) and his book *Orientalism*, published in 1978, that broke ground for more contemporary postcolonial analysis and study. Born in British occupied Palestine in 1935, Said grew up in Egypt and later the United States. Like Fanon, he came from a relatively privileged family background. He received his master's degree and Ph.D. from Princeton University in the field of literature and taught at Columbia University during most of his adult life.

With the publication of *Orientalism*, he became a leading critic of western depictions of the peoples and cultures of Asia, but particularly the Middle East in the 1980s. His central thesis in this book is that European writers, journalists, and scholars created the "Orient" in line with colonialist and racist ideologies; they portrayed the "Orient" in extremely negative and stereotypical ways. Eastern cultures, particularly those of the Middle East, were portrayed as violent, backward, and irrational. He asserted that these depictions were promoted in part to establish a picture of the "West" as civilized, cultured, and reasonable. On the other hand, the "Orient" allowed the "Occident" to create this imagery—to name them. Said attacked those colonized elites who not only allowed this creation but also internalized it. Such a depiction of the East and the Middle East was instrumental to the process of its colonialization.

Central to Said's own work is the rejection of any binary distinctions between the colonizer and the colonized, the West and the East. Such western fictions are rooted in the drive to make people into the "other" and into objects. At the same time he rejects the ideology of difference and the need for metanarratives promoted by the classical West. Said's work was influenced by Foucault in this regard and by the belief that there is an essential relationship between knowledge and power and that all knowledge is produced in situations of unequal relations to power.

Said agrees with Foucault's contention that no text can be understood apart from its political and social circumstances. Furthermore, writing itself is viewed as a systematic conversion of the power relationships between the controller and the controlled into written words. However, he is at odds with Foucault's insistance that oppressive power originates from below and is not determined through hegemonic rule. Foucault gives him nothing that he can use to assess the domination of one state by another, which Said sees as the basis of colonialism. Said instead turns to Antonio Gramsci because Gramsci expresses in his work the importance of political and cultural hegemony. *Orientalism* offers an example of how **cultural hegemony** works to reinforce the ruling ideology not through domination but rather through consent. And unlike Foucault, Gramsci holds out the possibility of revolutionary dissent and social change (Kennedy 2000, p. 32). Said endorses this position.

But for Said, the concept of Orientalism is discourse; it is not fact. It is inherently ideological, and it is an ideology that not merely controls those disempowered but is incorporated into their very being. The creation of Orientalism is an expression of the "will to power" over those so labeled. Said frequently uses a poststructural approach in his analysis. Where Foucault helps him to better understand power embedded in the text, Derrida assists him in deconstructing colonialism itself (Saksena 2005). Still Said is reluctant to subscribe uncritically to any systematic model for understanding texts. He often appears to promote humanism and many of the foundational tenets of the European Enlightenment, which puts him at odds with most poststructuralists (Siddiqui 2007, p. 69).

As a work of literary criticism and as poststructural analysis, *Orientalism* shows how powerful discourse helped shape colonialism. Through his analyses of various western literary texts, Said lays the groundwork for connecting postcolonial studies to contemporary theoretical analysis, particularly poststructuralism. Like other cultural theorists, he connects literary criticism to sociological analysis. But beyond this, *Orientalism* helps establish a research agenda for the field of postcolonial studies.

Much of Said's other work, but most notably *Culture and Imperialism* (1994), was a continuation of *Orientalism* in that it also used literature to examine the portrayal of nonwestern peoples. Not only does Said testify to the power of the exploited being seized in this way by a cultural elite, he also views this power as being used as a weapon against the oppressed. Said never assumes to speak for those who are or were oppressed by colonialism, yet he recognizes how Orientalists (scholars who study the East) have done this without hesitation.

Said identifies four typical elements of Orientalist discourse. These comprise the use of (1) generalizations; (2) confrontation, often through the use of binary oppositions such as "theirs" and "ours"; (3) sympathy; and (4) classification through "synchronic essentialism" wherein derogatory categories such as "Orientals" are developed and used as a means of control (1978, pp. 227–240). He also sees scholars of the East as complicit in western imperialism. Said's project was to show how such elements in literature helped to construct the reality of colonialism, or at least the perception of that reality. In his work he identifies the intellectual forces in culture that promoted brutality directed against native peoples. Through literary criticism he is able to reconstruct a history that promoted Empire and exploitation. Said draws from Dante, Shakespeare, Byron, Conrad, and others to make such points. He shows simultaneously how colonialism itself helped to fortify racism and articulate the "superiority" of the West. Said is adept at using his vast knowledge of western literature to recapture real political events.

The attacks on Said's work came from all sides of the cultural and political spectrum but particularly from Orientalists such as Bernard Lewis (1982) who used such words as *outrageous, absurd,* and *reckless* to describe Said's conclusions in *Orientalism.* Said was chastised for being hyperbolic by portraying nearly all western scholars, artists, and writers who wrote descriptions of the East as racist and supportive of the program of imperialism. He was berated for bad writing and poor scholarship. And he was criticized by those on the left for being reluctant to own the Marxian analysis that seemed to underlie much of his thinking or, worse, failing to recognize it. Still his work was groundbreaking and opened up dialogue on the Middle East in particular.

Much of Said's later life was taken up by his public political advocacy for the establishment of an independent Palestine and the rights of the Palestinian people. He became a public intellectual making television appearances and giving radio interviews. And all the while his work became essential to the burgeoning field of postcolonial studies.

GAYATRI CHAKRAVORTY SPIVAK: TALKING SUBALTERNS

Said insisted that he did not speak for those who were marginalized and exploited. To do so would be to occupy the same position of the Orientalists, whom he denounced. A question he posed was: Aside from resistance, can the colonized speak for themselves? Given the colonialists' destruction of their cultures and the Orientalists' distortions, he believed that this would certainly be problematic if not impossible.

Gayatri Chakravorty Spivak, a colleague of Said's at Columbia University and known for her translation of Derrida's *Of Grammatology* into English, also emerged as a powerful critic of colonialism and its methods. In her paper, which has become a canonical text of postcolonial theory, Spivak (1988) asks: "Can the Subaltern Speak?" *The **subaltern** is a term borrowed from the Italian activist and theorist Antonio Gramsci, who used it to describe the disempowered.

Like Said, Spivak believes that researchers on postcolonialism who speak for those who have been oppressed are active participants in the imperialism they say they deplore. Spivak takes aim at what has been called the Subaltern Studies group led by Ranajit Guha, an Indian-born scholar whose work focuses on South

Asia. Guha (1988, p. 35) and other scholars associated with his collective want to conduct systematic studies of the colonized, or subalterns, "to rectify the elitist bias characteristic of much research and academic work in this particular area." They want to give voice to the voiceless. Spivak was at one time part of this group.

In her paper, which has now become foundational to postcolonial studies, Spivak draws on poststructuralism and Marxian analysis to identify what she sees in this attempt of any elite group of intellectuals to give voice to the marginalized. She challenges this whole notion of the faceless marginalized "subject" and the ability of the privileged to have them speak with one voice. Translating the experience of a subaltern group into the discourse of another more powerful culture and using findings as sociological evidence are dangerous ventures. One's interrogation of a "subject" often changes that subject. One's creation of a research archive often invents truth. Like Said, Spivak sees such attempts as the violent imposition of another form of imperialism.

At the same time Spivak recognizes that no act of dissent or resistance on the part of the subaltern occurs separately from the dominant discourse. This discourse usually provides the linguistic framework and the conceptual categories with which the subaltern speaks. While she does not minimize the ability of the subaltern, she attacks what she views as the uncritical deployment of essentialism that characterizes much research on the oppressed. For Spivak, the creation of colonial history is a form of *epistemic violence* a form of palimpsest, or a document written over an original in which the original is erased but traces still show through. This form of violence quiets the subaltern.

The real need of any scholar wanting to better understand the postcolonial subaltern is to recognize culture as deeply embedded in deeply flawed history that has been written over innumerable times along with a multiplicity of trajectories, or fragmentation of subaltern groups. One needs to avoid the western liberal bias of attempting to translate one's findings into an easily comprehensive narrative. Even in a specific culture, there is not one subaltern, but many. Such fragmentation is not limited to class alone but also includes factors such as gender. While Spivak believes it is crucial to attempt to discover the traces of how oppression came to be, she contends that an examination of the lives of subaltern women can never be accurately exhumed using the language and tools of the logocentric elite. She recognizes the importance of the fragmentation of identities brought about through modern capitalism; however, she still believes in the possibility of a collective consciousness among various subaltern groups. She sees the need for what she calls *strategic essentialism*, which is temporary solidarity for the purpose of social action. This is not to say that all groups have common needs, but rather each subaltern group can defer specific goals (related to race, gender, etc.) in the short term for broader collective ones. At the same time, Spivak does not dismiss academic engagement with the colonized but sees the value of scholars as making space for the voices of the oppressed to be heard.

Throughout her work, Spivak weaves some significant interpretations of Marx, Foucault, and Derrida related to their understanding of the subaltern, or their attempts to do so. Poststructuralism allows her to challenge basic foundational elements of western imperialism. She uses Derrida to deconstruct Marxian analysis of imperialism and to find political value in it. She uses Marx to assess how subjects are created through capitalistic power in general and how this relates to subaltern labor in particular. She recognizes Marx's continued importance in assessing contemporary forms of imperialism and exploitation.

Unlike Derrida, Spivak confronts political issues, particularly the legacy of colonialism, straight on. She champions the voices of those most marginalized in the world. For her, the effects of colonialism did not simply vanish after the imperial powers relinquished political control. Important residues of social, economic, educational, and political structures were left behind. These structures have a tremendous impact on the lives of once colonized people everywhere.

HOMI BHABHA AND MARGINALIZED IDENTITY

Another important figure in the launching of contemporary postcolonial studies is Homi Bhabha, who was born in Bombay (Mumbai, India); was educated at Oxford; and is currently a professor of English and literature at Harvard. Bhabha's work involves issues of identity, agency, and national affiliation. Much more a poststructuralist than either Said or Spivak, his central project is to analyze what he refers to as postcolonial discourse. His work entails an examination of how colonized people have resisted the power of the colonizer. And it is one of his central theses that such power isn't as secure as it might appear from the outside, thus granting space for the colonized to resist. At these moments of resistance, western anxieties grow. He illustrates this through his use of literary and cultural analysis (Huddart 2006).

Another reason for such anxiety for the colonizer has been the seemingly heterogeneous nature of the world—its vast and frightening differences and the constant changes in its composition. For Bhabha, the colonizer's power rests in part on a type of fixity, a form of stereotyping, in terms of his construction of otherness. All distinguishable differences flow from such fixity constructed in the western text. But the world does not remain fixed. The colonized assumes an obligation to mirror back the colonizer's reflection. But the colonized does this in an exaggerated way. It is not respectful imitation. Bhabha believes that the colonizer looks at the colonized and perceives consciously or unconsciously a reflection of himself. But at the same time it is not himself. This mimicry of the colonizer by the colonized threatens his belief in his own superiority and invincibility. It is mockery and as such is often a destabilizing force. The observer also realizes that he has become the observed. Such a reflection is disquieting. This is a similar argument to that of Fanon in his first book, *Black Faces, White Masks* (1952). The mimicry is a mask hiding something quite sinister—the true nature of the colonized as an object of oppression and exploitation. Such a hiding is in essence a *veiled threat*. This reflection is what Bhabha refers to as doubling. This doubling is often present in colonial literature.

Bhabha makes the point that the colonial text is often transformed by the colonized simply in its reading. The colonizer cannot maintain control over the meaning of the text, and like any other narrative understanding, it assumes a negotiated meaning. In this sense he develops a linguistic model of resistance and agency. The colonial text contains the colonized voice. It is the subaltern speaking.

In Bhabha's poststructural approach, the colonial text does not say what it initially appears to say or what it might have intended to say. It occupies a position of hybridity. In this position is a disquieting recognition of the influence, if not the power, of the "Other". Likewise, hybridity subverts the purity and power of the colonial empire (Bhabha 1994, p. 88). In essence it is the antidote to the fixed properties of essentialism. It provides what Bhabha refers to as a *third space* that enables more than one position to emerge. This is the space of new forms of cultural meaning, or hybrid identities.

Bhabha rejects essentialistic identity politics because it is not sustainable in the changing world. Identity is never stable; it is always in flux. He sees the world and all societies comprised of networks of meaningful yet often complex interactions. Out of these interactions come these *hybrid identities* such as those found within the third space. These hybrid identities are transcultural and encoded with counterhegemonic agency. Hybrids have an ability to traverse two or more cultures and to mediate between them. He sees hybridity as the remedy for the hegemonic practice of the colonizer.

Bhabha sees postcolonialism and postmodernity as inextricably connected. Postcolonalism generally and hybridity in particular have transformed our understanding of what it means to be modern. For Bhabha (1994) it is nationhood and its ambivalence that signifies modernity. Space and colonialism are its trademarks. But postmodernity or, to use his term in discussing the colonized, *countermodernity*, stands in opposition to the notion of the modern nation and its imagined identity. Otherness becomes central to this new modernistic motif. The hybrid is no longer marginal but rather central.

For borrowing extensively from Lacan, Foucault, and Derrida, Bhabha has been criticized for his own Eurocentrism as well as for strident elitism. Still Bhabha's work is radical and creative. He has developed a perspective that allows the scholar to better understand the phenomena of postcolonialism and its postmodern significance.

THEORIES OF GLOBALIZATION

Where postcolonial theories often focus on issues of identity, cultural borders, diaspora, and transnationalism, they venture only modestly into the study of the material processes behind globalization and modernization. While many literary theorists assume a neo-Marxian position related to the effects of global capitalism, their work is often bound up in a poststructural review of text rather than social, political, and economic processes that such texts reflect. Theories of globalization as a sociopolitical process emerge primarily from the social sciences. Similar to cultural studies and postcolonial studies, global studies also has emerged as an academic field. But it is more embedded in the traditional social sciences and leans toward grand, developmental narratives.

The term *globalization* has many competing definitions in the academic community, but the word is often been used to describe a worldwide integration of economics, politics, and culture through a process of enhanced communication mechanisms and technological advances in production, media, and transportation services. This seemingly benign integration has been the source of a host of critical theoretical interpretations of the economic, political, and cultural outcomes it produces. Theories of globalization take many forms, but one can see some similar themes taken up in postcolonial theory. In fact there is relative affinity between these theoretical approaches.

For some, *globalization* has become a code word for new corporate imperialism—the exploitation and piracy of resources (natural and labor) in lesser developed nations by those corporate entities with considerable wealth and military power under their direct influence (Petras and Veltmeyer 2001). While neoliberal economists tend to place a positive spin on globalization as a rejection of tribalism and a welcoming of science and progressive secularism for the masses, and where they envision (with the help of free and open markets) improvements in health, education, hygiene, and the overall economic well-being of all world citizens, the vast majority of social theorists who write about globalization are not so optimistic. To a large extent, they share the more pessimistic sentiments of postcolonial scholars but do not usually share their methodologies. One primary reason for this is that globalization lends itself to vigorous social science research. And much of public policy is likely to be guided by such formula. Social scientists do not see what they do as liberating truth from text; rather, they seek "objective" factual information to discover trends and "laws." Structural Marxists and scholars, such as Immanuel Wallerstein, focus their work on world patterns and shifts, including social and economic projections. Many such theorists begin with Marx and his insights into capitalist imperialism and the abuses of colonial empires.

WORLD-SYSTEMS THEORY

Karl Marx was the first to refer to the global nature of capitalism characterized by rampant economic exploitation and colonialism. Capitalism did not end at a nation's borders. It was transnational. These ideas influenced a whole generation of twentieth-century scholars.

While the work of Immanuel Wallerstein is discussed in Chapter 2 as an example of structural analysis, it is important that we revisit the meaning of his work as it now relates to globalization. Wallerstein has been studying world geopolitical and economic processes since the early 1970s. He started his academic career at Columbia University as a specialist in African affairs and his theoretical perspective took shape during the political and cultural turmoil of the late 1960s. His most important work, *The Modern World-System*, was published in three volumes, the first in 1974, followed by volumes two and three in 1980 and 1989. This work was significantly influenced by Marx's writings on the international character of capitalism and by the writings of the French historian Fernand Braudel. Braudel (1902–1985) had written extensively on the nature of economic exchanges in European society between 1400 and 1800. Braudel contended that key nation-states worked to protect the interests of monopoly capitalists at the expense of everyone else, particularly those who were most marginalized.

Wallerstein's work is an attempt to explain important processes of modernization and globalization that began taking shape after the decline of European feudalism. To do so, he develops the concept of a world-system—a broad economic entity that has its own division of labor and is not constrained by political boundaries. This is a large unit of analysis that is in essence a self-contained social system with its own unique life span.

Wallerstein sees the world-system as having originated around 1500 A.D. with the collapse of European feudalism, new advances in technology, and the dynamic opening up of world markets. It is comprised of an international division of labor that has linked world regions and functions within this world capitalistic order. Wallerstein refers to three areas in this order: core, periphery, and semiperiphery. The core areas gain the most from this system and tend to dominate it. In the sixteenth century, Europeans established a division of labor in which industrial or capital-intensive production was a function of core countries, while peripheral areas provided low-skill labor and raw materials. Core areas have strong central governments, large armies, and extensive bureaucracies, which allow the local bourgeoisie to have control over the system. These core areas exploit the rest of the system. The periphery areas are most exploited. They tend to have weak central governments, are often controlled by powers outside their borders, and have weak laws related to labor protections. They are often rich in natural resources that are primarily exported to the core areas. The semiperiphery areas exist between these two extremes of exploiter and exploited. Frequently, these areas were once periphery and were mostly exploited. Their economies are weaker than those in the core areas but stronger than those in the periphery.

For Wallerstein, this is a very dynamic system that changes over time. Thus, he ventures into an historical analysis of the various stages and world events that account for its history of development, which we will not cover in this book. However, it is clear that Wallerstein sees this system of modern capitalism as predicated on exploitation wherein a very small group of people become rich at the expense of the many. Much of his model is based on what was called *dependency theory*, which advanced the notion that there were core states that exploited peripheral ones. But Wallerstein saw this much more as a dynamic process, as a function of a system or integrated network of global, transnational, capitalist institutions.

Wallerstein and other world-systems theorists migrated to the State University of New York at Binghamton and established the Fernand Braudel Center for the Study of Economies, Historical Systems, and Civilizations in 1976. This is a center for world-systems study. Joining them there in the late 1970s was an Italian scholar and political activist, Giovanni Arrighi. Like Wallerstein, Arrighi's earlier work had focused on economic development in Africa.

Arrighi (1994) begins his world-systems work by looking at what he sees as cycles of capital flows and accumulation and their geographic meaning over time. Like Wallerstein, his work is based in the groundbreaking work by Fernand Braudel. Arrighi's research into capital accumulation leads him to conclude that, while capitalism has a long history in the West, it was constituted by diffused activities until the rise of city-states in Italy and later the nation-states in Europe. And it is only then, with the advent of colonialist expansion and other policies of exploitation and accumulation, that capitalism took on its modern characteristics. In his theory the wealthiest states compete with one another for the world's resources—redistributing wealth from the poorest to the richest nations as it goes along. Unlike those who see the state taking a secondary position to unbridled capitalism, Arrighi, as did Braudel, sees capitalism merely as a function of the state. This is not market capitalism, but regulated and unregulated state-sponsored monopoly capitalism. These global flows of capital as well as its accumulation are determined by state and transnational policies, with the most powerful states representing the interests of their wealthiest classes, including the business class. This is the heart of the world-system, the system of the present time.

Arrighi sees redistribution outcomes as determined by state military power and coercive state influence over markets. Such power not only consists of protectionist methods related to trade and investments but is also aimed at blocking the influence of foreign culture. After years of successive cycles of capital accumulation came the rapid expansion of the capitalist world-system. But when such material expansion reached its limits, which it did around the 1970s, capital moved to the realm of high finance. Here there was room for greater expansion: financial expansion and credit expansion. Nation-states secured for their most powerful clients the most expansive opportunities. But this expansion also had limits and basically came to an end with the last great fiscal crisis. This is the current crisis of global capital.

Arrighi sees financial expansion as the last gasp of state capitalism. Financial expansion is merely a temporary fix, one that will result in hegemonic catastrophe because its unregulated expansion rests increasingly on precarious and shaky grounds. With the dismantling of Bretton Woods (the world economic agreements established by the Allied nations in 1944) and fixed exchange rates, the world becomes unstable. Capital is no longer fixed to real assets, which produces enormous risks and speculation.

Arrighi asserts that East Asia is certain to replace the West's hegemonic dominance. As it produces and gains access to capital, it embarks upon its own program of expansionism. But the old guard does not want to vacate its position of dominance and disparately attempts to hold on through all means necessary.

DAVID HARVEY AND THE SPATIAL FIX

David Harvey (discussed in Chapter 5) has been central to modern discussions of globalization. Like Arrighi, Harvey views globalization as a fix—as in a drug addict getting a fix, or to a problem being fixed in order to return it to a previous state of order, to be fixed in place so it is not out of control. In other words, a fix is not a solution but a stopgap measure. For Harvey, globalization is a fix used to resolve capitalism's inner crisis tendencies through geographical expansion. He views capitalism as addicted to geographical expansion in order to forestall its inevitable collapse. Just as it needs technological fixes to allow for expansion, it also needs space. In this sense, says Harvey, globalization, or the spatial fix, has been going on at least as far back as 1492.

Harvey cites Marx's fundamental law of capitalist development, which is "the annihilation of space through time." For Marx as well as for Harvey, capitalism needs to be fixed in space, whether it be in factories, roads, houses, water, transport, communications media, and the like. Only by fixing can the crisis be overcome. In the process, it must eventually destroy its old space to create new space. Harvey proposes that capitalism cannot survive without being geographically expansionary and that technological innovations in transportation and communication are necessary for such expansion to take place. He also contends that the modes of geographic expansion depend on its particular needs: fresh labor, new markets, raw materials, and/or new methods of production.

Marx and Harvey note that *overaccumulation* of capital, wherein there are surpluses of labor and/or capital, can have disastrous consequences such as the devaluation of both, and the elimination of potential profit. But to stave off this outcome, strategies need to be developed. One such strategy is to seek out a spatial fix, which can include opening new markets for the surplus by exporting work or capital to a new territory to start up new production. Thus, if the surplus is predicated on lack of local demand for commodities, demand needs to be found elsewhere. Where there is a surplus of capital and a shortage of labor (that can drive up costs), capital can be moved to places of labor surpluses. The effect of these strategies, however, is to replicate these built-in contradictions in capitalism and to impose them over an ever-expanding geographical range. Thus, in actuality, the fix is temporary.

But there is another aspect to the concept of fix that Harvey believes also compounds this crisis of capital. When capital itself is fixed or stays put, it tends to lose value over time. What he is referring to here is capital that is embedded in machinery, land, or other fixed assets that deteriorate over time and/or become obsolete. Also, capital can be locked up or committed to something (a project, let us say) from which it cannot be detached. These and other such fixes are responsible for much of what we call globalization.

Harvey makes the point that once space is saturated with capital, new space is required for capital to expand. He has spent much of his own work attempting to understand the creation of cities as centers of capital accumulation. New York, particularly Manhattan, and its expensive real estate values is a reflection of this. However, once capital is accumulated and fixed in a handful of urban centers, new spaces must be created for investment. Capital must always be on the move or it festers and disappears. He points to the early 1970s and the accumulation crisis that facilitated a more accelerated movement of capital, fixed and unfixed, across the globe. And often fixed investments carry with them high risk. Often they are highly speculative.

But capital investments produce uneven geographical development. This is primarily true because neoliberal economic policies mistakenly assume an equality over space and time due to self-regulating markets. This also leads to the inevitability of monopoly capitalism taking shape. In actuality, with the more dramatic flows of capital that go unregulated, the world has witnessed a greater gap between rich and poor and a greater concentration of capital in fewer hands. This is the process Harvey outlines as globalization.

Beyond this Harvey sees accumulation of capital and its expansion as being replaced by brute financial power as fictitious capital, speculation, and even fraud drive the competitive process. All of this results in what he refers to as accumulation by dispossession.

GIDDENS' THEORY OF GLOBALIZATION

While Anthony Giddens' work on modernity has been discussed in Chapter 5, his theory of globalization is taken up here. It is important note that Giddens approaches globalization as an aspect of modernization. For Giddens (1990, p. 64), globalization is a type of *stretching process* through which regions become networked across the earth's surface. This is the result of innovations in technology, which enhance both the speed of communication and the rapid spread of information around the globe. These improvements act to "collapse" the time-space continuum, so that time is no longer a function of place. What happens in one part of the world is often immediately felt in another part.

Giddens's notion of a time-space distanciation is a central component of both his theories of modernization and globalization. (1991, p. 21). Whereas in tradition-based societies, time and space had been inseparable, globalization has undermined this connection. Traditional life was much more insulated, with time being oriented toward particular cultural needs and more connected to nature. Much of the world was not based on the mechanical clock that measured hours and minutes. With the advent of modernization global there was a rapid spread of this type of abstract time across the earth that led to greater, more efficient, coordination of human activities. Inherit in this globalizing process is what Giddens calls "an emptying of time." In modern society, time is frequently associated with money, an even greater abstraction. Likewise, place loses its traditional significance as space replaces and commodifies place. Thus space is also emptied of its traditional significance. In many ways, Giddens' theory is an extension of Max Weber's notion of *disenchantment* brought about through increased secularization and market capitalism.

Giddens views the process of globalization as a natural consequence of modernity (in fact, it is the global spread of modernity), which will lead not only to the reconstruction of the modern nation-state but also to significant changes in economy and culture worldwide. He views the world capitalist economy, the nation-state system, world military order, and the international division of labor as four dimensions of globalization. These elements don't merely define global-ization but can also determine its strength and velocity as a development. All of these elements are interrelated. For instance, the world capitalist economy, which is to a large extent constituted by transnational corporate enterprises whose resources far exceed those of most nation-states, have headquarters based in par-ticular nation-states. But beyond this they are given vast leverage to make deci-sions affecting the very futures of those nation-states and others. However, notes Giddens, they cannot rival nation-states in two respects. The first is that of ter-ritoriality and the second is the direct control over the means of violence. To be safeguarded by the state, transnational corporations must act as its agents in some respects and recognize its sovereignty. Thus, the nation-state is the second dimen-sion of globalization. As such it establishes borders or boundaries and claims sov-ereignty within those boundaries. The state is the primary actor. The position and influence of the nation-state is not dependent on its wealth per capita, but on its military strength. The world military order, the third dimension, defends national sovereignty. Finally, Giddens turns to the international division of labor, which he sees as globalization's fourth dimension. Here he sees at work specializations that are globally distributed. Since World War II there has been a growing interdepen-dence of such specializations for research, finance, marketing, and production. This establishes, in a Durkheimian sense, an organically organized and cohesive globalism complete with its own culture.

This conflation of modernity and globalization is something other theorists find too Eurocentric in its orientation (Woodiwiss, 1996). Unlike Wallerstein or the postcolonial theorists, Giddens sees globalization as a potentially reward-ing process. He does not equate it with imperialism. But neither does he deny the unevenness and ecological problems associated with it. It has very different effects on different societies in the world. He sees the unemployment in the West due to outsourcing of jobs as a temporary matter. Such outsourcing will bring down prices and help consumers. He denies that corporations *control* this system. According to Giddens, much of globalization emerges from below. As evidence, he points to the work of nongovernmental organizations (NGOs). He embraces the neoliberal optimism of writers such as Thomas Friedman. He associates glo-balization with the birth of a new kind of individualism. In his book, *Runaway World* (2000), Giddens contended that globalization is a dialectical process that will pit fundamentalism against cosmopolitan tolerance. It is responsible for bringing down the Soviet Union and South African apartheid. He sees families around the world being democratized because of it, and women having their rights recog-nized. And while he does not dismiss problems associated with it, such as global warming and fundamentalist terrorism, he asserts that such risks provide the big-gest challenge to the changing world. Living with risk is critical to progress. There is no turning back. For Giddens, it is old-fashioned democratization that will be the tool to bring the runaway world under control.

THEORIZING EMPIRE: HARDT AND NEGRI

Where Wallerstein speaks of world-systems, Michael Hardt and Antonio Negri speak of Empire. The term *Empire* is frequently found in postcolonial theory, but here it means something else. Hardt, an American literary theorist from Duke University, and Negri, an Italian communist, accused terrorist, and political sociologist who has spent years in prison for his politics, combined forces to create a theory of a global system that aims to replace the core/periphery binary proposed by Wallerstein. Instead, Empire is a ***biopolitical machine***, a defused network of global power with identifiable but unruly flows of people, information, and resources. *Biopolitics* is a term they borrow from Foucault, but for them it means a governance that is all pervasive. Empire is a decentered and deterritorializing apparatus of rule that progressively incorporates the entire global realm within its open, "expanding frontiers" (Hardt and Negri 2000, p. xii). Hardt and Negri draw on the models and imagery put forth by Deleuze and Guattari. They speak of the "ubiquity" of power, and "flows" of energy. This is not traditional Marxist analysis but something else. Their analysis of globalization has been referred to as a vision of a postmodernized global economy (Munck, 2001). Empire comes to take the place of the nation-state. It has broken down boundaries and borders. It is not a consequence of the collapse of capitalism but is a result of massive heroic struggles that helped put an end to colonialism. And while capitalism might appear to be impervious to challenge, it is everywhere vulnerable to rebellion.

Hardt and Negri do not see this new system as a form of imperialism. No nation-state, no corporation, can act as a launching pad for an imperialist program today. They see these accusations of imperialism as nostalgic notions, ways of attempting to hold on to modernist thinking comprised of binaries such as good and evil. They take postcolonial theory to task for failing to see this new paradigm of Empire emerge. They view postcolonial theorists as content to critique a system that has failed to be effective a long time ago (Hardt and Negri 2000, p. 138). In fact, Hardt and Negri are critical of the antiglobalization movement, which they believe fails to come to terms with the fact that thinking locally, seeing oneself as an outsider, can never halt abuses in this global system. The left fails to recognize that the local is not outside the global, but rather constitutes a significant part of it—the most significant part. The globalizing process produces what is called the local, but it is a fiction. Empire is a non-place where boundaries are fictitious and flows of power transcend space. Any small-scale action will never be able to resist these power flows because Empire operates at all levels. It not only manages territory and populations, but also creates the very world it occupies. Any resistance must recognize itself as part of this Empire, which is not a bad thing. It must be global because it is. Just like Deleuze and Guattari, however, Hardt and Negri see revolutionary desire flowing through small groups that are capable of producing massive collective action. Insurgent energy is everywhere. Change is constant. They are extremely optimistic about a positive outcome.

In one sense Empire is the final stage of capitalism—its last gasp, so to speak. Hardt and Negri see it as a creatively destructive force. "[It] constructs its own relationship of power based on exploitation that is in many respects more brutal than those it destroyed" (2000, p. 43). All of humanity is, to some extent, absorbed or subordinated to networks of capitalist exploitation. Because of such brutality, Empire offers an enormous revolutionary potential. Hardt and Negri speak of a "multitude" that will move over and under the global landscape like "uncontainable rhizomes" (2000, p. 397). The rhizome metaphor is one they borrow from Deleuze and Guattari. The multitude is force of liberation and innovation, but does not include labor, as Marx and Engels imagined in the *Communist Manifesto*. Actually, the multitude is more abstract. Hardt and Negri use this term *multitude* to describe "productive, creative subjectivities of globalization" (2000, p. 60). For them, the multitude is the answer to Empire. It offers the possibility of democracy on a global scale.

ALEX CALLINICOS: GLOBAL IMPERIALISM

A radical social theorist, Alex Callinicos is a professor of politics at King's College in London. A self-professed Trotskyist, he has been highly critical of Anthony Giddens' position on globalization. He also takes exception to postcolonial theory and views it as some transmuted form of postmodernism. Callinicos' theory of imperialism embraces a Marxian view of globalization.

Callinicos' theory of imperialism is similar in many respects to that of Harvey's. Like Harvey (1989), Callinicos sees imperialism as constituted by two interconnected forms of capitalist competition: economic and geopolitical. Here Callinicos (2002) refers to investment competition, or "economic competition between capitals" and competition between states. These types of competition were historically separate and often opposed to one another; their total integration is the basis for the new imperialism. Today, geopolitical competition requires economic resources that can be generated only within the framework of capitalist investment. Thus, Callinicos views capitalism as the primary form of modern imperialism. The strength of such a construction of imperialism, as opposed to the more classical forms or the Third World-systems approach, is that it is open to assuming various configurations over time and space, and it integrates the geopolitical and economic strategies and therefore is nonreductionist. Finally, it underscores the importance of understanding competition.

Like others who take a similar view, Callinicos' position is predicated on several factors: (1) global capitalism is still responding to the economic crisis from overaccumulation in the 1970s; (2) this crisis in advanced capitalism comes from divisions among world trading centers in Western Europe, North America, and East Asia; and (3) despite the vast power of the United States compared to the others, significant conflicts of interests constantly give rise to geopolitical struggles. However, the United States remains the most important political and military power in the world. It maintains this position by flexing its military muscle in the Middle East and elsewhere. Its state power and influence are enormous.

Callinicos (2009) sees the United States as having constructed transnational and geopolitical space after World War II that helped to unify the capitalist world under its own influence. Capital and commodities flowed within this space with growing freedom. Rivalries lost the likelihood of becoming military conflicts as they had under the classical imperialist form. Callinicos borrows from economist Robert Rowthorne's notion of U.S. super-imperialism to describe the power the United States exerts over other capitalist states that puts them in the position of having little control over their own economic policies, especially those in conflict with American interests. The European Union was a response to U.S. super-imperialism; it was one point of resistance. Still the United States acts as the organizer of world capitalism to preserve its unity in the face of socialism, while it promotes a distinctly American brand of capitalism. The International Monetary Fund (IMF) and World Bank have become enforcers of the Washington consensus, giving the United States power to restructure lesser developed countries' economies to fall in line with the U.S. imperialist order. At the same time, the United States works diligently through its multinational corporations and military to control most of the world's natural resources.

Callinicos (2002, p. 260) takes exception to Hardt's and Negri's notion that a new form of imperialism, namely, Empire, describes the current condition. This contention concludes that neither the United States, nor any other state, is hegemonic in terms of imposing a world order. But Callinicos maintains that an Empire has not materialized and that imperialism, in its hegemonic form, remains a major force in controlling the world's resources.

DAVID HELD AND DEMOCRATIC GLOBALIZATION

David Held is a renowned social and political theorist. Educated in Britain, France, and the United States, he currently teaches at the London School of Economics. For Held, globalization is a deeply divisive process because it benefits some, hurts others, and often goes unrecognized by most people in the world; it is far from uniform global development (Held 1998, p. 11). He sees globalization as characterized not only by the stretching process outlined by Giddens but also by the development of new interregional and intercontinental arrangements of economic and social activities, along with increases in social interaction between states and societies.

For Held, globalization has ushered in greater democracy around the world, which has displaced autocratic regimes in a rapid order of succession since the mid-1970s. As evidence, he cites events such as the fall of the Berlin Wall and the release of Nelson Mandela from a South African prison. At the same time, democracy is challenged by financial power that has escaped national jurisdiction and control. He sees the sovereignty of nation-states being compromised, if not challenged, by increasing networks of interconnection overlapping jurisdictions, which is characteristic of this process. Held examines ways to increase democratic control in the face of rapid globalization. For him, the nation-state alone cannot provide democratic guarantees. He posits that democracy within some nations is inadequate; what is needed is democracy among all nations.

In the past few decades, the world has seen the rise of what Held refers to as a new *cosmopolitan elite*. This group is at home in the global arena and has more than adequate access to the institutions and organizations that constitute this new global order. It is distinctly different from the world's more marginalized groups in terms of its influence and ability to transform their own economic, political, and social circumstances by exerting control over and through these emerging networks and nodes of power. This hierarchy of access is the unevenness of which Giddens speaks. Held sees this unevenness as being associated with key factors in the globalization process: international trade, financial flows, decisions of multinational corporations, environmental conditions, and the proliferation of new organizations that manage transnational activities. These factors transform the nature and prospect of democratic political community.

Held promotes the need for what he calls *cosmopolitan democracy*, which entails the creation of democratic mechanisms that hold transnational institutions accountable. They do not replace nation-states but exist alongside them and can override state authority in spheres of transnational significance. Such institutions would have the authority to initiate projects that have regional or global implications, including pollution control, resource use and depletion, and regulation of trade and finance. Under this system, stakeholders would have input into important decision making.

Cosmopolitan democracy promotes what Held calls multiple citizenships, meaning that citizenship cannot end at a nation's borders. People need to recognize themselves not merely as citizens of their local communities but also as stakeholders in the wider regions in which they live. According to Held (1993, p. 40), constituencies need to be defined not simply according to a nation's borders but also according to issues in which they share a common interest—issues that cut across borders. While local nationalist cultures are certain to remain important in terms of personal identity, the rapid growth of transnational communications and flows of people, resources, and information challenge the strength of this identity.

Held sees the rise of a more heterogeneous global culture that confronts the rigid notion of national culture predicated upon geographic boundaries and space. He refers to this as cosmopolitan culture. Cultural products that circulate in the global economy change the traditional notion of national cultures; however, he refutes the assertion that this is a form of American imperialism. Nations that want to block the import of culture and cultural values from afar have difficulty doing so, given the information technology that is becoming more and more widely accessible. While Held views NGOs such as Green Peace and Amnesty International as having considerable impact, by and large he views the new global culture as being promoted and distributed through capitalist, corporate interests. He and other globalists predict a significant fracture in local nationalist cultures and the absorption of external interests and values. As the world shrinks, this becomes more and more inevitable.

Held suggests that individuals have increasingly complex loyalties and multilayered identities corresponding to the globalization of economic interests.

He links cultural changes back to global democratization—the liberalization of nation-states and the growth of human rights on an international scale.

UNBUNDLING TERRITORY: SASKIA SASSEN

Like David Held, Saskia Sassen looks to the emergence of new democratic institutions to confront the challenges of global change. A Dutch sociologist born in The Hague, Sassen is noted for her analysis of globalization and studies of international human migration. She has done considerable work on the relationship between space and power and has written extensively on the global city.

For Sassen (1998), globalization is seen as the unraveling of traditional concepts of territory associated with the nation-state. She views global cities, those most essential nodes in the international arena, as becoming transnational entities, and she sees key cities in the world as becoming denationalized. Sassen contends that globalization generally can be characterized as denationalizing and redrawing boundaries. Nationalism rested on imperial geographies, but with the advent of denationalization, which began toward the end of the twentieth century, intercapitalist rivalries came to be addressed in the economic rather than in the military domain.

Political nationalism may still prevail rhetorically and make these deep structural transformations illegible. But it needs to be distinguished from structural tendencies that make international competition today function primarily as a mechanism for denationalizing capital, while in the earlier phases it functioned as a logic for strengthening national capital and developing political nationalism (Sassen 2006, p. 140).

Like many global theorists, Sassen traces the origins of these new processes from the establishment of the Bretton Woods agreements in 1944 to a shift away from these policies in the 1970s. The Bretton Woods agreements opened the door to greater forms of denationalization. But she views the real tipping point that was most responsible for the global age as having come in the 1980s, which brought about major organizational and structural realignments within the states, between the states, and within the private realm.

More recent cross-border economic processes—flows of capital, labor, goods, raw materials, and travelers—have challenged the old notion of territoriality. The interstate system has been the dominant organizational form for the past century, but the advent of privatization, deregulation, and the opening up of sovereign states to foreign investment brought about the change. This change has rescaled territories. Global cities and regions (what Sassen refers to as subnational entities) come to play significant roles and often link national economies with global circuits.

Sassen describes such cities, and the strategic geographies that connect them as well as frequently bypass nation-states, as ***global domains*** connected by ***transboundary networks***. Living in these spaces offers the individual an ability to transcend state affiliation. She sees such places as "enabling" (Sassen 2004), out of which emerges a type of cross-border politics centered in localities yet connected digitally. These digital connections form the basis for the development of important new political institutions that can represent the underrepresented and challenge state power.

MANUEL CASTELLS' THE NET AND THE SELF

Manuel Castells is a sociologist and social theorist who teaches at the University of California at Berkeley. He has done extensive research in network theory, some of which was noted in Chapter 3 in this text. He uses the network paradigm to define the global trend toward a new form of capitalism, which he views as more flexible than older capitalist forms and yet more hardened in its goals. Still this new form of capitalism is being challenged around the world by social movements comprised of activists who seek to control and define their own lives and are actively working to protect the environment from assault and abuse. Castells' theory of globalization bears some resemblance to the concept of globalization advanced by Anthony Giddens.

According to Castells, since the 1990s the entire planet has become organized around networks of computers. These networks are at the core of information and communications systems and are at the heart of this new mode of finance capitalism. Governments, banks, human resources, universities, armies, media, industries, and the Internet are integrated in a massive technological web. Understanding technology is vital to comprehending how this system works. While technology is not a panacea for developing nations, it is essential for economic and social development. It provides the basis for globalization, which Castells views as primarily an economic process.

Castells (1999, p. 4) notes: "A global economy is an economy whose core activities work as a unit in real time on a planetary scale. Thus capital markets are interconnected worldwide, so that savings and investment in all countries, even if most of them are not globally invested, depend for their performance on the evolution and behaviour of global financial markets". Thus, Castells does not view globalization as encompassing the entire planet. In fact, most people are excluded from this technological system. The network includes only those things and people of value to its functioning. The extraneous—those who are incapable of contributing to its goals—remain outside.

Castells' primary assertion is that this system of networked connections, which is emerging as the dominant power in peoples' lives and has absorbed nation-states themselves, challenges the goals and values of liberal democracy. This system has become alienated from both the people who are outside it and the many who work within it. He views societies as being organized around a tension, if not an opposition, between what he calls the Net and the Self. The Net represents this system of networked organizations, a system that is replacing vertically integrated hierarchies as the dominant form of social organization. He frequently refers to this as a *space of flows*. The self represents the practices through which people attempt to reaffirm identity in an environment of constant change.

Space of flows is characterized by what Castells calls timeless time and place-less place. *Timeless time* occurs when the network is out of alignment in terms of its sequential ordering of activities, or the typical way in which the system operates. The space of flows is constantly disturbing the rational order of sequential events, thus dissolving time. Also, space of flows dissolves geographical distance, similar to Gidden's and Harvey's notions of the collapsing of time and space.

It will not be possible to detail Castells' decades of research and complex theoretical work on this process in this textbook, but it should be noted that Castells has produced three volumes detailing how this new information phase of capitalism works. The specifics of his theory are detailed in his trilogy, which he has titled, *The Information Age*. The first volume of Castells' trilogy, *The Rise of the Networked Society* (1996), focuses primarily on changing patterns of technology, production, consumption, and labor practices that come together to produce a new global network. This work is built on the theoretical foundations laid by Karl Marx and Max Weber. Here Castells promotes the value of empirical social science in his research by providing data to support his theoretical assertions. His second volume, *The Power of Identity* (1997), is dedicated to understanding the development of identity in the modern age of the Internet. He specifically looks at various types of social movements and identities that have emerged within this new system. He specifies three types: *legitimizing identity*, introduced by dominant institutions to exercise control over actors; *resistance identity*, formed by actors both neglected and oppressed through the system's logic of domination; and *project identity*, developed by those who aim at transforming society and who are primarily *not* excluded from the system. His third and final volume, *The End of the Millennium* (1998), is an attempt to integrate the work in his first two volumes by relating it to the events that transpired at the close of the twentieth century.

There has been considerable praise for this major contribution of Castells toward explicating the workings of the information society. The scope and breadth of his project has not really been matched. However, new social theory has become centered on culture and has raised significant challenges to the value of networking logic and structuralist thought. Castells' work comes at a time when theory is moving away from this sort of grand theoretical construction. While many see value in elements of his theory, as a whole, it is seen as overly weighty and remains outside much contemporary theoretical discourse.

ROLAND ROBERTSON AND WORLD CULTURAL THEORY

Considerably different from most of the theories of globalization offered in this text is the work proposed by Roland Robertson. Robertson is a lecturer in sociology at the University of Aberdeen in Scotland. Unlike the Marxist and neoliberal theorists who advance a materialist notion of globalization, Robertson (1992) assumes a more phenomenological approach. That is, he defines globalization not only as a "compression" of the world, but also as an "intensification of a consciousness of the world as a whole" (1992, p. 8). For Robertson, this involves the crystallization of four main components of the "global-human circumstance": societies (or nation-states), the system of societies, individuals (selves), and humankind. The crystallization takes the form of processes for, respectively, societalization, internationalization, individuation, and generalization of consciousness about humankind (Robertson 1992, p. 27).

Each unit in the emerging world order takes shape relative to the others that surround it. Thus, nations states are required to accept universal standards derived from common conceptions. As globalization does not create a common culture wherein all hold the same beliefs and values, actors perform on a global stage and compare themselves to other actors. Different groups interpret global values and standards differently. The outcome is both harmony and a incongruity.

Robertson recognizes that globalization as a process is nothing new and has little or nothing to do with modernization or, for that matter, imperialism. He presents his own view of the important stages of its development. In what has been called his minimal phase model, he identifies five distinct stages or phases of globalization. The first is what he refers to as the germinal phase, which lasted between the early fifteenth and the late eighteenth century. This was characterized not only by the development of strong national communities that displaced a transnational system, but also by the beginning of modern science, including modern geography. The second phase, or the incipient phase, extended from the mid-eighteenth century into the late 1870s. The emphasis was on the unitary state, formalized international relations, and citizenship. Agencies arose to deal with international issues, and there was a debate on the issue of nationalism versus internationalism. Phase three, the take-off phase, lasted between 1870 to 1925, and was characterized by the development of strong national identity and an emphasis on international coordination, with the establishment of mechanisms such as the international dateline, time zones, and the widespread adoption of the Gregorian calendar with seven-day weeks. Robertson asserts that a single international society emerged that has had a strong Eurocentric imprint. At the same time, strong emphasis is placed on competition between nations. The struggle for hegemony is what he identifies as the next phase, phase four. This lasted from the mid-1920s into the late 1960s and was distinguished by disputes and wars with conflicting conceptions of the world future. There was a greater crystallization of the Third World as a cold war raged between the Soviet Union and the West, and the United Nations became a central international forum. The final phase, phase five, he identified was called the uncertainty phase, which lasted from the late 1960s into the 1990s and perhaps beyond. With the collapse of the Soviet Union there is now only the capitalist model for the future that links the globe. The development of transportation and communication technologies accelerates and helps increase a global consciousness. It is this global consciousness, or *globality*, that intrigues him. This is the foundation for global culture.

Robertson cannot easily accept the notion that the economy is central to globalization. It is his contention that it is an important factor, but only one. He rejects the world-systems theorists as limiting themselves to issues of exploitation and dependency. Still, he does not deny the reality of any of this, only the importance it has been given in defining globalization. He views the globalized world as integrated but not harmonious. He advances his own theory of world culture. For Robertson, globalization as a process both connects and stimulates an awareness of this connection. Accordingly, the autonomy of individual actors is limited because they are required to develop an identity relative to the emerging global whole (Robertson 1992, p. 29).

Robertson turns to what he sees as the rapid expansion not only of globalizing tendencies but the simultaneous acceleration of local ones. He uses the term *glocalization* to describe this process (a term he derives from the Japanese *dochakuka*). "*Glocalization* is the interdependent interpenetration of the universalization of particularization, and the particularization of *universalism*" (Robertson 1992, p. 100). Robertson sees glocalization as a type of internalized globalization. It is how world events and globalizing processes play themselves out locally. It takes into consideration globalization's impact on unique localities—on their economies, politics, cultures, and human relations. It recognizes that the processes of globalization are experienced differently depending on where one lives. At the same time it traces the impact of local occurrences on the global arena. Such a way of thinking has opened up new avenues of research and new ways of reestablishing the locality as central to this process.

GEORGE RITZER AND MCDONALDIZATION

An important social theorist and author of numerous texts on social theory, George Ritzer has looked at significant structural and cultural dimensions of globalization. One of his central contributions in this regard has been his theory of McDonaldization (Ritzer 2008). This theory of global structural change posits that societies around the world are gradually taking on the characteristics of an American fast-food restaurant chain. Ritzer's thesis is primarily an extension of Max Weber's classical theory of modernization, which was developed at the beginning of the twentieth century.

For Weber, societies were moving from traditional societal forms to more rationalistic bureaucratic ones characterized by impersonality, a heightened division of labor, a proliferation of rules and regulations, efficiency, and a hierarchy of control. He observed an unprecedented degree of superficiality as traditional values began to take second place to performance and calculated outcomes. For Weber, decisions in modern life appeared to be based on instrumental reasoning in terms of an end-means schema. Ritzer refines Weber's hypothesis and updates it. He suggests that the form of the fast-food restaurant has come to epitomize what Weber was talking about. McDonaldization is a growing phenomenon affecting not only U.S. society but also global society as McDonald franchises are exported around the world.

What Ritzer means by McDonaldization is that key characteristics associated with businesses such as McDonald's restaurants become transplanted throughout societies. These characteristics include increased calculability, predictability, and the substitution of labor power with technology. Above all, it means standardization and the efficiency associated with it. Such measures signal the success not merely of fast-food businesses but also of things like education, media, and criminal justice. McDonald's has come to represent the power of U.S. capital to impose its values and culture on the rest of the world. But the power of McDonald's as a representative of the United States to inflict this type of standardization on other nations is often met with great resistance (Turner 2010). Still its successes outweigh its losses.

An interaction between economics and culture is central to Ritzer's notion of McDonaldization. While his theory emphasizes the cultural, he acknowledges that economics, particularly profitability, is the engine behind its global spread. In a sense, this theory seems to support Robertson's notion of glocalization. As McDonald's and its techniques might very well be the influence to launch the development of similar, yet indigenous chains, around the globe.

Ritzer believes that McDonaldization influences not only the development of culture in the United States but also its development around the world because its techniques are exported and applied accordingly. This certainly is the case related to fast-food meals and eating fast-food in general. Not only a new way of eating, but also a type of eating that could undermine family and communal traditions is introduced. In fact, such establishments might very well displace more local ones. As these efficient and hyperrational techniques are applied to other cultural institutions such as education and health care, its influence might be felt powerfully as modes of exchange that were once very personal are depersonalized and, as Weber implied, dehumanized.

McDonaldization offers a new means of consumption. In fact, it is having an impact on how people around the world consume. But again, such models must take into consideration local culture or they are frequently bound to fail. Still Ritzer sees McDonaldization as a form of U.S. cultural imperialism. McDonald's and other similar franchises have expanded enormously in the last decade around the globe. Although individual franchises might adapt to the national menu and style of service, the operating procedures remain the same everywhere. Finally, it appears that while the number of American food franchises around the world is proliferating, more a sign of "invasion" is the vast number of McDonald-like clones springing up around the world. "The emergence of local variations on American consumption mechanisms reflects an underlying change—the McDonaldization of those societies" (Ritzer and Malone 2001, p. 108).

POSTMODERN GLOBALIZATION

The attempts to discern what constitutes globalization are too numerous to review here. Elements of globalization discussed earlier in this chapter give some sense of what it is. People have approached it from a variety of perspectives. Still, the word *globalization* is used to signify what appear to be significant changes that have

Spivak, Gayatri Chakravorty. 1988. "Can the Subaltern Speak?" in Cary Nelson and L. Grossberg, eds., *Marxism and the Interpretation of Culture*. Urbana, IL: University of Illinois Press.

Turner, Byran. 2010. "McDonaldization: The Major Criticisms," in Greorge Ritzer, ed., *The McDonaldization Reader*, 3rd edn. Thousand Oaks, CA: Pine Forge Press.

Wallerstein, Immanuel. 1974. *The Modern World-System, vol. I: Capitalist Agriculture and the Origins of the European World-Economy in the Sixteenth Century*. New York/London: Academic Press.

Wallerstein, Immanuel. 1980. *The Modern World-System, vol. II: Mercantilism and the Consolidation of the European World-Economy, 1600–1750*. New York: Academic Press.

Wallerstein, Immanuel. 1989. *The Modern World-System, vol. III: The Second Great Expansion of the Capitalist World-Economy, 1730–1840's*. San Diego: Academic Press.

Woodiwiss, Anthony. 1996. "Searching for Signs of Globalization," *Sociology*, Vol. 30, No. 4, pp. 799–810.

CHAPTER 9

Gender and Queer Theory

While feminist theory is an extension of feminism and feminist activism into the theoretical realm, gender theory does not emerge from any social movement or political struggle; it is an interdisciplinary field, *a hybrid*, that analyzes the phenomenon of gender. Neither feminist theory nor gender theory is exclusive of the other, and at times both tread the same intellectual terrain. Queer theory is more closely aligned with the study of gender and sexualities. Like gender theory, however, it has deep roots in feminist discourse, and like feminism emerges from identity politics and social activism. Although gender theory and theories of sexuality existed within fields such as anthropology, sociology, biology, psychology and psychoanalysis for many years, with the advent of the linguistic turn and the feminist movement in the 1970s, these theories claimed their independence from the natural and social sciences.

Today all of these are rich fields of intellectual inquiry and find expression in film, literature, and the social sciences. Perhaps much of the reason for this rests with their utilization of poststructural paradigms. With the linguistic turn of the 1970s, there was a definite movement away from essentialist thought and gravitation toward social constructionism. Where early theories of gender and sexuality often assumed that sex and gender were inherently connected, this is far less the case today.

Gender and queer theory are separated here for presentation purposes only. Keep in mind that these two frames of analysis (often along with feminist theory) are frequently integrated. Some university departments combine all three, or at least two of the three.

GENDER THEORY

The origin of the word *gender* presents a theoretical dilemma. *The Oxford English Dictionary* locates its etymology in the concept of *genus* or *kind*, which signals an inherent difference. At face value, this is an essentialist approach in which biology is destiny. Today, most contemporary theorists see gender as a cultural product, not a biological one. That is, modern theory does not look at gender categories as discrete and inflexible. While the establishment of gender distinctions appears to be cross-cultural, how these categories are constructed can differ widely. Gender is traditionally defined as characteristics that seem to distinguish males from females in a particular culture. But this is built on the assumption that there are only two genders and that sexuality is binary. Sociologists have long distinguished gender from sex, assigning to the concept of gender those characteristics that are socially ascribed and to sex those that are associated with innate biology. As one secures a more sophisticated understanding of gender theory, one begins to comprehend the great complexity of something once deemed so simple.

The study of gender has been an important subfield of sociology since the early 1900s. Well before second wave feminism, sociologists had written not only about gender and gender inequality but also about gender identity and sexuality (Heap 2003; Salerno 2007, pp. 68–86). Much of this early research was buried in various studies of marriage and family. In anthropology, researchers such as Margaret Mead (1935) made significant contributions to studying gender in non-western societies, revealing the strong influence culture had on gender and sexual practices. An important starting point for more contemporary gender theory was Simone de Beauvoir's *The Second Sex* (1949), wherein she posits: "One is not born a woman, one becomes one." Here one can see her keen understanding of the relationship between gender construction and feminist theory relative to the oppression of women.

BIOLOGICAL DETERMINISM

Few scholars today are likely to subscribe to a rigid essentialist approach to gender; however, most do recognize the influence that the biological exerts on the social. Because male and female bodies comprise different hormones, anatomical structures, and chromosomes, it would be unlikely that these have absolutely no impact on what we call gender. We know that parts of the male brain develop differently from that of the female brain. Scientific studies indicate that the gonadal hormones androgen and estrogen have significant influences over regions of the brain that correspond to sex differences. And scientists have concluded that brain regions are important in deciphering nonverbal cues, such as the ventral frontal cortex, are morphologically different between genders (Wood, et al. 2008). The more contemporary position in which the biological and the social are recognized as important to gender construction is represented by Lisa Elliot (2009), who in *Scientific American*, wrote: "The early appearance of any sex difference suggests it is innately programmed—selected for through evolution and fixed into our behavioral development through either prenatal hormone exposure or early gene expression differences. On the other hand, sex differences that grow larger through childhood are likely shaped by social learning, a consequence of the very different lifestyle, culture and training that boys and girls experience in every human society."

The nature versus nurture debate is, for the most part, over in sociology, and it is obvious that each individual is affected by genetics, innate potentialities, hormones, and a whole array of psychological and social conditioning factors. Just how much genetics alone is responsible for difference in gender is questionable, given the recent research on neuoplasticity of the brain in biological development. Melissa Hines, in her book *Brain Gender* (2004), concludes that any such differences between men and women are a matter of degree and not kind. She describes a variety of questionable research practices that seem to have an agenda. She quotes from studies ranging from Moir and Moir's *Why Men Don't Iron* (2000) to Simon LeVay's study (1993, pp. 57–61) that contends that men's distaste for child care is related to their limited fetal exposure to androgen. LeVay is a Harvard-trained neuroscientist who has done research into explaining the differences between homosexual and heterosexual men by measuring average size between the third interstitial nucleus of the anterior hypothalamus (INAH3). His finding that it is twice as large in straight men as it is in gay men leads him to conclude that homosexuality is prenatally determined. He also found that the INAH3 was the same size for women as for gay men.

Eleanor Maccoby and Carol Jacklin (1974) did extensive research into studies that professed to show a relationship between sexual biology and gender characteristics. Their work revealed that widely held stereotypes often impinge on a scientist's objectivity in this work. In their research, they identified several common problems: (1) overreporting of the significance of findings or an exaggeration of positive results, (2) disagreement in results when data are obtained in different ways, and (3) limits because of situational differences.

While evidence reveals differences between men and women in select personality traits such as nurturance and assertiveness on standardized personality tests (Feingold 1994), it remains questionable as to the source of these differences. But it is important to note that the contemporary social theory leans heavily toward environmental influences.

Linda Nicholson, a professor of women, gender, and sexuality studies at Washington University, has advanced the concept of *biological foundationalism*. While she dismisses biological determinism and sees gender as primarily socially constructed, she also views the body as a rack upon which cultural attributes are cloaked. While men and women are not the same in different cultures, they do share behavioral attributes that intersect across time and space (Nicholson 1995).

Donna Haraway (1989), a poststructural science historian, has illuminated in her work the strong ties among ideology, politics, and science throughout history. She sees the construction of binary and exclusionary divisions between biological categories leading to or being responsible for the misguided "scientific" division between male and female, as well as that between human and animal, or machine and human. Gender theorists see in her work a welcome attack on the traditional categorical divisions developed in the biological sciences.

GENDER SOCIALIZATION

A few scholars still see gender as significantly innate and related to the difference in physiology and biochemistry of the male/female binary. However, most contemporary gender theorists are dismissive of this line of reasoning, arguing that for humans biology is not destiny. They believe that as learning animals, children are socialized or conditioned to take on particular traits and patterns of behavior associated with the gender they have been assigned in their society based on their genitalia, and that so-called biological predispositions do not, in themselves, determine outcomes.

Judith Lorber, professor emerita of sociology and women's studies at The Graduate Center and Brooklyn College of the City University of New York, has done considerable work in this area of gender socialization. For Lorber (1994, p. 13), "[g]ender is so pervasive that in our society we assume it is bred into our genes. Most people find it hard to believe that gender is created and recreated out of human interaction, out of social life, and is the texture and order of that social life."

Lorber's work is an important starting point for beginning any discussion of contemporary gender theory. Her work very much evolves from the interactionist sociological tradition wherein our social interactions are seen to create our social realities. Perhaps this is a solid bridge to even more modern discussions of social construction and its role in the production of gender. Still, Lorber does not need to draw from poststructuralism to make her points. For Lorber, while birth is the point at which assignment of gender begins according to the child's genitalia, we now recognize that such a social assignment is, in fact, prenatal.

Many parents want to know and do learn, the sex of their children before they are born. The naming of children, assignment of dress, as well as the modeling of gender roles is something parents do as part of parenting. Every society classifies girl and boy children. These classifications are seen as the socially acceptable categories and each is usually assigned different responsibilities. "Personality characteristics, feelings, motivations and ambitions flow from these different life experiences, so that the members of these different groups become different kinds of people" (Lorber 1994, p. 15). Basic institutions in society such as media, education, and religion all bolster such binaries. In some religions, different induction rituals exist for boys and girls. In most cultures, language itself is gendered, as is the way it is used.

Gender itself becomes institutionalized in society. Gender assigns distinct social statuses and different rights and responsibilities. All of this is conditioned through social interactions with other boys and girls, other females and males.

Lorber posits that, in almost every encounter, people "produce gender." And gender norms and expectations are enforced through what sociologists call sanctions, both formal and informal. Peers often single out gender-inappropriate behavior for comment or ridicule. Most people voluntarily go along with societal proscriptions for gendered behavior, attitudes, and beliefs because such norms are sewn into the fabric of human social relations. To be gendered, and gendered in the particular ways of one's sociocultural surroundings, seems natural.

The term *differential socialization* has been applied to gender to emphasize how one is conditioned in any binary-gendered society to take on male or female characteristics. But what characterizes "male" and "female" change across cultures and within cultures over time. Michael Kimmel (2000, p. 4), who has extensively studied various types of masculinities around the world, has noted that there appears to be a generally accepted idea that the differences *between* male and female are much greater than the differences that exist within each category alone. In contrast, however, he finds the differences *between* men and women are not as significant as the differences *among* men and women. He also contends that, when examined closely, perceived differences between male and female turn out to be differences based less on gender than on differences in the social positions that men and women occupy. For Kimmel (2000, p. 4), "gender difference is a product of gender inequality and not the other way around. In fact gender difference is the chief outcome of gender inequality, because it is through the idea of difference that inequality is legitimated."

MASCULINITIES AND FEMININITIES

If men (or males) signify a hegemonic grouping of individuals who exercise control over society, then one must stand ready to define what then constitutes being a man. The definition proposed by a number of theorists is that there is never only one masculinity. Just as it means different things to be a woman in different cultures, in different ethnicities, and in different social classes at different times, being a man is likewise variable. This is not to ignore the privileges granted to men in nearly all societies in terms of access to power, education, and wealth. And in western societies aren't white males usually given exceptional advantages? Just as it is important to understand which specific characteristics constitute "white" racially, it is important to understand the traits ascribed to "nonwhite" in order to devalue them. This tells us a lot about the society in which we live. It is similarly important to acknowledge how masculinity and femininity are uniquely and culturally constructed according to other respective status categories. For example, black males differ from white males who differ from Asian or Arab males. Each culture and class has a matrix around which femininities and masculinities are formed. Similarly, one might ask: are lesbian femininities different from heterosexual femininities?

It should be clear that, just as there are different types of heterosexual female and male constructions, there are unique types of homosexual male and female constructions. Neither heterosexual nor homosexual is a homogenous grouping of people. The same can be said about queer identities. There are different expectations and different constructions associated with each type. But how does one construct these categories?

As long ago as 1929 (at least fifty years before contemporary theorist Judith Butler wrote about it), the idea that gender was a performance was posited by the noted psychoanalytic theorist Joan Riviere. Riviere was a founding member of the British Psychoanalytic Society and was an analyst herself—one of the few professional psychoanalysts to be analyzed by Sigmund Freud. Her paper, "Womanliness as Masquerade," appeared in the *International Journal of Psychoanalysis*. It presents the case of a woman (some have suggested it was Riviere herself) who gives a scholarly paper at an academic conference and feels obliged to flirt with male colleagues in order not to challenge their masculinity. She goes on to state that being a woman is always a masquerade. Later taken up by Judith Butler, the whole notion of ***performativity*** as essential to gender provides a more comprehensive theoretical overview of this phenomenon. One is not innately gendered; rather, one *performs* gender in a variety of different ways. The notion that gender is simply a performance speaks to several things, among them the power of a society to impose particular views of gender onto individual actors through coercion, socialization, and violence; the power of social institutions to divide populations in arbitrary ways for the purpose of organizing and controlling people's social and sexual behaviors; and the individual potential to discard gender altogether as a personal identifier.

GENDER AND PSYCHOANALYSIS

Freud's work on gender is considered, for the most part essentialist, having its roots in biology. However, his ideas on gender and sexuality were not quite as traditional as one might think. Although he confessed to understanding men better than women, he constantly posited the notion that sexuality and gender were separate from one another, that gender development was influenced by parents, and that gender identity was a "delicate negotiation between desire and identification" (Freud 1905; Barden 2001, p. 115). His position on homosexuality was quite radical for his time. Because of his conflicting statements, some claim that he saw it as a perversion, but he never did. He recognized the power of society to impose the label of perversion on sexual behavior it deemed inappropriate. And although we could go into detail on his notion of the Oedipal and Electra complexes, this exploration would lead us astray from our consideration of *contemporary* social theory. But it must at least be said that he viewed the family and the society surrounding it as powerful influences on both sex and gender.

Those who followed Freud, who took up the calling of psychoanalysis, brought a unique array of perspectives to the discussion of gender and sexual issues. Sociologist Nancy Chodorow (see Chapter 6) was responsible for applying the object relations theories of Melanie Klein to gender socialization. Although we have dealt with them before in other contexts of theory, Juliet Mitchell, Jessica Benjamin, Julia Kristeva, and the French poststructuralist feminists have all contributed to the advance of gender theory. So have an array of poststructuralist and postmodernist theorists—some of whom we looked at in Chapter 6.

For Jacques Lacan (1973), sexual identity is not based on biological difference or any other innate factor, but it is primarily learned through identification and language. In other words, it is strictly social. He views masculinity and femininity as symbolic positions, not biological classifications. Like Freud, he believes that a child becomes a sexed object; she or he is not born one. Both see this as related to what Freud called the castration anxiety born out of Oedipal desire. This was the male child's fear of his penis being castrated by his father. But both men saw this working quite differently. For Lacan, it was not the basis for sexual identity, as it was for Freud. For Lacan, both girls and boys were led by it to identify with the father. According to his theory, the individual's sexual identity is always a rather precarious matter, a source of perpetual self-questioning. Anatomy does not determine one's sexual identity but only influences it on a symbolic level.

GENDER, SEXUALITY, AND POSTSTRUCTURALISM

While Michel Foucault did not engage in significant discussions of gender in his writings, his impact has been widely felt in contemporary feminist theory, queer theory, and gender theory. His three-volume study of a history of human sexuality in the West had a significant impact on scholars; after reading it, they abandoned biological models of sex and gender and subscribed to a more discursive paradigm that revealed the power behind sexual proscriptions and prohibitions (Foucault 1978, 1985, 1988). Central to his work was the notion that culture precedes nature. In this regard, his contributions carry considerable weight in contemporary discussions of gender.

The challenging element in his notion of culture as a starting point is that this form of "genealogy" pushes us to subscribe to a non-essentialist worldview—one that is inherently relativistic. The power of this position in looking at gender becomes obvious. He proposes that sexual nature is constructed through discourse. It is comprised by an array of articulated characteristics that are grouped together and which are given *fictitious unity*. Also, sex is seen as arbitrary and contingent component of identity.

Foucault makes the point that sexual identity is a created phenomenon. It is constructed through historic discourse and discriminatory power relations. He dismisses the notion that one's sex is foundational to identity and also rejects the essentialist assumption that shared identity is the basis for community. He wants to move beyond identity politics but at the same time he recognizes that identity is a social construction. He sees liberation through breaking away from the artificial confines of ascribed sexuality (Foucault 1978, p. 157). Foucault urges us to reject the gender binary and look toward a new configuration of gender that is rhetorical and therefore interpreted differently by different people. Above all, he sees neither gender nor sex as static and absolute; instead, he views both as interactive processes of identification (McCallum 1996, p. 91).

Foucault asserts that sex and gender are bound up in power and resistance as well as in the production of knowledge and truth. He is most interested in the ways regimes of power produce discourses on sexual perversion, pathology, delinquency, and criminology and in the new subjects emerging from these discourses. He views gender as a product of such regulatory practices. He challenges all discourses that have helped to establish categories that limit and punish people. For Foucault, gender is deployed as a mechanism of such limitation. The only way he sees to counter this is through pleasures, the body, and knowledge in its multiple forms. That is he tries to undo categories.

While some feminists have claimed Foucault is insensitive to issues of gender, citing his failure to even recognize this term, other theorists have given him the benefit of the doubt and interpreted his use of the term *sexuality* to often stand as a surrogate for *gender* (de Lauretis 1987; McCallum 1996; Butler 1999). And the usage of *gender* and *sex* in the French language suggests that his use of *sex* for *gender* might not be a gross misinterpretation (McCallum 1996, p. 84).

JUDITH BUTLER AND THE LIMITS OF GENDER

Judith Butler is one of the most important contemporary theorists of gender and human sexuality. Educated in philosophy at Yale University in the 1980s, her work has come to represent an innovative yet distinctly American application of poststructural theory to gender and queer studies. Among her most important works have been *Gender Trouble: Feminism and the Subversion of Identity* (1990) and *Bodies That Matter* (1993). While we have already touched upon some of her ideas in feminist theory, it is also important to see her writings as encompassing more than feminist theory. Her work challenges foundational notions of identity and is frequently in conflict with mainstream feminist thought and traditional notions of gender and womanhood. Her positions make her one of the most radical anti-essentialists working in social theory today.

Butler argues that all categories of both sex and gender are socially constructed through power and discourse. She views distinctions between male and female, as well as gay and straight, as culturally constituted. Neither gender nor sex is a category with ontological integrity. Both are fragments of identity, and both are performative. She takes issue with other theorists, including French feminists, who propose that the notion of woman is a universal concept. For Butler, it is a cultural invention. She rejects the notion that the construction of gender is predicated on what seems to be the biological imperative of one's sex. She fully subscribes to Foucault's proposal that discourse comes before biology and that biology is only a particular type of discourse. It is as socially constructed as gender.

Butler's notion of role performance applies to both genders. There is a tacit collective agreement as to how we perform gender in society to produce and sustain polar opposite genders. While Butler understands that how we perform gender will also be filtered through screens such as ethnicity and class, she recognizes that those who do not abide by society's expectations in these matters will be punished or marginalized. Gender performance is highly ritualized and regularized through societal norms and threats. These help perpetuate the rituals of gender and gender splitting.

Butler sees things such as drag performance to be a purposeful exaggeration of gender traits often used to undermine the binary system. Such performance is sometimes a form of resistance. We are always performing, however. Unlike many poststructuralists who resign themselves to having no choice, Butler sees performance itself as choice. By choosing an alternative type of gender behavior, gender trouble (which is the title of her book), we can work to undermine the binary. She views identity as free floating and not connected to essence. It does not emerge from an innate biological program but rather is a personal invention.

Judith Butler's theoretical work on identity and sexuality frequently crosses over into psychoanalysis. Drawing creatively on Freud's work on mourning and melancholia, Butler proposes that oedipal attractions help to form the basis of identity and sexuality in children, but not exactly as envisioned by Freud. She sees in Freud's discourse recognition of a need to repress one's erotic attraction to the parent of the opposite sex and then identify with the parent of the same sex. But in this process of identification with the same-sex parent, there must be a complete repression of any sexual attraction to this parent, this object of identification, despite the deep attachment and desire. Butler posits that there is a psychic cost for this denial, what she calls *heterosexual melancholia*: the unconscious longing for an erotic connection with those of the same sex. This is the price paid for stable conflict-free heterosexuality and a socially acceptable gender identity. And while this melancholia haunts its victim, from the depths of the unconscious it remains consciously elusive. In this way, homosexuality remains taboo and a symbol of cultural and personal failure.

QUEERING SOCIAL THEORY

What we today call queer theory is a relatively recent phenomenon. At one time the word *queer* was used as a derogatory term to describe someone who was gay. Similar to the word *nigger*, it has had a powerful ideological and political history associated with human abuse and discriminatory practice. But with the recent struggles for gay, lesbian and transgender rights, the word was adopted by activists working for progressive social change who wanted to call into question traditional labels. *Queer* remains a term unaligned with any specific identity category and is often used to break down categorical divisions, particularly related to sex and gender. It focuses on mismatches among sex, gender, and desire (Jagose 1997).

While queer theory has its roots in the struggle for human rights, particularly in the movements of gay and lesbian activism in the 1970s, it has a distinctly different tone. It is especially influenced by poststructural analysis and constructionist thought. It rejects civil rights strategies subscribed to by an older generation of gay and lesbian activists in favor of a politics of carnival and transgression (Gamson 1996, p. 400). Here, the word *queer* is not used as an identity (to substitute for gay or lesbian, or something else) but rather is used as a critique of inflexible identity. Such theory was significantly influenced by the work of Michel Foucault, but it did not enter the academic world until the 1990s. A spin-off from feminist and gender theory, it is also rooted in LGBT (Lesbian, Gay, Bisexual and Transgender) studies. But its focus has been away from essential categories such as gay and lesbian and more toward fluid notions of both sexual desire and gender identity.

Queer theory remains something many thinkers have written about but few have fully embraced epistemologically. Steven Seidman (1994, p. 174) writes extensively on this topic and has looked at the struggle of queer theory to find acceptance among those who view human sexuality in binary terms. Thus, queer theory is critical of a heterosexually focused society while also challenging much of homosexual theory and discourse.

Gay and lesbian theory of the late 1970s focused primarily on homosexual identities and the meaning of homophobia. Politically, much of this theory was oriented toward legitimizing homosexuality, or at least defending it from more reactionary positions that considered it deviant. Seidman (1996, p. 8) notes that a good deal of early lesbian feminist and gay liberationist theory aimed at challenging the dominant view of homosexuality as deviant by asserting its normalcy. But things began to change in the late 1980s.

Seidman (2008, pp. 236–240) draws a clear distinction between identity theories of the 1970s offered by activists such as Adrienne Rich and Jeffrey Weeks, which provided the political and theoretical foundation for gay rights activism, and later queer theory. Adrienne Rich is a poet, lesbian, and feminist activist who became marginalized when the women's movement moved toward the political right to shore up its conservative constituents. She saw lesbianism as both a political as well as a personal identity. As the women's movement began to distance itself from gay rights and lesbian issues, Rich wrote her now classic essay, "Compulsive Heterosexuality and Lesbian Existence," which appeared in 1980. The essay argues that heterosexuality is a violent political institution that establishes male dominance over women economically, sexually, and physically. In the essay, she views heterosexuality as politically institutionalized and directed against the freedom of women to be with women except in those ways designated by men. Rich became an important figure in the lesbian movement. Likewise, British sociologist Jeffrey Weeks, who was an active member of the Gay Liberation Front and a founding member of the Gay Left Collective, wrote extensively on homosexual politics and gay identity in Britain. In his work, he argues for political activism as a means of achieving sexual liberation.

GAY AND LESBIAN IDENTITY THEORY

Against the powerful social institutions in the West (e.g., medicine, religion, criminal justice, and psychiatry) that historically stigmatized homosexuality as a form of deviant sexuality, it was primarily the fervent political struggles for liberation and against social oppression that helped create to positive gay and lesbian identities in the 1970s and 1980s. Identity was foundational for social theorists who attempted to explain the meaning of homosexuality.

Most immediately related to the gay and lesbian liberation movements was identity politics. The struggles for gay and lesbian rights helped to provide a base for an openly gay identity in the 1970s. John D'Emilio's groundbreaking work provides important insights into the origins of contemporary gay and lesbian identities and the power that social events had in this construction. For D'Emilio (1983), the struggle against homophobic culture and politics, the battle against discrimination, and the horrors of the AIDS epidemic of the 1980s all contributed to the nurturing and establishment of a more cohesive gay and lesbian community as well as to the strengthening of gay politics and culture.

However, these rigid or fixed identities had their limitations, too. As noted previously, Steven Seidman (1996), who was active in the gay rights struggles of the late 1960s and early 1970s, sees a division between contemporary queer theory and theories that emerged from the LGBT movements. He contends: "The notion of homosexuality as a universal category of the self and sexual identity was rarely questioned in homophile, lesbian feminist, and gay-liberationist discourses" (Seidman 1996, p. 8). Seidman (2002) proposes that the need for a politically cohesive community was critical to the struggle for gay and lesbian rights. But as more people found it possible to emerge from their closeted sexuality in the 1980s and 1990s, this changed. Part of this change was a rejection of the notion that one's sexual identity as straight, gay, bisexual, lesbian, or transgendered would always be the most essential component of one's identity; that sexuality, gender, and sexual preference were unchanging and stable components of the self.

An essentialism was foundational in much of this older identity position. The change that took place was both a generational and a cultural movement away from this position. Not only was the change to become manifest in contemporary social life, but also in the development of more contemporary theory. Especially with the advent of the sex and gender discourse of Michel Foucault and Judith Butler, and with the work of theorists like Jeffrey Weeks and Steve Seidman, theory was to change. Jeffrey Weeks uses the deconstruction of sexuality as the central theme of his classic text, *Sexuality and Its Discontents* (1989). For Weeks, "[t]here is no essence of homosexuality whose historical unfolding can be illuminated. There are only changing patterns in the organization of desire, whose specific configuration can be decoded" (Weeks 1995, p. 6).

Steven Seidman has suggested that sexuality as a social construction became an important link to queer theory in the 1990s, which was considerably less structured and less essentialist than theory that focused on the development of gay identity. But for him and others who came out of the gay liberation movement, there is a problem in relegating sexual identity, or sexual orientation to a secondary position. There is a depoliticizing and ahistorical tone to much of the new constructionist position, which in some ways seem to accommodate to easily to modern society's need to erase differences.

EVE KOSOFSKY SEDGWICK AND THE QUEER FRONTIER

Although Judith Butler is one of the most renowned contributors to queer theory, Eve Kosofsky Sedgwick (1950–2009) helped to pioneer the field. And she did this during the height of the Reagan–Thatcher years. Sedgwick was a professor of literature at both Duke University and the Graduate Center of the City University of New York. She was among the first literary scholars to deconstruct literary works, art, and film to unveil their homoerotic content. She discovered sexual subtexts woven through classic literary texts, including works of William Shakespeare, Charles Dickens, Jane Austin, T. S. Eliot, and others. Sedgwick saw her initial project as unearthing these hidden messages—many of which were related to same-sex love. Her work centered on attempting to understand the various kinds of sexual desire and how these have been constructed by culture over time. Sedgwick argued that sexuality and desire are not innate but rather are carefully crafted and well-managed social constructions. Like Foucault, she saw these categories or labels (man, woman, homosexual, heterosexual, lesbian, bisexual, and transexual) not as natural categories but as constructs established by hegemonic and patriarchal power aimed at control.

In *Between Men: Male Homosocial Desire* (1985), a study of nineteenth-century English literature, Sedgwick uncovers the pervasiveness of men's same-sex bonds. Sedgwick encourages us to revisit classic texts to better understand how men have expressed a homosocial desire for other men throughout history. By *homosocial desire*, she means not homosexual desire, but a category that can include friendship, camaraderie, mentorship, closeness, alliance, and the like. In fact, homosocial male bonding often includes a hatred and fear of homosexuality. *Obligatory heterosexuality* is a significant aspect of such male alliance. Thus, she sees homosocial desire as a type of oxymoron used to describe close same-sex bonds at the expense of opposite sex connection and at the same time intense homophobia. Sedgwick uses it in her study of male relationships.

Sedgwick (1985) proposes that socially acceptable male-to-male relations, including the intensity of feeling and types of desire, have changed with time. Part of what she assesses is what might and might not count as sexual in terms of such relations. She sees these relationships as shaped by power in a Foucauldian sense. She sees homosocial and homosexual as far more dichotomous for men than they are for women. For women, there is more of a continuum than some distinct separation. She proposes in her work that homophobia and "obligatory heterosexuality" is very much part of the system of patriarchy. It is both a political and an ideological system, and it is the same system whose rules and regulations repress and limit women. She views this homophobia as "tightly knit into the texture of family, gender, age, class, and race relations" (Sedgwick 1985, p. 4). She contends that if our society ceased to be homophobic it would lead to dramatic changes in our economic and political structures. She proposes that sex is deeply enmeshed in ideology, which works to maintain inequality. In fact, viewed historically, what constitutes sex is more ideological than anything else.

Sedgwick's book, *Epistemology of the Closet* (1990), is one of the founding texts in queer theory. Here, she calls into question not merely the gender binary, but also the meaning of sex itself. Working with important texts of European and American writers such as Henry James, Marcel Proust, and Oscar Wilde, she describes a genealogy through which sexual identity becomes central to personhood in much the same fashion that gender had been. For Sedgwick, sexuality is particularly important in societies obsessed with sex and the so-called evils of homosexuality and practices such as sodomy.

Sedgwick challenges the language and categories established to enforce some system of sexual and gender classification and control. She rejects the associated connection between gender and sexual preference and reaches beyond the simplistic categories used to stereotype and immobilize. Sexuality, gender, and desire constitute an enormous range of human individuality. Sedgwick contends that those who have been marginalized and compartmentalized through the system of heterosexist control and domination have often been made politically ineffective because of their own unique biases, ignorance, and identity politics. She sees latching on to labels of sexual difference (such as "gay," "transgendered," "lesbian," and "queer,") as self-defeating in the long run. Such organization around the concept of homosexuality, gay or lesbian, is the appropriation of a prison for the sexual self—a prison constituted by a system of knowledge based on exclusion, isolation, and oppression.

As a student of literature, Sedgwick recognizes the extent to which writers felt it necessary to hide their deepest homoerotic sentiments in their art. As a critic, she is able to deconstruct the messages present in the works of some of the world's greatest authors and the lengths to which they went to hide their sexual identities and preferences. She discusses the system of the closet, which helped to establish inflexible identities, a system that came about because of panic based on the very real concern of vicious and brutal attacks.

Sedgwick died at the age of 58 in 2009, and left behind an enormous body of work that helped lay the foundation for more contemporary queer theory. She was sensitive to the issues of nonheterosexual love and relationships and the scars left by radical conservative bigotry. Her work emphasized moving away from the inflexible frame created by hegemonic patriarchy for nonheterosexual love.

THEORIZING TRANSGENDER

According to sociologist Sally Hines (Hines and Sanger 2010, p. 1) at the University of Leeds, the label *transgendered* "denotes a range of gender experiences, subjectivities and presentations that fall across, between and beyond stable categories of 'man' and 'woman.' 'Transgender' includes gender identities that have, more traditionally, been described as 'transsexual,' and a diversity of genders that call into question an assumed relationship between gender identity and the presentation of the 'sexed body.'" Hines shows that the early history of sexuality, especially the study of non-normative sexual practices, frequently viewed gender diverse practices as contrary sexual feeling, or what the medical profession then called sexual inversion. Cross-dressing and cross-living practices were viewed as aberrant sexual behaviors. In the early part of the twentieth century, however, a number of leading sexologists such as Hirschfeld and Ellis distinguished gender practices from sexual ones.

In 1923, the German physician and sexologist Mangus Hirschfeld (1868–1935) used the term *transsexualism* to describe the condition of patients he had seen suffering because they felt that their bodies did not reflect their gender identities or sense of sexuality. While many psychologically identified with the "opposite sex" and wanted to be considered part of that group, a smaller number felt locked into the wrong body, a body alien to them and their feelings. Hirschfeld was the first to supervise sex-reassignment surgery in 1930, where the body of the patient was modified. Harry Benjamin (1885–1986), a German-trained endocrinologist working closely with Alfred Kinsey in the United States, studied transgender and transsexual phenomenology and helped identify and secure help for individuals dealing with these issues. A scale devised by Benjamin showed varying intensities of transgendered feeling. The highest intensity were those who desired that their bodies be modified through sex reassignment surgery (SRS); other levels include those who might benefit from hormonal treatment or those who were content living out a gender that was opposite to the one they were culturally assigned because of their innate biological appearance. However, these categories remain contentious, as does the definition of the word *transsexual*.

None of this discussion, reflects the pathology which has been ascribed to sexual and gender differences throughout history, nor to the persecution and suffering of people who have been labeled as sexually or genderedly non-normative. The medicalization of gender and sex has been connected to this history of modernity and its essentialistic focus on control through typologies and repair.

The term *transgender*, as a catchall for a vast array of male and female body-gender variant individuals (including self-identified transsexuals and transvestites), is relatively new and did not enter the lexicon until the 1990s (Valentine 2007, p. 4). Sally Hines finds transgender practice and discourse as instrumental in moving gender theory away from the gender binary and for the robust emergence of queer theory. But she also sees transdiscourse as having destabilized the politics that promoted a subscription to sexual identities and stereotypes.

SEXED BODIES

While the discourse on bodies owes much to feminist theory, it is necessary also to discuss the concept of the *sexed body* as it relates here to issues of gender and queer theory. Stephanie Turner (1999, p. 458) has noted: "The powerful relations that provide normative guidelines for gender behavior also provide normative guidelines for the material aspect of the body: in other words, how it is made."

(This notion that the body is a social construction was discussed in Chapter 6). It is important to recognize not simply that the body is defined, but also who has the power to define and control it, and why has been it defined differently throughout time and across cultures. In fact, it is the social definition of the body, or what the body should be, that makes the body an important signifier. Beyond this, the body is physically modified, marked, conditioned, and controlled in all cultures, leading not only to a sexed body but also to a cultured one.

Associating character with the human body has a long tradition in the social sciences, dating back to modes of character analysis. Phrenology (determining one's character by measuring head shape and contours) and other pseudosciences were means used to systematize this understanding. But well before this, physical appearance was a means of separating what some believed to be humans from nonhumans, and devils from angels.

Male and female bodies are treated differently at birth and are often physically modified in ritualistic practices. But in terms of more contemporary gender socialization, sociologist Karen Martin (1994) at the University of Michigan has examined how the child's understanding of the gender binary is formed at an early age and how her or his body is conditioned to construct it. In looking at the public preschool programs in the United States, Martin found a "hidden curriculum" that transforms children who are similar in bodily comportment, movement, and practice into stereotypical boys and girls—children whose bodily practices differ. She noted five ways in which this was achieved: dressing up, permitting certain relaxed behaviors or requiring formal behaviors, controlling voices, verbal and physical instructions regarding the child's body by the teacher, and permitting select physical interactions among children. For Martin, this institutionally based treatment of "docile bodies" helps create gender differences and makes them appear to be innate.

The issue of the gendered body is especially significant for intersexed people, many of whom have had their bodies surgically modified to fit the accepted male/female binary. In contrast, other self-identified *intersexed* individuals reject the gender binary and want their bodies to signal their unique identity. In her study of how intersexuals relate to their bodies, Turner found that many envision a wholly new intersection of sex and gender, a sort of third sex that evades gender determination. Because of the political and intellectual foundation laid down by feminist, gay, lesbian, transgender, and queer activists, intersexed people also have a basis for resisting being forced into so-called normative binary categories. In recent years, an intersex intellectual and political movement has emerged to politically resist policies demanding gender and sexual rigidity, expressing the right to be seen and treated for who they are rather than as sexual categorical misfits (Epstein 1990). This movement has connected to and energized others that demand sexual and gender reform.

KEY TERMS

biological foundationalism A concept advanced by Linda Nicholson to suggest that the body is a rack (as in a clothing store) on which attributes of gender are hung.

differential socialization The male/female socialization of children based on the gender binary.

fictitious unity Foucault's notion that one's sexual nature is socially constructed through key characteristics that are grouped together.

heterosexual melancholia The unconscious grieving of self-defined heterosexuals for their unfulfilled homosexual longings and feelings.

homosocial desire A term used by Eve Sedgwick to describe a non-sexual longing for affection and the close company of people of the same sex.

intersexed An anatomical condition in which people have no clearly defined set of male or female genitalia or possess an atypical combination of both features.

obligatory heterosexuality The social, cultural, and political attempts to control peoples' sexual orientation and actions by prohibiting all but heterosexual relations.

performativity As applied to gender, the notion that all gender is a performance.

sexed body How the body is marked or processed to reflect a particular gender.

SOURCES

Barden, Nicola. 2001. "The Development of Gender Identity," in S. Izzard and N. Barden, eds., *Rethinking Gender and Therapy: Changing Identities of Women*. Philadelphia, PA: Open University Press.

Butler, Judith. 1993. *Bodies That Matter: On the Discursive Limits of Sex*. New York: Routledge.

Butler, Judith. 1999. *Gender Trouble: Feminism and the Subversion of Identity*. New York: Routledge.

de Beauvoir, Simone. 1949. *The Second Sex*. New York: Vintage Books.

de Lauretis, Teresa. 1987. *Technologies of Gender: Essays on Theory, Film and Fiction*. Bloomington, IN: University of Indiana Press.

D'Emilio, John. 1983. *Sexual Politics, Sexual Communities: The Making of a Homosexual Minority in the United States 1940–1970*. Chicago: University of Chicago Press.

Elliot, Lisa. 2009, September. "Girl Brain, Boy Brain," *Scientific American*, Vol. 20, Electronic format.

Epstein, Julia. 1990. "Either/Or-Neither/Both: Sexual Ambiguity and the Ideology of Gender," *Genders*, Vol. 7, pp. 99–142.

Feingold, A. 1994. "Gender Differences in Personality: A Meta-analysis," *Psychological Bulletin*, Vol. 3, No. 116, pp. 429–456

Foucault, Michel. 1978. *The History of Sexuality: An Introduction*, Vol. 1. New York: Vintage Books.

Foucault, Michel. 1985. *The Use of Pleasure: The History of Sexuality*, Vol. 2. New York: Vintage Books.

Foucault, Michel. 1988. *The Care of the Self: The History of Sexuality*, Vol. 3. New York: Vintage Books.

Freud, Sigmund. 1905. "Three Essays on the Theory of Sexuality," in J. Strachey, ed., *The Standard Edition of the Complete Psychological Works of Sigmund Freud: Vol. VII*. London: Hogarth Press.

Gamson, Joshua. 1996. "Must Identity Movements Self-Destruct: A Queer Dilemma," in S. Seidman, ed., *Queer Theory/Sociology*. Cambridge, MA: Blackwell.

Haraway, Donna. 1989. *Primate Visions: Gender, Race and Nature in the World of Modern Science*. New York: Routledge.

Heap, Chad. 2003. "The City as a Sexual Laboratory: The Queer Heritage of the Chicago School," *Qualitative Sociology*, Vol. 26, No. 4, pp. 457–487.

Hines, Melissa. 2004. *Brain Gender*. New York: Oxford University Press.

Hines, Sally, and Tam Sanger. 2010. "Introduction," in S. Hines and T. Sanger, eds. *Transgender Identities: Toward a Social Analysis of Gender Diversity*. New York: Routledge.

Jagose, Annamarie. 1997. *Queer Theory: An Introduction*. New York: New York University Press.

Kimmel, Michael. 2000. *The Gendered Society*. New York: Oxford University Press.

Lacan, Jacques. 1975. *Encore*. Paris: Seuil.

LeVay, Simon. 1993. *The Sexual Brain*. Cambridge, MA: MIT Press.

Lorber, Judith. 1994. *Paradoxes of Gender*. New Haven, CT: Yale University Press.

Maccoby, Eleanor, and Carol Jacklin. 1974. *The Psychology of Sex Differences: Vol. 1*. Stanford, CA: Stanford University Press.

Martin, Karin. 1994. "Becoming a Gendered Body: Practices of Preschools," *American Sociological Review*, Vol. 63, No. 4, pp. 494–511.

McCallum, E. L. 1996. "Technologies of Truth and the Function of Gender in Foucault," in S. Hekman, ed. *Feminist Interpretations of Michel Foucault*. University Park, PA: University of Pennsylvania Press.

Mead, Margaret. 1935. *Sex and Temperament*. New York: William Morrow.

Moir, Anne, and Bill Moir. 2000. *Why Men Don't Iron: The New Reality of Gender Differences*. New York: Harper-Collins.

Nicholson, Linda. 1995. *Social Postmodernism: Beyond Identity Politics*. Cambridge, England: Cambridge University Press.

Rich, Adrienne. 1980. "Compulsive Heterosexuality and the Lesbian Experience," *Signs*, Vol. 5, No. 4, pp. 631–660.

Riviere, Joan. 1929. "Womanliness as Masquerade," *International Journal of Psychoanalysis*, Vol. 10, pp. 303–313.

Salerno, Roger. 2007. *Sociology Noir*. Jefferson, NC: McFarland.

Sedgwick, Eve Kosofsky. 1985. *Between Men: English Literature and Male Homosocial Desire*. New York: Columbia University Press.

Sedgwick, Eve Kosofsky. 1990. *Epistemology of the Closet*. Berkeley: University of California Press.

Seidman, Steven. 1994. "Symposium: Queer Theory/Sociology: A Dialogue," *Sociological Theory*, Vol. 12, No. 2, pp. 166–177.

Seidman, Steven. 1995. *Sexuality and Its Discontents*. New York: Routledge.

Seidman, Steven. 1996. "Introduction," in S. Seidman, ed., *Queer Theory/Sociology*. Cambridge, MA: Blackwell.

Seidman, Steven. 2002. *Beyond the Closet: The Transformation of Gay and Lesbian Life*. New York: Routledge.

Seidman, Steven. 2008. *Contested Knowledge: Social Theory Today*. Oxford: Blackwell.

Strozier, Robert M. 2002. *Foucault, Subjectivity and Identity*, Detroit, MI: Wayne State University Press.

Turner, Stephanie. 1999. "Intersex Identities: Locating New Intersections of Sex and Gender," *Gender and Society*, Vol. 13, No. 4, pp. 457–479.

Valentine, David. 2007. *Imagining Transgender: An Ethnography of a Category*. Durham, NC: Duke University Press.

Weeks, Jeffrey. 1989. *Sexuality and Its Discontents: Meanings, Myths and Modern Sexualities*. London: Routledge.

Weeks, Jeffrey. 1995. *Invented Moralities: Sexual Values in the Age of Uncertainty*. New York: Columbia University Press.

Wood, Jessica, Dwayne Heitmiller, Nancy Andersen, and Peg Nopoulos. 2008. "Morphology of the Ventral Frontal Cortex: Relationship to Femininity and Social Cognition," *Cerebral Cortex*, Vol. 18, No. 3, pp. 534–540.

CHAPTER | **10**

Race Theory

O ne of the more obvious features of contemporary social theory is its relative weakness on issues dealing with the matter of race. Although entire
categories of new theory have been devoted to culture, postcolonialism,
feminism, and sexuality, one of the central problems confronting modern and postmodern societies is the powerful persistence of racism. The importance of race is
frequently obscured by a leveling of issues of gender, race, and class—where race
is but one element in a hierarchical chain of signifiers. The notion of race has some
presence in all of these new categories of theory, but it rarely occupies a central
place of importance.

Before second wave feminism, the civil rights movement of the 1960s dealt
with issues of racial exploitation and oppression. As a model social movement
that was successful in bringing about an era of radical political reform in many
industrialized nations, civil rights activists opened an avenue for other movements promoting the civil rights of minorities. It helped spark the second wave
of the women's movement, various aboriginal and indigenous rights movements
(including the Native American and First Nation movements), as well as the gay
liberation movement. It provided an organizational model that was to be emu-
lated not only by groups fighting discrimination and social injustice around the
world, but also by organizations struggling for other types of reform—antiwar,
environmental, labor, and economic.

RACE AND THE ENLIGHTENMENT PROJECT

Most of classical sociology is silent about race. But when it speaks, it embarrasses
itself. Embedded in western philosophy and social thought, especially modern
western philosophy, are elements of racism that helped to shape European discourse and build empires. This is recognized in the postcolonial theory of today.

G. W. Friedrich Hegel (1837), who had one of the most profound influences on Marx and other modern philosophers, subscribed to a racist perspective. In his *Philosophy of History* (see *Vorlesunger uber die Philosophie der Geschichte*, 1970) he writes:

> The Negro as already observed, exhibits the natural man in his completely wild and untamed state. In this character there is nothing that reminds one of the human. This is perfectly corroborated by the extensive reports of the missionaries. Therefore, the Negroes get the total contempt of human beings . . . This character is not capable of development and education. The Negro is destined to end up a slave (p. 122).

Sociology and anthropology, which grew out of the European Enlightenment, were filled with essentialist racist theory, most of which was grounded in natural science or the science of biology. The whole notion of race was an Enlightenment invention.

Immanuel Kant, who proposed the existence of universal moral imperatives, developed a theory of race stratification, which also gave a justification for the enslavement of African peoples who he described as being incapable of developing a higher sense of moral reasoning. Montesquieu (1689–1755) touted the scientifically grounded notion of Negro inferiority, as did Schopenhauer (1788–1860). The defense of slavery as well as the holocausts visited upon indigenous peoples around the world was viewed as natural modes of progress (Winant 2000, p. 174). For the European colonizer "there was an assumption that darker non-European races were always immoral, promiscuous, libidinous and always desired white people" (Loomba 1998, p. 158).

Much of early race theory was grounded in religious beliefs and myths, including the notion of how races were constructed by God. While people were sometimes classified or grouped according to the physical characteristics and cultural affiliation in antiquity, it was not until the nineteenth and twentieth centuries that attempts were made to codify scientifically these human groupings and systematically assign to each group particular character traits and place them on a scale of evolutionary development. The emergence of physical anthropology and evolutionary biology had much to do with this.

Although race was primarily an invention of Enlightenment science, the existence of races or subspecies of homo sapiens could never be proven scientifically. Elazar Barkan locates the origin of the term *race* in eighteenth-century zoology and shows how it was later applied to humans by Johann Friedrich Blumenbach (1752–1840), who was a German medical doctor and an anthropologist. But Blumenbach was only one of many to engage in race science, which became extremely popular in colonial nations in the nineteenth and twentieth centuries. Samuel George Morton (1799–1851), a biologist and a professor of anatomy at the University of Pennsylvania, became a primary spokesperson for touting the so-called scientific evidence for the racial superiority of whites and the inferiority of other races, all of which he invented in his classification system. Howard Winant (2000, p. 172) has explored this history of the relationship between race and science and the development of colonial empires: "The onset of global economic integration, the dawn of seaborne empire, the conquest of the Americas, and the rise of the Atlantic slave trade were all key elements in the genealogy".

THE SOCIAL CONSTRUCTION OF RACE

Modernity is where race is codified and integrated into a system of cultural, social, and political discourse. It is where a taxonomy of races was developed. Race became a set of physical features, and it came to represent how such features were associated with culture and character. Culture and race here became intertwined. Race was thought of as cultural or national category—always comparing unfavorably to the race of the most dominant, powerful group. Jews, Irish, Italians, and Albanians were all considered races in certain parts of the world. Any human grouping could be made into a subspecies—made into a race. While some subscribe to the notion that racism emerges from a reaction to racial character, it is more obvious today that racism creates race through the process of social, physical, and cultural division.

Although the development of race as an essentialist category is connected to the origins of modern science, some enlightened thinkers saw race as a social construction. "The negro is 'with us' not as an actual physical being of flesh and blood and bones, wrote the black physician and abolitionist James McCune Smith in 1852, "but a hideous monster of the mind" (Dain 2002, p. xi). W. E. B. DuBois (2009) was among the first social theorists to address race as a fictitious concept when he wrote *Dusk of Dawn: An Essay Toward an Autobiography of a Race Concept* (first published in 1940). Both men understood race's relationship to power and domination and to its place in social discourse. Their words did not dominate the rhetoric because their insights were not seen as valuable in justifying the interests of empire, capitalism, and global domination.

Stephen Jay Gould's important book *The Mismeasure of Man* (1981) tells a history of race research in the nineteenth and twentieth centuries and its failure as science. This did not mean, however, that essentialist race theory was unsuccessful politically, economically, and socially. Wars, slavery, genocides, and colonialism have all used race as a justification. Gould's book was published in the 1980s, when attempts were still being made to associate race with intelligence in order to block the development of educational and social programs aimed primarily at poor black minority populations in the United States and Britain. Today, the meaning of race is no longer the meaning assigned to it in the nineteenth or even the twentieth century. Race as a category is always morphing into something else.

But one of the most important aspects of the contemporary notion of race is not that people still suffer from racism today (which they do), it is that all people are racialized. People are still assigned a race, even if it is mixed race, in the society in which they live, just as much as people are assigned a gender. While race might not have as much to do with color today as it once did, it still exists in many forms. And according to that assignment, according to the place and time in which one lives, one is accorded more or less privilege because of it. However, just as gender and sexuality are important signifiers, so are race and class. These important social constructs combine to influence everyone's material life as well as everyone's perspective on that life.

This point is made clearly in Ruth Frankenberg's book, *White Women, Race Matters: The Social Construction of Whiteness* (1993). While this book actually was written to address the race issue that arose between white women and women of color in the women's movement, Frankenberg's analysis goes far beyond this. In this book she calls for a closer study of whiteness, which she concludes has three important dimensions: (1) it is a location of structured advantage or race privilege; (2) it is a "standpoint," a place from which white people look at themselves and others in society; and (3) it often refers to cultural practices that are hardly ever remarked upon.

Nonwhite racial groups have often changed over time and space. Throughout history, certain groups deemed racially nonwhite, such as the Jews or the Irish, have been admitted to the exclusive club of whiteness (but frequently with an asterisk after their names). However, whiteness has remained viable despite its minority status in the world. As Frankenberg (1993, p. 1) notes, both materiality and discourse are always connected. And the discourse of whiteness remains palpable as its power to oppress.

An entire discipline of "whiteness studies" has emerged over the past decade aimed at examining how whiteness as a social construction is used to organize power and promote inequities. The study recognizes what some refer to as the variegated notion of whiteness and how that which constitutes this label changes to promote particular group interests. A brief discussion of this area of theory will be presented later in this chapter.

RACE AND THE LINGUISTIC TURN

Elements of poststructuralism and postmodernism can be traced back to Hegel, Kant, Marx, Freud, Nietzsche, Saussure, Barthes, and a host of other Enlightenment and post-Enlightenment white male European thinkers discussed here and in other textbooks. These contemporary paradigms have affected much of the current social thought. Relatively few theorists have used these approaches to understand race, and far fewer black social theorists than white have embraced these paradigms. In Derrida's method of deconstruction in particular, and in his contention that there is "nothing outside of the text," there often appears to be a neglect of issues of race and social justice. Political change through social action has little play here. Yet deconstruction helps give creditability to the notion that the power of race rests in its linguistic construction and dissemination and not merely its application. As Foucault might suggest, it is the authoritative formulation of race in art, literature, philosophy, and the social sciences that becomes the source of oppression and violence.

Henry Louis Gates is a prominent literary critic and scholar who is also a professor of literature at Harvard and the director of the W. E. B. DuBois Institute for African and African American Research. He has attempted to understand how race is constructed in literature and art. His writings on race in literature, which have been criticized by many in the African American community, draw generously from poststructural theory. *The Signifying Monkey* (1988) is perhaps his best known work in this regard.

Gates asserts that race is a signifier—a significant yet contentious container of meaning. Race has been written into existence in an effort to mark particular populations and thus subordinate them in accordance with these markings. Portrayals of race in literature and in art have all attempted to naturalize and legitimate the racialized body as an innately inferior one. By a *racialized body*, Gates means a body that is given race through discourse. While race pretends to be an objective term of classification, in fact it is a trope—a rhetorical figure of speech that becomes an interpolation. He notes: "Race has become a trope of ultimate irreducible difference between cultures, linguistic groups, or adherents of specific belief systems which—more often than not—have fundamentally opposed economic interests" (Gates 1985, p. 5). By examining the trope of race, by deconstructing it, Gates hopes to expose the notions of difference inscribed therein and by doing this expose the "hidden relations of power and knowledge inherent in popular and academic uses of 'race'" (Gates 1985, pp. 5–6). He capitalizes on the notion of trope in his other works (Gates 1986, 1988) moving it to various points in history to ascertain various constructions and readings of "Negroes" and "black people" in literature and art.

Gates focuses on the use and control of language by white elites in the historic construction of race. In American slave society, reading and writing were the skills denied by law to slaves and their children. And to teach a slave to read was met with harsh, often institutionalized, punishment. The legacy of this certainly can be found in both the economic condition of people of color, and in the stratified racial inequalities in education today. Racism is often hidden and Gates wants people to read between the lines.

Gates' failure to move further left in his analysis as well as his attachment to continental poststructural theory, rather than Marxist analysis or some modified form of it, is seen by many of his critics as an escape from the materiality of race. His outspoken rejection of *Afrocentrism*, which comes from (as he suggests) a total refusal to capitulate to the forces of racism in society, has also made him unpopular in some circles—especially among those who find incongruity between poststructuralism and the black experience.

A strong opposition to the poststructuralist paradigm as it relates to the issue of race comes from Joyce Joyce (1987, p. 340), a professor of English and African American literature at Temple University. In an essay highly critical of Gates, she notes: "Black poststructuralist critics have adopted a linguistic system and an accompanying world view that communicates to a small, isolated audience. Their pseudoscientific language is distant and sterile; these authors evidence their powers of ratiocination with an overwhelming denial of most, if not all senses. Ironically, they challenge the intellect, 'dulling' themselves to the realities of the central communicative function of language". Joyce asserts in her work that she sees Gates and others as withdrawing from a commitment to struggle. Literary theorist and Professor of Literature at NYU, Robert Young, (2001), in his critique of Gates, makes the same charge by suggesting that Gates' work deemphasizes the lived experience of black people.

Young attacks Gates for subscribing to a postmodern discourse that promotes the notion of race as a fiction and, in doing this, engages in a denial of many of the harsh realities of race in society today. And he criticizes Gates for adhering to postmodern theorizing while asserting that this theory "is not much good at exploring relations between identity and political agency" (p. 337). Young praises Cornel West for rejecting this paradigm.

Cornel West (1994, p. 65) sees poststructuralism as a diversion for young black intellectuals. West suggests that, while poststructuralism promotes a leftist form of skepticism, it also adopts an "incessant interrogation of power-laden discourses in the service of neither restoration, reformation, nor revolution . . . and provides a sophisticated excuse for ideological and social distance from insurgent black movements for liberation". He promotes in its stead a version of pragmatism and a return to the ideals of Dewey.

CORNEL WEST: THE SIGNIFICANCE OF RACE

One of the world's most prominent public intellectuals as well as an important social theorist who has dealt extensively with the topic of race is Cornel West. West received his Ph.D. in Philosophy from Princeton University, where he came under the influence of Richard Rorty, the renowned American philosopher and a proponent of contemporary pragmatism.

West's book *Race Matters* (1993) gave him recognition as an important academic and public commentator on the issue of race, particularly in the United States. His theoretical work is very much a rejection of the poststructuralist/postmodern critique, although he does attempt to take elements from Foucault and integrate them into his own analysis of racism in contemporary society. He has spent time developing a perspective he calls ***prophetic pragmatism***, which he believes can counter the pessimism and nihilism he associates with postmodern thought.

For West (1993a), postmodernism appears to be culpable in the destruction of western metaphysical traditions, which he feels is both positive and negative. It is positive because it recognizes the errors in Enlightenment thinking; it is negative because it undermines peoples' sense of power, autonomy, and a quest for moral purpose. Above all, West is a humanist and identifies himself with the black humanist tradition.

Prophetic pragmatism is a theoretical position that emerges from African American liberation theology and, as West sees it, combines the work of Ralph Waldo Emerson, John Dewey, William James, and W.E.B. DuBois. The fact that these philosophers are all American is no coincidence. It is his hope to construct a model in philosophy that runs counter to the current continental posture—one that is uniquely American and imbued with Christian values. To this end, he calls on past American progressives who he believes helped provide the United States with prophetic sensibilities. As someone who identifies himself as both African American and a progressive socialist, he also wants to promote a form of pragmatism that is meaningful to the African American community.

West (1989) sees the classical American pragmatism of Dewey as promoting cultural pluralism, democracy, and individuality as central norms. He sees it as a deployment of future-oriented instrumentalism in the service of social action and democratic ideals. He sees such a philosophy as grounded in a religious faith, or at least in sympathy with the moral ideals that religions, particularly Christianity, espouse. He views religious traditions, particularly the Judeo-Christian-Islamic tradition, as providing a basis of communal life necessary to the defense of moral values in the face of major social change through globalization. He associates with this tradition both tolerance of difference and respect for diversity. He frequently asserts "We are all made in God's image" (West 1989; 1993, 93–94). He wants to see this new turn toward prophetic pragmatism include a focus on religious sensibilities and practices. Thus, prophetic Christianity needs to provide a foundation for meeting the existential demands of a changing world, serving as what he terms an enabling tradition, very much as he sees prophetic black Christianity doing for black communities. And while West is attracted to Marx, his work essentially reflects a theological orientation toward social equality and justice.

West's prophetic pragmatism has been challenged by a number of thinkers, including Rorty (1991) himself, who views it as outside the original intent and confines of American pragmatism. Rorty sees particular difficulty with West connecting pragmatism to prophesy, which Dewey saw as a mode of discovery in the service of democracy. But West has clarified his idea over time. He suggests:

> [P]rophetic pragmatism is a particular historicist interpretation of American pragmatism put forward after such developments as the decolonization of Third World peoples, the second wave of feminism, and the collapse of American apartheid; it is a specific historicist philosophic intervention into our postmodern moment after the rise of analytic philosophy, structuralism, deconstruction, and Western Marxism. The 'prophetic' in prophetic pragmatism refers to both the Protestant sources of the philosophical movement and my own attempt to be true to the blues notes in American history (its own forms of evil and death and its wrestling with tragicomic darkness). . . . [T]he prophetic has little or nothing to do with prediction. Instead, it has to do with identifying, analyzing, and condemning forms of evil and forging vision, hope, and courage for selves and communities to overcome them. Radical democracy is visionary plebodicy—the grand expression of the dignity of the doxa of the suffering demos (West 1993, pp. 350–351).

West's contributions to contemporary discourse on matters of race have been constant and significant. Like bell hooks, he combines scholarship with activism and has inspired people both inside and outside of academic life.

POSTMODERN RACE THEORY

W. Lawrence Hogue (1996), professor of modern thought and literature at the University of Houston, suggests that postmodernism problematizes race categories, meanings, and identities by decentering, shifting away from something that was taken for granted. Race now becomes only one in a constellation of factors associated with identity of more or less importance, depending on the time and/ or place. Therefore, the postmodern world challenges individuals who seek their identity primarily through race because the factors that determine race are constantly in flux—as is the definition of race itself. Race is now constructed through what Hogue refers to as "a nostalgic reconstitution of a center that does not exist" (1996, p. 20). Given the advances in communications technologies, people are no longer exotic. They can no longer be perceived to comprise subspecies. With the development of mass culture, the world has radically changed. Postmodern theorists see a blurring of categories wherein race, gender, sexuality, and class are *floating signifiers*.

Just as people of color frequently borrow and incorporate cultural forms from one another as well as from the so-called white community, white people incorporate cultural forms from those who are nonwhite. Hogue recognizes that this does not mean an end of racism, but rather he sees race becoming one of many factors that comprise one's identity. It is not merely written on the body but also in the psyche. Hogue asserts: "The supposed elimination of differentials stemming from postmodernity . . . does not mean that people of color have achieved full equality in the United States . . . [people] are still discriminated against . . . still experience police brutality because of the color of their skin color" (Hogue 1996, p. 21). Also, most people still carry around deeply embedded stereotypes based on skin color. This is the paradox of postmodernity.

In her critique of postmodern theory, bell hooks claims that, while postmodern theory often privileges an abstract notion of otherness, it often fails to resonate with most people of color in the West or around the world. It has already been suggested here that there is an inherent Eurocentric, male, white, middle-class bias built into the paradigm. It carries assumptions about the European Enlightenment and high modernism, often at the expense of ignoring other enlightenments, thus making the theory itself unappealing. Its references are extensively European. Although it espouses a philosophy of inclusion, most people in the world and conditions under which most people live are not represented by it. Hogue is an exception, but otherwise little postmodern theory has emerged from the black intellectual community.

bell hooks (1990) has made the point that black people are often ignored in the construction of postmodern theory and that white postmodern theorists fail to recognize the connection between the black experience and critical thought about culture and aesthetics. She believes this is bound to turn away people who are neither recognized by nor are included in postmodern discourse. And the language of postmodern discourse itself has been exclusionary, unfriendly, and self-absorbed. It also fails to separate the politics of otherness from the politics of racism.

Yet hooks believes much in postmodern discourse can serve the interests of people of color. This is especially true in its work on identity, particularly the notion of blackness, which is something that has been (at least in part) imposed on black people by those who exert power over media. She contends that the postmodern critique of *essentialism* and contended notions of authenticity are quite powerful. In fact, she sees critiques raised against postmodernism by those favoring an Afrocentric position as frequently a defense of black essentialism and a retreat into isolation. hooks notes:

> Postmodern culture with its *decentered subject* can be the space where ties are severed or it can provide the occasion for new and varied forms of bonding. To some extent ruptures, surfaces, contextuality and a host of other happenings create gaps that make space for oppositional practices which no longer require intellectuals to be confined to narrow, separate spheres with no meaningful connection to the world of every day. Much postmodern engagement with culture emerges from the yearning to do intellectual work that connects with habits of being, forms of artistic expression and aesthetics, that inform the daily life of a mass population as well as writers and scholars (1990).

bell hooks also sees postmodern theory as opening up the opportunities for critical dialogue with others who have been marginalized by creating a new space for critical exchange, a place that can perhaps be the location of critical resistance and radical happenings. The notion of the *borderland* exemplifies such space. It is a space that is both physical and imaginary.

Gloria Anzaldua grew up in the borderlands between Texas and Mexico and was a sixth generation *Tejana* (Texan of Mexican descent), *Chicana* (woman of Mexican descent), and a self-identified *Mestiza*—a word she creates to designate someone who exists in a third place beyond binaries, belonging everywhere and nowhere. This is a person of mixed and conflicting identities. She views the Texas borderlands as a postmodern space. For Anzaldua, borders between countries do not create barriers but rather they engender a form of hybridity—something new that mixes them. Anzaldua (1999) has written extensively on the intersections among race, gender, sexuality, and culture. She points to the complexity in the lives of people of color who are expected to occupy many different categories that are *in between*. Certainly, there is an echo of W. E. B. DuBois notion of *double consciousness* here. She contends: "As a lesbian, I have no race, my own people disclaim me; but I am all races because there is the queer of me in all races" (p. 80) and "I am cultureless because, as a feminist, I challenge the collective cultural/religious male-derived beliefs of Indo-Hispanics and Anglos; yet I am cultured because I am participating in the creation of yet another culture, a new story to explain the world and our participation in it, a new value system with images and symbols that connect us to each other and to the planet" (pp. 80–81). For Anzaldua, the borderland is both metaphorical and geographic, a place where things mix and blend. It is a place of liberation.

WHITENESS STUDIES

The social construction of race has been a significant component of contemporary race theory. Often seen as a trope in the linguistic sense—as an empty signifier that is often used to mean different things at different times—race remains a powerful instrument of oppression throughout the world.

Over the course of the past decade, an entirely new field of race study has emerged. Its focus is on whiteness. The concern here is on social construction of whiteness as a race category. White studies, rather being a reaction to black studies, attempt to understand how whiteness as a racial category has been used as an instrument of oppression and exclusion. Questions raised by white studies scholars are frequently related to matters such as: What constitutes whiteness? How is this category used as a means of discrimination? Historian Peter Kolchin (2005) has examined the development of the new field of whiteness studies. While he generally finds too much emphasis on American versions of whiteness and a lack of historiography that would place whiteness in the context of European empire, he recognizes how it has refocused scholars and theorists on the morphology of race and the importance of whiteness as an ideological construct used to support slavery and other forms of economic and social oppression.

Studies in whiteness vary significantly and range from social science to literary criticism. (Biological essentialism seems at long last out of favor.) And while most students of race see whiteness are socially constructed as blackness, some try to figure out exactly who white people are and what they are like culturally—a rather bold undertaking.

Timothy Barnett (2000), a professor of English at Northeastern Illinois University, makes several observations on the findings or propositions advanced by students of white studies in literature. Such qualities are seen as essential to the idea of whiteness and have been used historically to establish and maintain white dominance in English studies. These qualities include (1) the seeming invisibility of whiteness, which promotes whiteness as normal and thus invisible through coded discourse on race; (2) the promotion of whiteness as unraced, which hides its political and economic interests; (3) the suggestion that whiteness somehow represents the opposite of otherness and that the other is always raced, always part of a closed tribal network living outside the normative of the unraced; (4) the idea that whiteness is not tied to skin color per se but it is related to the notion of race (which it has primarily invented) without being one; and (5) the idea that whiteness reserves for itself the ultimate power to define race according to its political, social, and economic interests. In his groundbreaking book *How the Irish Became White* (1995) Noel Ignatiev, who is both a civil rights activist and a Marxist scholar, has looked at the Irish Catholic experience in the waves of emigration to the United States in the eighteenth and nineteenth centuries. While the Irish came to the America to escape caste, harsh oppression, and discrimination, they were totally unfamiliar with the notion of race determining social position. As Ignatiev points out, however: "[T]hey adapted to it in short order" (p. 2). The Irish and Free Blacks often occupied the same slums, sometimes intermarried, and developed a common culture of the disenfranchised, but the Irish were to leave behind their nonwhite status and were allowed access to white citizenship and greater participation in white society. They would go from targets of discrimination to beneficiaries of the oppression against black people who were their friends and neighbors. But how did they become white? How were they able to make this transition in racial status? Ignatiev's hypothesis is that the price for becoming white was to join in and frequently lead the attacks on black people. Discrimination became a way of gaining advantage over their closest competitors in the labor market. By becoming white and identifying blacks as other and lesser, the Irish underclass gained powerful political and economic advantages that they, their children, and grandchildren would all benefit from.

Ignatiev, who teaches at the Massachusetts College of Art, has written for and promoted a website and publication known as *Race Traitor*. The journal promotes the notion that "treason to whiteness is loyalty to humanity" (see http://academic.udayton.edu/race/01race/traitor.htm). Noel Ignatiev, Dayton Law School professor Vernellia Randall, and others who advance this position have been attacked for hating white people. Their counterclaim is that they merely oppose race identity and white privilege associated with it.

CRITICAL RACE THEORY

A perspective that appears to be making inroads with a wider nonacademic audience, but one focused on issues of race and inequality, is Critical Race Theory (CRT). Less of a theoretical position than a political one, CRT is a stream of theoretical propositions and ideas that originated with the civil rights lawyers and legal activists in the 1970s. While this category of theory grew out of American legal academic conferences and paper presentations, its origins can be traced to the Critical Legal Studies (CLS) movement founded in 1977 at a legal conference at the University of Wisconsin at Madison. This grouping of organizers consisted of people who had been legally trained in the 1960s, some of whom had been active in the civil rights movement in the United States. While the initial aim of these scholars has been to attack the racial inequities that exist within and throughout the legal system, they also challenge the system itself, particularly the legal thinking that provided a basis for racist court decisions and legal procedures. Legal scholar Alan Hunt (1987, p. 5) called CLS "a movement in search of a theory." Some of the founders of critical legal studies broke away because they considered it too narrowly focused and concerned only with "incremental change" (Peters 2005, p. vii).

Richard Delgado, a founder of critical race theory and a former professor of law at the University of Pittsburgh Law School, has written extensively in this field. In opposition to poststructural theory, Delgado (Delgado and Stefancic 2000, pp. xvi-xvii) contends that critical race theory is built on a set of basic insights, including, (1) racism is normal and not aberrant in U.S. society, (2) laws that treat whites and blacks alike can remedy only the more extreme forms of injustice, and (3) white elites will tolerate racial social change only when it serves their own interests.

Another of the field's founders is Derrick Bell, a legal scholar, civil rights activist, and former Harvard Law professor. Bell is respected as one of the primary contributors to the notion of *interest-convergence*. In an article that served as a foundation to critical race theory, he argued that the U.S. Supreme Court decision of *Brown v. Board of Education* as well as the civil rights reforms of the 1960s were not as much products of liberal judges or an Enlightened American public but rather were necessary to burnish the tarnished image of the United States in the rest of the world and to avert racial unrest at home. When advances no longer served the interests of white elites, they were halted (Bell 1980).

The real challenge encountered in critical race theory is its attempt to integrate **humanism**, Marxism, critical theory of the Frankfurt school, American pragmatism, poststructuralism of Lacan and Foucault, deconstruction of Derrida, gender theory of Butler, and postmodern thought and apply all of this to social issues and to law and legal matters pertaining to race. Therefore, its central weakness is not having a particular theoretical perspective at all. Its apparent strength is its areas of study: law, white racism, and the impact they have on society and issues of social justice. Still, it has been made clear that practitioners of CRT see themselves as both scholars and moral activists as opposed to intellectuals and liberal reformers. Their aim is to bring about racial equality through social change (Ladson-Billings and Donnor 2000).

Much of critical race theory focuses on the production and reproduction of white hegemony through an institutionally racist legal system. It insists on recognizing the validity of the experiential knowledge of people of color. A primary research method therefore is narrative or counter storytelling. Accordingly, it is proposed that white narratives support white racial hegemony. A "stock" story justifies the world as it is by perpetuating inequality under a regime of "contested white supremacy," which could mean something like relating a story that would show how affirmative action discriminates against white people. In **counter storytelling**, researchers collect stories from people who have been discriminated against in employment or education, thus exposing the hidden racism in the stock story. According to sociologist Christopher Schneider (2004, p. 93): "Their hope is that stories of black and brown persons can reach readers and listeners and help bridge the gap between their worlds and those of others." Presenting these alternative realities as truth is a challenge that critical race theorists face because their efforts are often thwarted by counter storytelling in white-dominated media. Not finding much acceptance in the realm of poststructural discourse, CRT has found acceptance in a field that it helped to establish—critical race pedagogy (Taylor, Gillborn, and Landson-Billings 2009).

CRT has sprouted many branches: Critical Race Feminism (CRF), Latino Critical Race Studies (Lat Crit), Asian American Critical Race Studies (Asian Crit), American Indian Critical Race Studies (Tribal Crit), Critical Race Pedagogy (CRP), and Critical White Studies (CWS). All have generated research, conferences, and publications. CRT has easily entered into scholarly discourse and has met with varying degrees of success around the world. Like its predecessor black studies (which has not been able to sustain the appeal as it had in the 1960s and 1970s), it is part social movement and part academic project. But unlike black studies, CRT's intellectual interests and focus appear significantly broader. Much of it is an attempt to reach nonacademic audiences, so it is usually written in accessible prose. Still, its efforts to use theoretical paradigms developed by Europeans has been considered by some as racially conciliatory.

AFROCENTRIC THEORY: MOLEFI KETE ASANTE

Afrocentrism is a discourse of reaction to Eurocentrism and the intractability of racist white supremacy in American and European societies. As a field of research and theory, it emerges from a variety of sources, but its purpose is to reveal the hidden history of African culture and its importance to the world. It rejects the trajectory of what it considers to be white social theory.

Molefi Kete Asante, a professor of African American studies at Temple University, is credited with being one of the leading contributors and exponents of Afrocentric research, which posits that Africa is the cradle of all civilization. Asante is American born (his birth name was Arthur Lee Smith), and he was schooled at Oklahoma Christian College and the University of California at Los Angeles, from which he received his doctorate in communications studies. He has been a prolific author and a controversial thinker.

Afrocentrism is chiefly an American phenomenon, having emerged from the black power struggles in the 1960s and the eventual development of black studies programs at universities across the United States. Asante's first book, *Afrocentricity: The Theory of Social Change* (1980), was an attempt to move black studies away from an inherently white perspective and to help formulate a new way of understanding the experience of African descendants. Afrocentric theory is not as much interested in exploring the concept of race, and appears to accept race as an essentialist category. Its struggle here is to confront white racism on its own terms. Having its start in the 1960s, its goal is to restore a mode of black pride to a people dehumanized and oppressed by as system of institutionalized white power. And as Asante notes (2008, p. 33), "Afrocentricity is a paradigm based on the idea that African people should re-assert a sense of agency in order to achieve sanity".

According to Asante, the Afrocentric view is a *constructural adjustment* to black disorientation, decenteredness, and a lack of agency. The Afrocentrist asks the question, "What would African people do if there were no white people?" (Asante 2009, p. 33). Its goal as a paradigm is to remove Europe from the center of African reality. Its standpoint is to see black people "as subjects and not as objects, basing all knowledge on authentic interrogation of location" (Asante 2007, p. 15).

Asante proposes that a primary assumption of this theory is that it recognizes that "all relationships are based on centers and margins" and that only when black people see themselves as central to their own history will they be able to recognize themselves as active agents of change. One way to achieve this is through what Asante calls marking. By *marking*, Asante means creating a bond between oneself and other black people by identifying, or marking, heroes of black culture such as Franz Fanon or Malcolm X (1997). This theory recognizes that the consciousness of most black people is false and is based on the consciousness of the powerful white elite, which is the primary source of black oppression. It also proposes that most white history is also false and covers up the important contributions of Africans to human progress and culture. African civilization is rich in history that has been denied by white Europeans and Americans.

Asante (2008, p. 34) identifies five characteristics of the Afrocentric method: (1) locating all phenomena to be studied in psychological time and space; (2) recognizing the diverse, dynamic, and changing nature of all phenomena, including the investigator and that being investigated; (3) using cultural criticism that examines the ethnological use of words in order to "locate" the author; (4) uncovering the masks concealing the rhetoric of power in order to understand how myths create place; and (5) locating imaginative systems of power. All of this is to be applied to textual analysis.

He proposes that Afrocentrism is humanistic and is inherently opposed to postmodernism and notions of radical individualism and social constructionism. It is strongly communal and collective in nature, thus proposing that there is an African community and experience that unites all black people who live on in Africa and who have left the continent. It is only through recognizing this unity that white racism can be addressed meaningfully.

Afrocentric theorists purposefully avoid engaging with poststructural race theory, most of which they tend to discard out of hand as white theory, or theory utilizing a Eurocentric perspective. Clarence Walker (2001), a professor of history at the University of California at Davis, has been highly critical of this perspective in terms of what he views as its deeply flawed understanding of history and its application.

POST-RACE THEORY: PAUL GILROY

If race is a trope, if it is a fiction, why would it have material importance? The reason is expressed most clearly in the work of Paul Gilroy (whose work on postcolonialism has been discussed in Chapter 7). While agreeing that race is a construct, Gilroy also concedes that it enacts a powerful influence on people's lives and has real, tangible consequences—consequences that can result in genocide. This notion of a post-racial society is an important element in the work of social constructionists (Nayak 2006).

Certainly there is a type of utopianism here in saying that race will or may come to an end, or even that it has come to an end. However, few social theorists would ever make this claim. What some do claim is that race is no longer viewed as an essentialistic phenomenon and, as such, it is what discourse makes of it. It is malleable—a floating signifier. The linguistic turn of which Foucault and Derrida spoke was in part a profound recognition that words are enormously powerful constructs. Gilroy (2000) has observed that we are living in a time of profound transformation in the way in which race is both perceived and acted on. Yet he warns that many other elements of our identity are now being challenged. Unlike many other scholars of a more traditional bent, he welcomes race's dissolution.

Gilroy's earlier work, *The Black Atlantic* (1993), helped advance the notion of the *diaspora* as a substitute for examining race through national frameworks, which he contended were inadequate for forming significant identities. Such a concept allowed for a more critical appraisal of the historical and experiential difference between location and belonging. It was a concept that could unify people of African descent from all over the world. It allowed one to discard the hyphenated illusion of national identity. In that same work, Gilroy rejects contemporary Afrocentrism as akin to a mythical racist ideology void of sound methodology and penetrating thought. He equates it to European beliefs of racial and ethnic superiority and subtle forms of fascism.

In attacking race as an illusionary signifier void of any validity, Gilroy draws on the poststructural and postmodern work of theorists ranging from Michel Foucault to Donna Haraway, as well as biologists and social scientists, to support his contention. He steadfastly rebuffs any authenticity of race. He sees race-thinking as dehumanizing, not only for those who become targets of discrimination, but also for those who engage in using it to their advantage. This brings him to reject the commercialization of multiculturalism, too, which he believes helps to divide people and perpetuate illusions of otherness where none exists. He sees the commercialization of race, but particularly blackness, as an advertising and public relations distortion of reality and perpetuation of racist myths in the service of oppressive capitalism. His work is evidence of a strong undercurrent of Marx and poststructural thought.

The struggle to put an end to race as a signifier of consequence once and for all is something Gilroy views as a critical challenge. It is one that must not only overcome what he sees as the resistance in white society to letting go of a powerful tool of control and oppression, but must also come to terms with important figures in what he sees as the so-called black community as well as a new conservativism he observes emerging in middle-class black life. Racial categories have been imbued with much personal and historical meaning and to give up race will be a significant challenge. He stands alongside feminist and queer theorists who view gender and sexual categorizations as closely linked to global oppression. But Gilroy calls for a rejection of all identity politics and has embraced a movement toward a more individualistic cosmopolitanism.

KEY TERMS

Afrocentrism A political and theoretical movement developed by scholar/activist Molefi Asante. It places African ideals at the center of any analysis and attempts to uncover the true history, not only of Africans but also their world prominence that has been covered over by white historians and scholars.

borderland Indicating something (a space, a place, an idea, a symbol, or even a way of life) that is located between two or more distinct areas of identified meaning, which develops a marginalized character or way of life of its own.

constructural adjustment A term used by Afrocentrists to describe their efforts to reveal hidden white social obstacles to black agency in order to reenergize it.

counter storytelling Calling into question a narrative presented as true, which is actually biased from a white perspective, by presenting in its place an alternative narrative reflecting the black experience.

decentered subject The object of decentering (a postmodern term), which means calling into question the subject's stability and true meaning by challenging its foundation.

diaspora The geographic scattering of a group of people who share a common culture or place of origin.

double consciousness A term used by W. E. B. DuBois to describe understanding the world (particularly white society) through the eyes of the dominant group and also understanding it as an outsider or member of an outcaste group.

essentialism The proposition in race studies that race is innate and determines a variety of social outcomes. Also, a term that is applied generally to mean that in nature are discoverable, essential elements of every object.

floating signifiers A term in semiotics to mean a word or sign that is empty and can be made to mean various things.

humanism In the context of social theory, humanism can be either focusing on the values associated with human beings, or a more formalized notion that humans reflect certain inherent characteristics that set them above all other species.

interest convergence A belief that progressive change occurs for African people in white society only if it serves the interests of white elites.

marking In Afrocentric theory, the process of identifying black heroes in order to promote the achievements of people of African descent and to help provide a basis for black community.

Mestiza A world invented by Gloria Anzaldua, an American activist and poet, who sees the Mestiza as a third space that exists outside two places (between borders of countries, for example) but gains its identity from both. This notion is close to the concept of hybridity, which represents various cultural, sexual, and social identities within one person.

prophetic pragmatism A concept developed by Cornel West that represents a combination of the American philosophic pragmatism of Dewey and the Christian notion of prophetic humanism often evident in black churches. West sees prophetic pragmatism as a means of achieving greatness as a culture.

racialized body The concept that bodies are socially ascribed a race based on physical features.

SOURCES

Anzaldua, Gloria. 1999. *Borderlands: The New Mestiza/La Frontera.* San Francisco, CA: Aunt Lute Books.

Asante, Molefi Kete. 1980. *Afrocentricity: The Social Theory of Change.* Chicago, IL: Third World Press.

Asante, Molefi Kete. 1997. Fall. "Afrocentricism and World Politics: Toward a New Paradigm," *African American Review.* Electronic format.

Asante, Molefi Kete. 2007. *An Afrocentric Manifesto*. Malden, MA: Polity Press.

Asante, Molefi Kete. 2008. "Afrocentricity," in V. Pariello, ed., *Encyclopedia of Social Problems*. Thousand Oaks, CA: Sage.

Barkan, Elazar. 1992. *The Retreat of Scientific Racism*. New York: Cambridge University Press.

Barnett, Timothy. 2000. "Reading 'Whiteness' in English Studies," *College English*, Vol. 63, No. 1, pp. 9–37.

Bell, Derrick. 1980. "Brown v. Board of Education and the Interest Convergence Dilemma," *Harvard Law Review*, Vol. 93, pp. 518–533.

Dain, Bruce. 2002. *A Hideous Monster of the Mind: American Race Theory in the Early Republic*. Cambridge, MA: Harvard University Press.

Delgado, Richard, and Jean Stefancic. 2000. *Critical Race Theory: The Cutting Edge*. Philadelphia, PA: Temple University Press.

DuBois, W. E. B. 2009. *Dusk of Dawn: An Essay Toward an Autobiography of a Race Concept*. Piscataway, NJ: Transaction Press.

Frankenberg, Ruth. 1993. *White Women, Race Matters: The Social Construction of Whiteness*. London: Routledge.

Gates, Henry Louis. 1985. "Writing 'Race' and the Difference It Makes," *Critical Inquiry*, Vol. 12, No. 1, pp. 1–12.

Gates, Henry Louis. 1986. *Race, Writing and Difference*. Chicago: University of Chicago Press.

Gates, Henry Louis. 1988. *The Signifying Monkey: A Theory of African American Literary Criticism*. New York: Oxford University Press.

Gilroy, Paul. 1993. *Black Atlantic: Modernity and Double-Consciousness*. Cambridge, MA: Harvard University Press.

Gilroy, Paul. 2000. *Against Race: Imagining Political Culture Beyond the Color Line*. Cambridge, MA: Harvard University Press.

Gould, Stephen Jay. 1981. *The Mismeasure of Man*. New York: W. W. Norton.

Hegel, Georg Wilhelm Friedrich 1970. *Vorlesunger uber die Philosophie der Geschichte*. Trans. by M. Mies Frankfurt: Suhrkamp.

Hogue, W. Lawrence. 1996. *Race, Modernity, Postmodernity: A Look at the History and Literatures of People of Color Since the 1960s*. Albany, NY: SUNY Press.

hooks, bell. 1990. "Postmodern Blackness," *Postmodern Culture*, Vol. 1, No. 1, Electronic format.

Hunt, Alan. 1987. "The Critique of Law: What Is 'Critical' About Critical Legal Theory," *Journal of Law and Society*, Vol. 14, No. 1.

Ignatiev, Noel. 1995. *How the Irish Became White*. New York: Routledge.

Joyce, Joyce. 1987. "The Black Canon: Reconstructing American Literary Criticism," *New Literary History*, Vol. 18, No. 2, pp. 335–344.

Kolchin, Peter. 2005. "Whiteness Studies: The New History of Race in America," *Journal of American History*, Vol. 89, No. 1.

Ladson-Billings, Gloria, and Janel Donnor. 2000. "The Moral Activist Role of Critical Race Theory Scholarship," in N. K. Denzin and Y. Lincoln, eds., *The Sage Handbook of Qualitative Research*, 3rd ed. Thousand Oaks, CA: Sage.

Loomba, Ania. 1998. *Colonialism/Postcolonialism*. London: Routledge.

Nayak, Anoop. 2006. "After Race: Ethnography, Race, and Post-race theory," *Ethnic and Racial Studies*, Vol. 29, No. 3, pp. 411–430.

Peters, Michael A. 2005. "Editorial," in Z. Leonardo, ed., *Critical Pedagogy and Race*. Malden, MA: Blackwell.

Rorty, Richard. 1991. "The Philosopher and Prophet," *Transition*, Vol. 52, pp. 000–000.

Schneider, Christopher J. 2004. "Integrating Critical Race Theory and Postmodernism: Implications for Race, Class, and Gender," *Critical Criminology,* Vol. 12, No. 1, pp. 87–103.

Taylor, Edward, David Gillborn, and Gloria Landson-Billings 2009. *Foundations of Critical Race Theory in Education.* New York: Routledge.

Walker, Clarence E. 2001. *We Can't Go Home Again: An Argument About Afrocentrism.* New York: Oxford University Press.

West, Cornel. 1982. *Prophesy Deliverance: An Afro-American Revolutionary Christianity.* Louisville, KY: Westminster John Knox Press.

West, Cornel. 1989. *American Evasion of Philosophy.* Madison: University of Wisconsin Press.

West, Cornel. 1993. *Race Matters.* New York: Vintage Books.

West, Cornel. 1993a. *Prophetic Thoughts in Postmodern Times.* Monroe, ME: Common Courage Press.

West, Cornel. 1993–1994, Winter. "The Dilemma of the Black Intellectual," *Journal of Blacks in Higher Education,* No. 2, pp. 59–67.

Winant, Howard. 2000. "Race Theory Today," *Annual Review of Sociology,* Vol. 26, pp. 169–185.

Young, Robert. 2001. "The Linguistic Turn, Materialism and Race: Toward an Aesthetics of Crisis," *Callaloo,* Vol. 24, No. 1, pp. 334–345.

Index

A

Actor network theory (ANT), 33
Adorno, Theodor, 6, 23, 78, 86, 92, 134,
    139–141, 146
Afrocentric feminist theory, 114. *See also* Feminism
Afrocentrism, 143, 202, 210–212
Agency, 10, 31, 33, 69
    and structure, 35–37, 98, 146
Agger, Ben, 65–66, 79–80, 84, 85
Ahistoricism, 142
Ahmed, Sara, 85, 127
Akbar, Ahmed, 174–176
    globalization from below, 175
Alain-Miller, Jacques, 76
Alexander, Jeffrey, 28
Alford, C. Fred, 57
Althusser, Louis, 24–25, 36, 46, 64–65, 69, 135–136
    Ideological State Apparatus, 25
    ideology, 76
    interpellation, 25, 40, 135, 147
    Repressive State Apparatus, 25
Amadiume, Ifi, 125
Anderson, Perry, 133
Androcentric, 116, 128
Ang, Ien, 144–146
Anthropology, 199
    cultural anthropology, 33
    functionalism in, 16–17
    hermeneutic anthropology, 55
    structural anthropology, 23, 24
Antiglobalization movement, 163, 175
Anzaldua, Gloria, 206–207
    Mestiza, 206
Aristotle, 35
Arrighi, Giovanni, 158–159
Art, 5, 85, 142, 192, 202
    modern art, 87

Asante, Molefi Kete, 210–211. *See also* Afrocentrism
Authenticity, 101, 205

B

Background assumptions, 51
Bakhtin, Mikhail, 90, 134
    carnivalesque, 134
Barkan, Elazar, 199
Barnett, Timothy, 207
Barthes, Roland, 25–27, 34–35, 63, 65, 70, 76, 100, 132,
    135, 201
Bateson, 17
Battaille, 26
Baudrillard, Jean, 100–102
    symbolic value, 100
    use and exchange value, 100
Bauman, Zygmunt, 29, 58, 97–100
    liquid modernity, 99
Beauvoir, Simone de, 11, 106, 181
Bell, Derrick, 208–209
Benjamin, Jessica, 108, 121–122, 185
    Hegel's influence, 121
    Lacan, 122
Benjamin, Walter, 6, 132, 141, 146
Berger, Peter, 47
Bergson, Henri, 8–9, 56
Bertalanffy, Ludwig van, 18
Bhabha, Homi, 155–156
    doubling, 155
    hybrid identity, 156
Binary oppositions, 22, 23, 40, 64, 118–119, 127
    gender binary, 186, 188, 189, 194
Biological determinism, 181–183
    biologism, 108, 128
Biological foundationalism, 182, 194
Biologism, 108, 128. *See also* Biological determinism
Biopolitics, 163, 176

Black studies, 209–210
Blau, Peter, 16, 30–31
Blumenbach, Johann Friedrich, 199
Blumer, Herbert, 45, 46
Body, 53, 96, 118–120
    and consciousness, 9
    and culture, 119
    female, 75, 119
    intentionality of, 53, 60
    racialized body, 202, 213
    sexed body, 193–194
    and wisdom, 5
Body without Organs (BwO), 95, 102
Borderland, 206, 212
Bordo, Susan, 119–120, 126
    Cartesian philosophy, 126
    Enlightenment thought, 126
Bourdieu, Pierre, 37–38, 58
    Habitus and Field, 37–38, 58–59, 98
Bourgeoisie, 2, 3, 101, 141, 158
Braudel, Fernand, 158, 159
Brecht, Bartolt, 132
Bretton Woods agreements, 159, 167
Bricmont, Jean, 79
Butler, Judith, 5, 119–120, 125–127, 139, 185, 187–188,
    190, 191, 193
    heterosexual melancholia, 188
    performance, 187
    and postmoderenism, 125

C

Callinicos, Alex, 164–165
Capital accumulation, 29–30, 159, 160
Capitalism, 3, 38, 95, 117, 157, 160. *See also* Late
    capitalism
    Althusser on, 25
    boundaries, 78
    and culture, 133, 140, 141, 142
    and Empire, 163
    and feminism, 107, 111, 116–117, 125
    global, 156, 157–160, 163, 164, 168
    Marx on, 3, 38
    and postmodernity, 94, 95, 101
    as a revolutionary force, 78
Carnivalesque, 134, 147
Carnivalization, 90, 102. *See also* Bakhtin, Mikhail
Castells, Manuel, 32, 168–169
Center for Contemporary Cultural Studies (CCCS),
    132, 134, 147
Césaire, Aimé, 150
Chicago school, 33, 45
Chodorow, Nancy, 108, 120–121, 123, 185
Chomsky, Noam, 23, 79

Civil rights movement, 10, 198
Cixous, Hélène, 75, 108, 110, 118–119
    l'ecriture feminine, 118
Coleman, James, 31
    Coleman Report, 31
Collective conscience, 17
Collective consciousness, 53, 154
Collins, Patricia Hill, 112–116, 143
    additive approach, 114
    Afrocentrism and feminism, 114
    matrix of oppression, 116
Colonialism, 151
Commodification, 3, 12, 78, 88
Comte, Auguste, 2, 14
Conflict theory, 19, 38–39
Connectedness, 70–71, 97, 99, 173
Conscious/consciousness, 5–6, 25, 53
    and body, 9
    collective consciousness, 53, 154
    double consciousness, 109, 128, 143, 206, 213
    false consciousness, 4, 13, 24, 77, 109, 141
Constitutive reflexivity, 89, 102
Constructionism, 35–36, 80, 90
    versus essentialism, 36
    of race, 200–201
Consumerism, 99, 119, 133, 134
Cooley, Charles Horton, 70
Corporality of consciousness, 53, 59
Cosmopolitan democracy, 166, 176
Counter storytelling, 209, 213
Critical Legal Studies (CLS) movement, 208
Critical race theory, 207–210
Cultural materialism, 137, 147
Cultural turn, 66–69, 150
Culture/culturalism, 132–147. *See also* Popular
    culture
    black cultural studies, 143–144
    depthlessness of, 142
    and economics, 172
    and feminism, 137–139
    and human activities, 136
    and postmodernism, 92
    and race, 200
    and social theory, 146–147
    working-class culture, 136
Culture industry, 137, 144, 145, 147

D

Decentered subject, 63, 206, 213
Decolonization, 151, 176
Deconstructionism, 63–66, 79–80, 81, 108
Deep structure, 16, 23, 40, 67
    and network analysis, 32

Deleuze, Gilles, 93–95, 100, 163. *See also* Deluze and Gattari
Deluze and Gattari, 93–96, 163
  aborescence, 93, 102
  Anti-Oedipus, 93–95
  Body Without Organs, 95
  deterritorialization, 95
  flows, 95
  reactive and productive desire, 94
  rhimzones, 93–94
Delgado, Richard, 208
D'Emilio, John, 190
Dependency theory, 158, 176
Derrida, Jacques, 10, 39, 63–66, 69–70, 72, 75, 108, 119, 153, 154, 156, 201, 212. *See also* Deconstructionism
Dewey, John, 43, 45, 47, 203, 204
Dialectical materialism, 132, 147
Diaspora, 143, 212, 213
Diasporic culture, 143, 144, 147
Différance, 64, 81
Dilthey, Wilhelm, 44, 45
Di Stefano, Christine, 126
Double consciousness, 109, 128, 143, 206, 213
Doubling, in colonialism, 155
DuBois, W. E. B., 11, 43, 109, 143, 200–201, 203, 206
Durkheim, Emile, 1–3, 10, 14, 16–18, 28, 38, 53, 54
Dworkin, Andrea, 107
Dystopianism, 142, 147

E

Eagleton, Terry, 92, 139–141
  ideology, 140
  literary criticism, 140
Ebert, Teresa, 127
Einfühlung, 45, 59
Elliot, Lisa, 181–182
Emirbayer, Mustafa, 33
Empire, 163–164, 199–200
Empiricism, 46, 53, 66. 146
Emplotment, 35, 40
Enlightenment Project. *See* European Enlightenment
Epistemic violence, 154, 176
Essentialism, 40, 190, 205–206, 213
  versus social constructionism, 36, 40
  strategic essentialism, 154, 177
Ethnomethodology, 51–52, 59
European Enlightenment, 2–3, 5, 21, 40, 56, 84, 97, 126
  Enlightenment Project, 21
  and modernity, 87–88, 91, 98
  and race, 198–200

Exchange theory, 16, 17, 77
  and rational choice theory, 30–31
Exchange value, 100, 103

F

False binaries, 118, 145
False consciousness, 4, 13, 24, 77, 141
  proletarian false consciousness, 109
Fanon, Frantz, 150–151
  Algeria, 151
Fascism, 94, 97, 133, 212
Fausto-Sterling, Ann, 127
Felski, Rita, 85, 126–127
Femininities, 184–185. *See also* Gender
Feminism, 106–127
  and cultural studies, 137–139
  French feminism, 108–109, 113, 118
  institutional ethnography, 109–111
  lesbian feminism, 122–124
  life-based feminism, 117
  Marxist influence on, 107
  neoliberalism, 117
  postcolonial feminism, 124–125
  postmodernism and postfeminism, 125–127
  poststructuralism, 71–75, 118–120
  psychoanalytic, 120–122
  and race, 112–116
  radical feminism, 107, 108, 128
  retraditionalizing, 139, 148
  socialist feminism, 116
  standpoint theory, 111–112, 128
  and structuralism, 107–109
  second wave, 106, 116, 122, 127, 128
  third wave, 127, 129
Fischer, Claude S., 32
Flax, Jane, 126
Floating signifiers, 85, 205, 211, 213
Flows, of desire, 95–96, 103
Foucault, Michel, 5, 10, 23, 25, 27, 52, 63, 66–69, 72, 152, 154, 156, 186–187, 190, 209, 212
  and feminist theory, 117
  fictitious unity, 186
  Fragmentation, 90, 97
Frankenberg, Ruth, 200, 201
Frankfurt school, 6–7, 13, 57, 70, 76, 78, 112, 132, 134, 137, 146, 147, 209
  culture industry, 137
Fraser, Nancy, 108, 116–118
  identity politics, 117
  redistributive justice, 117
Freud, Sigmund, 5–6, 21, 66, 72, 76, 96, 108, 185, 201
  feminist theory, 107, 122
  gender, 185

Freud, Sigmund (*continued*)
  Interpretation of Dreams, 6
  and Lacan
  and Nietzsche, 5
  the unconscious, 96
Friedan, Betty, 113
Friedman, Thomas, 162
Functionalism, 38. *See also* Structural-functionalism
  and anthropology, 16–17
  neofunctionalism, 28
Fundamentalism, 162, 174–175

G

Garfinkel, Harold, 51–52, 99, 109
Garvey, Marcus, 144
Gates, Henry Louis, 201–203
Gay Left Collective, 189
Gender, 180, 181. *See also* Queer theory
  binary of, 186, 188, 189, 194
  biological determinism, 181–183
  gay and lesbian theory, 189–191
  limits of, 187–188
  and performance, 188
  and psychoanalysis, 185–186
  sexed bodies, 193–194
  and sexuality and poststructuralism, 186–187
  socialization, 183–184
  transgender, 192–193
General Systems Theory, 18
Giddens, Anthony, 6, 29, 36–38, 88–89, 161–162, 164, 168
  time-space distanciation, 88, 103, 161
Gift exchange. *See* Exchange theory
Gilroy, Paul, 143–144, 211–212
  diasporic culture, 144
  transnational character, 143
Global domains, 167, 176
Globalization, 29, 156–157. *See also* World Systems Theory
  from below, 175–176
  democratic, 165–167
  and Empire, 163–164
  global imperialism, 164–165
  global theory, 28–29
  incipient phase, of globalization, 170
  international division of labor, 162
  McDonaldization, 171–172
  minimal phase model of, 170
  and modernization, 161–162
  postmodern, 172–174
  resistance, 174–176
  as a spatial fix, 159–161
  and territories, 167–168
  world capitalist economy, 162

Glocalization, 171, 176
Goffman, Erving, 17, 46, 109
Goodwin, Jeff, 33
Gould, Stephen Jay, 200
Gouldner, Alvin, 46
Gramsci, Antonio, 133–134, 135, 152
  hegemonic culture, 133
  Prison Notebooks, 133
Grands récits (grand narratives), 80, 89, 97, 103
Guattari, Felix, 93–95, 163. *See also* Deluze and Guittari
Guha, Ranajit, 153–154

H

Habermas, Jürgen, 7, 86–88, 91
Halbwachs, Maurice, 56
Hall, Stuart, 132, 133–137
Haraway, Donna, 120, 127, 182, 183, 212
  cyborgs, 120
Harding, Sandra, 111–112
  Foucault, 111
  standpoint theory, 112
Hardt, Michael, 163–164. *See also* Hardt and Negri
Hardt and Negri, 163–164
  biopolitical machine, 163
  Empire, 163
  nonplaces, 163
Harvey, David, 29, 91–93, 159–161, 173
  over accumulation, 160
Hassan, Ihab, 89–91
Hegel, G. W. Friedrich, 2, 6, 26, 46, 71, 109, 146, 199, 201
Hegemony, 133, 134, 147, 152, 176
Hegemony struggle phase, of globalization, 170
Heidegger, Martin, 7, 9, 45, 48, 53, 64, 112
Held, David, 145, 165–167
  cosmopolitan elite, 166
  cosmopolitan democracy, 166
Hermeneutics, 43–44, 60
  ethnomethodology, 51–52
  hermeneutic circle, 55, 60
  social life, textual understanding of, 54–56
  symbolic interaction and life-world, 46–48
  and phenomenology, 58–59
Heteroglossia, 134, 147
Heterosexuality, 189. *See also* Gender
  and male dominance, 122–123
  melancholia, 188, 195
  obligatory heterosexuality, 191, 195
Hines, Sally, 182, 192, 193
  transgender theory, 192
Hirschfeld, Mangus, 193
Hoggart, Richard, 132

Hogue, W. Lawrence, 204–205
Homans, George, 15, 18, 30
Homophobia, 123, 190, 191
Homosexuality, 188, 190. *See also* Gender; Queer theory
Homosocial desire, 191, 195
hooks, bell, 112–116, 205–206
    on French feminists, 113
Horkheimer, Max, 7, 23, 70, 78, 146
Horney, Karen, 120
Husserl, Edmund, 6, 8, 47–48, 51, 59
Huyssens, Andreas, 92
Hybridity, 145–146, 147, 156, 206
    hybridization, 90
    identities, 156, 177

I

Ideal type, 49, 60
Identity, 11, 98–99, 101, 145–146, 166
    black identity, 143
    hybrid identities, 156, 177
    legitimizing identity, 169
    marginalized identity, 74, 99, 155–156, 192
    politics, 116, 117, 128, 190
    project identity, 169
    resistance identity, 169
    sexual identity, 186, 190, 192
Ideology, 24–26, 36, 57, 76–78, 80, 81
    culture and, 135–136, 140, 141, 145
    Ideological State Apparatus, 25
    and racism, 143
Ignatiev, Noel, 207–208. *See also* White Studies
Imaginary, 70, 71, 95, 142
Imperialism, global, 164–165
Interest-convergence, 208–209, 213
Interpretative theory. *See* Hermeneutics
Intersexed individuals, 194, 195
Intersubjectivity/intersubjective, 8, 35, 49–50, 53–54, 56, 60, 122
Irigaray, Luce, 72–73, 108, 113

J

Jakobson, Roman, 23
Jameson, Fredric, 91–93, 138, 141–142
James, William, 43, 203
Jeffreys, Sheila, 124
Joissance, 118
    excess jouissance, 78, 81
Joyce, Joyce, 202

K

Kant, Immanuel, 2, 46, 77–78, 91, 199, 201
    and the sublime, 77–78

Kellner, Douglas, 173, 176
Kimmel, Michael, 184
Kinsey, Alfred, 193
Klein, Melanie, 120–121, 185
Kolchin, Peter, 207
Kristeva, Julia, 73–75, 108, 113, 127, 185
    third space, 127
Kula Ring Exchange, 1617
Kundera, Milan, 79

L

Labial "lips, " 73, 81
Lacan, Jacques, 6, 10, 26–28, 52, 63, 65, 69–74, 76, 93, 108, 119–120, 125–126, 156, 185, 187–188
    and feminism, 106, 108, 117, 122
    Imaginary, 70, 142
    mirror stage of life, 70–71
    Name of the Father, 71
    Real, 76
    Symbolic, 78, 117
Laing, R.D., 107, 108
Language, 8, 39, 70, 71. *See also* Linguistic turn
Late capitalism, 92–93, 142, 147, 173. *See also* Captalism
Latour, Bruno, 33
Lefebvre, Henri, 95, 100
Legitimation, 37, 99
Lemert, Charles, 79
Lesbian feminism, 122–124, 128. *See also* Feminism; Gender
Le temps modernes, 52–53
LeVay, Simon, 182
Levinas, Emmanuel, 56–58
Levi-Strauss, Claude, 9, 16, 17, 23–27, 29, 46, 54, 66, 70, 135
Lewis, Bernard, 153
LGBT (Lesbian, Gay, Bi and Transexual) studies, 189. *See also* Gender
Libidinal economies, 75, 96
Life-world, 48, 49, 50, 51, 60, 87
    intersubjective life-world, 49
Linguistic turn, 7–10, 40. *See also* Language
    and psychoanalysis, 26
    and race, 201–203
    and structuralism, 21–24
Liquid modernity, 99–100
Logocentric oppression, 75, 81
Lorber, Judith, 183–184
Lorde, Audre, 113, 123
Luckmann, Thomas, 47
Lukács, Georg, 111, 141
    false consciousness, 141
Luhmann, Niklas, 19–20

Lyotard, Jean-François, 91, 93, 95–97, 100
   Libidinal economy, 96

M

Maccoby, Eleanor, 182
Machines, of bodies, 95, 103
Male body, 119
Malinowski, Bronislaw, 15, 16–17
Mandela, Nelson, 165
Mannheim, 56
Marcuse, Herbert, 23, 70, 78, 100
Marginalized identity, 74, 99, 155–156, 192
Market system, 30, 38, 77, 86, 99, 173
Marking, 210–211, 213
Martin, Karen, 194
Marx, Karl, 1–4, 6, 7, 10, 17, 23–24, 29, 38, 56, 66–67,
      76, 86, 96, 97, 100, 201
   Marxism, 54, 141
Marxist Theory, 65, 66, 74, 77–78, 154, 169
   and capitalism, 3–4
   and critical theory, 6
   class struggle, 3
   culture, 132–134
   feminism, 109, 112, 116, 117
   humanism, 54, 135, 147, 209, 213
   ideology, 3
   material culture, 3–4
   Marxism, 54, 141
   structuralism, 4, 24–25
Masculinities, 184–185. *See also* Gender
Matrix of oppression, 116, 128
Mauss, Marcel, 17, 18, 30, 54
McDonaldization, 171–172
McRobbie, Angela, 137–139
   post-Marxism, 138
   post-feminist masquerade, 139
   postmodern theory, 138
Mead, George Herbert, 39, 45, 47, 70, 89
Mead, Margaret, 181
Merleau-Ponty, Maurice, 52–54, 58, 64–65,
      96, 110
Merton, Robert, 15, 28
Mestiza, 206, 213
Metanarratives, 97, 151
Milibrand, Ralph, 133
Mitchell, Juliet, 107–108, 185
Modernity, 87, 103
   consequences of, 88–89
   discontents of, 85–86
   and postmodernity, 89–91
   as a project, 86–88
   and race, 200

Mohanty, Chandra Talpade, 124–125
   and Marxism, 125
   globalization, 125
Moi, Toril, 127
Montesquieu, 2, 199
Moral reasoning, 87
Morton, Samuel George, 199
Moses, Clair, 108
Motherhood, 123, 125
Mothering/parenting system, 121
Multiculturalism, 144, 148, 212

N

Narratology, 33–35
Nationalism, 167
Nation-states, 88, 96–97, 159, 162, 165, 173
Naturalism, 47, 53, 65
Negri, Antonio, 163–164. *See also* Hardt
      and Negri
Neoliberalism, 116, 117
Neo-Marxian feminist theory, 107
Neo-Marxism, 11
Networks, 16, 40
Network analysis, 31–33, 40
New Left, 7, 133, 134, 141, 148
New Left Review, The, 7, 133
Nicholson, Linda, 182
Nietzsche, Friedrich Wilhelm, 3, 4–5, 46, 67, 91, 94,
      96, 146, 201
Nonwhite racial groups, 201

O

Object relations, 8, 70, 120–121, 128, 185
Objet petit-a, 78
Obligatory heterosexuality, 191, 195
Occupy Wall Street, 176
Oedipal complex, 94, 185
Oppressive power, 68, 152
Orientalism, 151–154
Otherness, 56–57, 98, 113
   and colonialism, 155, 156
   and feminism, 127
   and racism, 205, 212
Overaccumulation of capital, 160, 164, 177

P

Pareto, Vilfredo, 17–18, 31
   Pareto Circle, 18, 30
   Pareto optimum
Parle-etre, 27, 40
Paris Uprising, 10

Parsons, Talcott, 15, 17–19, 20, 26, 28, 46, 135
    action theory, 18–20
    AGIL, 18–19
Patriarchy, 108, 114, 122, 123
Performance, 90
    and gender, 185, 187–188
Performativity, 185, 195
Phallocentric logic, 127, 128
Phallocentrism, 71, 72–73, 75, 81
Phallus, 72, 118, 128
Phenomenology, 8–9, 13, 46–54, 60, 96, 99. *See also*
        First philosophy
    status of, 58–59
Phrenology, 194
Pierce, Charles, 43
Plato, 36, 49
Pluralism, 98
Popular culture, 69, 133, 134. *See also* Culture/
        culturalism
    globalization of, 144–146
    and poststructuralism, 76–79
Positivism, 7, 23, 47, 53, 115
Postcolonial theory, 150–156
    and feminism, 124–125
    marginalized identity, 155–156
    subaltern studies, 153–155, 177
Postfeminism, 125–127, 148
Postfeminist masquerade, 139, 148
Postfordism, 93, 173
Post-Foucaultianss, 69
Postmodernism/postmodernity, 80, 84–102,
        103, 142
    as a condition, 91–93
    and globalization, 172–174
    legacy of, 102
    Ludic postmodernism, 127
    and psychoanalysis, 93–95
    and race, 203, 204–206
    radical postmodernism, 100–102
    without modernity, 89–91
Post-race theory, 211–212
Poststructuralism, 10, 13, 23, 38–39, 63–82
    and cultural turn, 66–69
    deconstructionism, 63–66
    end of theory, 80–81
    and feminism, 71–75, 118–120
    in the new millennium, 79–80
    and popular culture, 76–79
    and race, 202–203
Poststructuralist Marx theory, 4
Power, 67, 68
    Foucault's notion, 67, 81
    and knowledge, 67, 68, 152, 202

oppressive power, 68, 152
    and truth, 5
Pragmatism, 43, 46, 204
    prophetic pragmatism, 203–204, 213
Presence, 53, 64
Producer, 134
Productive desire, 94, 103
Project identity, 169
Prophetic pragmatism, 203–204, 213
Propp, Vladimir, 34
Psychic life, 5–6, 27, 71
Psychoanalysis, 5–6, 95
    and feminism, 107
    and gender, 185–186
    and linguistic turn, 26
Psychoanalytic criticism, 141
Psychologism, 47

Q

Queer theory, 123–124, 125, 180, 188–192. *See also*
        Gender

R

Race/racism, 143–144, 198–212
    Afrocentric theory, 210–211
    critical race theory, 208–210
    and Enlightenment, 198–200
    feminism and, 112–116
    and linguistic turn, 201–203
    and postmodernism, 203, 204–206
    post-race theory, 211–212
    significance of, 203–204
    social construction of, 200–201
    trope of, 202
    whiteness studies, 206–208
Racialized body, 202, 213
Radcliffe-Brown, Alfred, 15, 17, 46
Radical postmodernism, 100–102
Rational choice theory, 30–31, 40
Reactive desire, 94, 103
Real, 70–71, 142
Reason, 3, 4–5, 67–68, 87. *See also* European
        Enlightenment; Postmodernism/postmodernity
Reductionism, 48, 58
Reflexivity, 37, 59, 90. *See also* Giddens, Anthony
    constitutive reflexivity, 89, 102
Reich, Wilhelm, 7, 94, 107, 108
Reification, 40
Rhimzones, 94–95, 164. *See also* Deluze and Gattari
Rich, Adrienne, 122–123, 189
    and capitalism, 123

Ricoeur, Paul, 35, 54–56
Ritzer, George, 171–172
    McDonaldization, 171
Riviere, Joan, 139, 185
Robertson, Roland, 169–172
    global human circumstance, 170
    glocalization, 171
Rorty, Richard, 203, 204
Rousseau, Jean-Jacques, 2
Rules, and actions, 37

S

Sadomasochism, 121
Said, Edward, 150, 151–153. *See also* Orientalism
Sameness, 56–57
Sartre, Jean-Paul, 7, 11, 46, 52, 141
Sassen, Saskia, 167–168
    global domains, 167
    transboundary networks, 167–168
Saussure, Ferdinand de, 8, 22–23, 64–65, 201
Schleiermacher, Friedrich, 44
Schneider, Christopher, 209
Schopenhauer, Arthur, 199
Schutz, Alfred, 47, 48–52, 99, 110
Scientific knowledge, 97, 111
Scientism, 7, 13
Sedgwick, Eve Kosofsky, 191–192
    obligatory heterosexuality, 191
Seidman, Steven, 189, 190
Self, 57
Selfless states, 90
Self-recognition, 70
Semiotics (semiology), 22, 25–27, 41, 74, 100, 137
Sexed body, 192, 193–194, 195
Sexual identity, 186, 190, 192
Sexual inversion, 193
Sexuality, 191–193. *See also* Gender; Heterosexuality;
    Homosexuality
    and communication, 118
    depressive sexuality, 75
    and discourse, 67
    female sexuality, 75
    and feminism, 127
    and gender. 180, 181, 185, 186–187
    and queer theory, 190
Shared identity, 56, 186
Shared meaning, 20
Signs, 23–26, 40, 100–101
    signified, 23, 39, 40
    signifier, 23, 27, 39, 40, 65
Signification, 37
Sign value, 100–101
Simmel, Georg, 44, 45

Simulacra, 101, 103
    third order of, 101
Skinner, B. F., 30
Slavery, 143
Smith, Adam, 3
Smith, Dorothy Edith, 109–111
    double consciousness, 109
    institutional ethnography, 110
Smith, James McCune, 200
Social cohesion, 17, 53, 54
Social imaginary, 55, 60
    of ideology, 56
    of utopia, 56
Social order, 16, 20, 30, 88, 137
Social Network Theory, 32
Social theory, defined, 1–13. *See also individual entries*
Sociopolitical imaginaire, 56, 60
Sokal, Alan, 79
Space, and capital, 160–161
Space of flows, 169, 177
Spencer, Herbert, 2, 14, 15, 28
Spivak, Gayatri Chakravorty, 150, 153–155
    strategic essentialism, 154
    subaltern, 154
Standpoint theory, 111–112, 128, 129
Stein, Arlene, 123–124
    queer theory, 123
Strategic essentialism, 154, 177
Structural anthropology, 23, 24
Structural-functionalism, 17, 28, 46
Structuralism, 9, 13, 14–39
    and capital accumulation, 29–30
    failure of, 28–29
    and feminism, 107–109
    habitus and field, 37–38
    and linguistic turn, 21–24
    narratology, 33–35
    and network analysis, 31–33
    structural intimacies, 20–21
    structuration, 36–37
    structure/agency divide, 35–36
    rational choice and network theory, 30–31
    of twentieth-century, 15–16
Structuralist Marx theory, 4
Structuration theory, 36–38
Structure, 41
    and agency, dualism, 35–37, 41, 98, 146
    of feeling, 137
    of language, 8
Subaltern studies, 153–155, 177
Subjective knowledge, 9, 108, 129
Subjectivity, 57
Sublime, 77
Substratum, 16

Symbolic interaction, and life-world, 46–48
Symbolic interactionism, 43, 45, 89
Symbolic order, 71, 72, 74, 117, 129, 139, 142
Symbolic value, 100, 103
Systems theory, 18–19, 20, 24
    world systems theory, 28–29, 41, 157–159

T

Taken-for-granted life-world, 48
Take-off phase, of globalization, 170
Temporal existence, 64
Text, 75, 79, 152
Textual readings, 44, 54–56, 65
The-Name-of-the-Father, 71, 82
The Net and the Self, 168–169
"They" relationship, 50, 60
Third space, 127, 156, 177
Thomas, W. I., 39, 45
Thompson, Edward P., 133, 135
"Thou" relationship, 50, 60
Timeless time, 169, 177
Time-space distanciation, 88, 103, 161. *See also*
    Giddens, Anthony
Titchener, Edward B., 21
Totalism, 97, 98
Tracers, 64, 82
Transboundary networks, 167–168, 177
Transdisciplinarity, 11–12, 13
Transgender, 192–193
Transnational character, 143, 148
Transnationalism, 156, 177
Transsexualism, 193
Trust
  and modernity, 88
  and social order, 20
Truth, 65, 67
  Foucault's notion, 67, 81
Turner, Stephanie, 193, 194
Typifications, 49, 50, 60
Tyrannical reason, 67, 82

U

Uncertainty phase, of globalization, 170
Unconscious/unconsciousness, 13, 21, 22, 24
  and ideology, 141
  and linguistics, 27, 70
  power of, 5–6
Use value, 100

V

Vacancy chains, in organizations, 32
Verstehen, 44–45, 49, 60
Virtual world, 82, 101
Voltaire, 2
von Mises, Ludwig, 47–48
  Vienna circle, 48

W

Walker, Clarence, 211
Wallerstein, Immanuel, 28–29, 157–158
  Africa, 157
  core and periphery, 158
  World Systems theory, 157–158
Weber, Max, 2, 3, 10, 44–45, 49, 51, 56, 86, 87,
    112, 169
  ideal type, 49
  Verstehen, 44–45
Weeks, Jeffrey, 189, 190
West, Cornel, 203–204
Whannel, Paddy, 134
White, Harrison C., 32
White Studies, 201, 206–208
Williams, Raymond, 133, 136–137, 138–139
  cultural materialism, 137
  Marxism, 138
Winant, Howard, 199–200
Wittgenstein, Ludwig, 21–22
Wolf, Virginia, 11
Women's movement, 10, 11, 71–72, 106
Words, 8, 70, 211
  and context, 22, 26–27, 39, 64
World cultural theory, 169–171. *See also*
    Culture
World military order, 162
World systems theory, 28–29, 41, 157–159. *See also*
    Globalization; Systems theory
  core areas, 158
  periphery areas, 158
  semiperiphery areas, 158

Y

Young, Robert, 202–203

Z

Žižek, Slavoj, 76–79, 80